BUILDING *the* RESILIENT SCHOOL

OVERCOMING THE EFFECTS OF POVERTY WITH A CULTURE OF HOPE

ROBERT D. BARR & EMILY L. GIBSON

Solution Tree | Press

a division of
Solution Tree

555 North Morton Street
Bloomington, IN 47404
800.733.6786 (toll free) / 812.336.7700
FAX: 812.336.7790

email: info@SolutionTree.com
SolutionTree.com

Visit **go.SolutionTree.com/schoolimprovement** to download the free reproducibles in this book.

Printed in the United States of America

Library of Congress Cataloging-in-Publication Data

Names: Barr, Robert D., author. | Gibson, Emily L., author.
Title: Building the resilient school : overcoming the effects of poverty
   with a culture of hope / Robert D. Barr, Emily L. Gibson.
Description: Bloomington, IN : Solution Tree Press, [2020] | Includes
   bibliographical references and index.
Identifiers: LCCN 2019053667 (print) | LCCN 2019053668 (ebook) | ISBN
   9781947604131 (paperback) | ISBN 9781947604148 (ebook)
Subjects: LCSH: Poor children--Education--United States. | Poor
   children--United States--Psychology. | School improvement
   programs--United States. | Resilience (Personality trait)--United
   States. | Hope--Social aspects--United States. | Motivation in
   education.
Classification: LCC LC4091 .B367 2020 (print) | LCC LC4091 (ebook) | DDC
   371.826/94--dc23
LC record available at https://lccn.loc.gov/2019053667
LC ebook record available at https://lccn.loc.gov/2019053668

Solution Tree
Jeffrey C. Jones, CEO
Edmund M. Ackerman, President

Solution Tree Press
President and Publisher: Douglas M. Rife
Associate Publisher: Sarah Payne-Mills
Art Director: Rian Anderson
Managing Production Editor: Kendra Slayton
Production Editor: Alissa Voss
Content Development Specialist: Amy Rubenstein
Copy Editor: Jessi Finn
Proofreader: Mark Hain
Text Designer: Kelsey Hergül
Cover Designer: Abigail Bowen
Editorial Assistants: Sarah Ludwig and Elijah Oates

Dedication

This book is dedicated to Dr. Clemmye Jackson of the Ames, Iowa Public Schools. She battled throughout her career for equity and opportunity for students of color and students of poverty. She represents all that is good about hope and resiliency. Clemmye, this book is for you.

—Bob Barr

This book is dedicated to one of my greatest sources of hope and resilience, Jay Girard, who supported the many long days and nights dedicated to its writing. Thank you for understanding when I suddenly "disappeared" into words and ideas, even mid-conversation!

—Emily Gibson

Acknowledgments

This book could have never been written without the help of people spread out over the entire United States, all deeply dedicated to improving the education of our most needy students. All have made an impact on me and my work.

First and foremost is Tom Hagley Jr., chief of staff of Vancouver Public Schools in Washington State. No other person has been so open and helpful and supportive in our work on resilient schools. He was, in fact, the first person with whom Emily Gibson and I first shared a one-page definition of our ideas regarding the resilient school and who took the time to think about that idea, returning it with valuable edits and comments. His response started us down this long road to resilience. There are others in Vancouver who were instrumental in our work. First, former superintendent Jim Parsley, surely one of the truly great school leaders of my generation, who invited me into the Vancouver Public Schools district during the 1980s and even put me on a retainer. Thanks to Karla Schlosser, now retired and living the good life, who heard me and Emily speak one day, and in the coming weeks hired Emily into the district and hired us both to provide Culture of Hope professional development to eight Title I schools. It was our work with the staff of these eight schools that first opened the door of community outreach to me. Karla always called Emily and me "rock stars." Can't get any better than that.

Next, there is a wonderful group of Kentucky educators who invited me into their state, welcomed me, and helped me learn about poverty and education. Over the years, I have spoken dozens of times at state conferences in Kentucky, working in schools all over the state and even presented twice to the legislature at combined House and Senate Education Committee meetings. First and foremost, thanks to Rhonda Caldwell, executive director of the Kentucky Association of School Administrators, who knows more about poverty and education that most anyone else. What a one-person force for better education for all kids. Once, years ago, Rhonda was worried about her daughter, who was teaching in the ruins of the bombed-out, post-Katrina ghost town of New Orleans. When she learned that I would be speaking at a conference in New Orleans, she asked me if I would visit her daughter's school and check on her. When I got there, I learned no taxis would even go into the "no-man's land" where her school was located behind a twelve-foot barbwire fence. It is the only time I had to go undercover to get into a school, and I came away with easily one of the greatest stories of personal dedication and bravery I have ever known. Thanks, Rhonda, for what you have done to help me learn about Kentucky, but also what you have done for the kids in your state.

Also in Kentucky, I must thank Barbara Kennedy, who taught me about state politics and outstanding teachers when she was a leader at the Kentucky Department of Education. Melissa Goins, the division director of the state office of Family Resources and Youth Services helped me learn about community outreach where it all started. Special thanks to Ryan Scott, the local elementary principal in Morganfield, Kentucky, who introduced me to the six-foot, eight-inch-tall county sheriff. The two of them hosted a county-wide symposium on poverty and invited me to speak. Everyone was there that day: city council members, juvenile judges, business leaders, educators, and community leaders. The day seemed to open up the highly charged and very mixed attitudes regarding poverty, and within two weeks of my presentation, Scott was asked for his resignation by the school superintendent. He was, of course, sought after by other schools and is now back at work serving poor kids. And last, but far from least, thanks to Karla McCarty, who invited me into the Johnson County School District where I first encountered high-poverty schools filled with hope and resiliency, and often joined me in presentations at professional meetings all over the country.

Special thanks to Dan Rea of Georgia Southern University and the director of the National Youth at Risk Conference held annually in Savannah, Georgia. It is because he invited us to present at the conference year after year for more than twenty-five years that has so filled up our professional work with contacts all over the South. It is also where I first met Leigh Colburn and Linda Beggs, from Marietta, Georgia, who introduced us to the powerful idea of seeking the voices of students to help define the services of an outreach center. The two are doing incredible work, including a new book for Solution Tree.

In Boise, Idaho, a special thanks to Stacey Roth, administrator of student programs and enthusiastic advocate for poor students and families in her district. Her guided tour of Garfield Elementary, the neighborhood school near my home, just transformed my understanding of what a first-rate family and community outreach program would look like. Both the outreach center at Garfield and the one at the Frank Church Alternative High School in Boise provided so much for the content of this book.

First at Boise State University (BSU) and later in Shasta County, California, thanks to my dear friend and professional colleague Sue Huizinga, who is the epitome of a dedicated professional, who has spent her career opening the doors of opportunity to students of color and poverty through the federally funded TRIO Program. She never gives up, she never shifts down; she is always full speed ahead. I must thank Scott Willison, the former Boise State director of the Center for Multicultural Education, and Bill Parrett, director of the BSU Center for School Improvement, which is funded for more than seven million dollars to help schools better serve the children of poverty. I count both Scott, who died way too early in his life, and Bill as dear personal and professional friends. Both touched my life in so many powerful ways and made me a better educator and researcher.

Emily and I were invited to work in the Longview School District in Washington, where we met the remarkable Jill Diehl. She gave us an opportunity to speak at a large community meeting in the evening and the next day to speak to the entire school district. Amazingly, she purchased a copy of *Building a Culture of Hope* for the entire district! Longview is an incredible school district with schools well on the way to becoming resilient.

I must also thank the Solution Tree team. First and foremost, I must recognize the support and assistance of the remarkable Douglas Rife, who is always open to new ideas and an incredible sounding board. I'm not sure what we would have done without his enduring encouragement. He has gone out of his way to hear me speak and then always debriefs with me in the most positive way. How Douglas loves a good story! Who else do you know with such a fine mind and an elegant manner, and who still loves country music. He is a wonder to behold. Thanks also to Rian Anderson for the great book cover and his willingness to work with us over and over again until the final masterpiece, and to Kelly Rockhill and her crew in the marketing department. Special thanks also to Alissa Voss, our wonderful, talented, patient, and supportive editor. She made our book so much better than the manuscript that she first received, and she was always willing to take a late-night call or email and immediately make a change in the text. Alissa has been a delight to work with. Last of all, special thanks to Jeff Jones, CEO of Solution Tree, who welcomed me into his publishing family when he first bought the business and took a gamble on me with a book contract. Thanks for his friendship and his support over all of these decades and all of my books. I feel deeply grateful to all of the professionals at Solution Tree who have supported my work, improved my ideas, and encouraged my vision for better schools.

—Bob Barr

The journey launched by *Building a Culture of Hope* is the journey that led to *Building the Resilient School*. The educators, school and district leaders, and education professionals we crossed paths with during professional development and presentations reinforced the Culture of Hope. My work as an instructional coach, intervention specialist, social-emotional learning specialist, and teacher in schools in Clearlake, California; Vancouver, Washington; and Bend, Oregon, vastly expanded my understanding of the needs of today's high-poverty, high-trauma students and the staff who teach them. Providing professional development, hopscotching across the United States, further informed and motivated my research into staff resilience and secondary trauma.

While it just isn't possible to mention all who played a part in the writing of this book, in addition to some of the dedicated professionals and friends who Bob mentioned in his acknowledgements—including Jill Diehl, Karla Schlosser, Sue Huizinga, Tom Hagley, and Dan Rea—I wanted to share a few additional significant contributors to our ideas.

First, the staff at Silver Rail Elementary School in Bend, Oregon. Since 1992, I had wondered if there was a school that would ever "fit" me (or perhaps a school I would fit with). In 2018, when I interviewed for a job at Silver Rail over the phone from Salem, Massachusetts, at the end of a three-month cross-country bicycle ride, I had a feeling that this might be the place—and it is. Silver Rail is truly building and becoming a resilient school, and I am delighted every day that I get to help with this building and becoming. Thank you, Tammy Doty and Stephanie Jensen—you are an administration team that fills all with hope and optimism and resilience. And thank you to the staff, which is continually open to new ideas and growth.

Second, Travis Boeh, principal of McLoughlin Middle School in Vancouver, Washington. McLoughlin is one of the eight schools we worked with in Vancouver, and when Travis welcomed me into his school to work on alternative programs for students with lagging behavior and academic skills, he opened a door to the writing of this book. Thank you, Travis, for trusting me to run with the CARE Academy, for it is in that work that I began to better understand trauma, resilience, and the impact of student trauma on staff. The CARE Academy and the ER (Engagement Room) are models of what can be, potentially, when we put students' needs first. I believe you will realize your vision and build a resilient school.

Third, Leigh Colburn and Linda Beggs of the Centergy Project. I actually met Leigh long before Bob, when she reached out to me after one of my first presentations on the Culture of Hope in 2013. After a staff book study, an action research project, and four years of work interviewing students, the Marietta Student Life Center was born, and soon after, the Centergy Project in collaboration with Linda Beggs. It has been a most rewarding experience to see where Leigh and Linda's work has taken them, and to know we played a small part in launching their part of the resilient school movement!

Finally, to the communities of eastern Oregon, where I have seen how a full-court communitywide press, led by the United Way of Deschutes County, can begin to make a dent in the sources of trauma caused by poverty. Rather than responding to the outcomes of poverty and the traumas caused by the lack of resources, the executive director, Ken Wilhelm, and his team dedicated their efforts to actions that reduce and eliminate the sources of poverty and trauma in families, like housing insecurity, food insecurity, lack of child care availability, availability of well-paying jobs, and mental health care shortages. We see this as a rallying cry across the nation, to build resilient communities. I am ever grateful to have landed in central Oregon and to be able to make my small contribution to the incredible work being done here.

—Emily Gibson

Solution Tree Press would like to thank the following reviewers:

Dawn Billings
Founder, School Synergy, LLC
Salem, Oregon

Rosa Isiah
Director of Elementary and
Instructional Supports
Norwalk-La Mirada Unified
School District
Norwalk, California

Sue Kimmet
Counselor
Southside Elementary and
Grammar #2 Elementary
Elko, Nevada

Summer Pannell
Associate Professor
University of Houston-Victoria
Victoria, Texas

Table of Contents

Reproducible pages are in italics.
Visit **go.SolutionTree.com/schoolimprovement** to
download the free reproducibles in this book.

About the Authors xvii

Introduction
Poverty: Our Greatest Challenge 1
    Poverty: An Ever-Growing Epidemic. 3
    Resilience: The Antidote to Despair 4
    Our Aim: A Look at the Chapters Ahead. 6

part one
Understanding Poverty 9

Chapter 1
Poverty: On the Outskirts of Hope 11
    The Need for Educators to Understand the Effects of Poverty. 12
    The State of Poverty in the United States 14
        Who Are the Poor? 16
        What Are the Challenges of Poverty?. 17
        What Are the Reasons for the Continuing Poverty Epidemic?. 20
    The Role of Hope in Ending Poverty. 26
    Conclusion. 29
    Next Steps *30*

Chapter 2
An Invisible Barrier: The Impacts of Poverty on Teaching and Learning 31
    Lack of Academic Preparation 32
    Absenteeism, Illness, and Interrupted Education 34
    Learning Loss Over School Breaks 36
    Adverse Childhood Experiences and Behavior Challenges 37
    Learned Helplessness 40
    The Role of Executive Function Skills in Ending Poverty 43
    Conclusion 46
    Next Steps 48

Chapter 3
An Unanticipated Challenge: The Detrimental Impacts of Poverty on School Staff 49
    Staff Turnover and Attrition 50
        Factors Related to the Teacher Shortage 53
        Teacher Job Satisfaction and Morale 54
        High Morale as a Form of Optimism 56
    Staff Exposure to Trauma 57
        Secondary Traumatic Stress 58
        Disrupted Learning Environments—A Primary Trauma 63
    Conclusion 66
    Next Steps 67

part two
Introducing the Resilient School 69

Chapter 4
The Research: Studying Resilient Students and Resilient Schools 71
    Research on Resilience in Youth 73
    Key Protective Factors for Resilience in Youth 73
        Internal Protective Factors of Resilience 75
        External or Environmental Protective Factors of Resilience 78
        The Self-Righting Capacity of Learners to Build Resilience 81
    Research on Poverty and Resilience in Education 82
        Developmental Risk Factors and Assets 83
        Trauma and Stress Neuroscience 84
        High-Poverty, High-Performing Schools 84

Childhood Trauma and Adversity 84

Social-Emotional Needs of the Whole Child 85

Needs of Families. 85

School Staff Attrition, Job Satisfaction, and Morale. 85

A Whole-School Model: The Search for an Effective Framework 86

The Framework Must Educate the Whole Child 87

The Framework Must Address Social-Emotional Needs 87

The Framework Must Be School- or Districtwide 87

The Framework Must Produce a Trauma-Sensitive School. 88

The Framework Must Lead to Relational and Professional Support for
   Staff Working in High-Poverty, High-Trauma Communities. 89

The Framework Must Lead to a School Filled With Hope and Optimism. . . 89

The Framework of the Resilient School 89

Conclusion 91

Next Steps *93*

Chapter 5
The First Cornerstone of the Resilient School: Addressing Students' Academic Needs . . . 95

Academic Essential 1: Visionary Leadership. 98

Academic Essential 2: Effective Teachers and the Power of We 99

Academic Essential 3: Data, Assessment, and Accountability. 100

Academic Essential 4: Rigorous, Aligned Curriculum for All 102

Academic Essential 5: Progress Monitoring and Remediation. 103

Academic Essential 6: Extra Time for Instruction and Support 105

Preschool and All-Day Kindergarten. 106

Before- and After-School Programs 106

Enriched Summer Programs. 106

Early Family Intervention and Support 107

Academic Essential 7: Targeted Reading and Mathematics. 108

All Students Literate by the End of Third Grade 108

A Focus on Mathematics 108

Restructured Learning Time. 109

Academic Essential 8: Positive Interpersonal Relationships 109

Caring Relationships and Mutual Respect 109

High Expectations and Positive Reinforcement 110

Trauma-Sensitive Relationships 111

Academic Essential 9: Parent and Guardian Involvement 112

A Welcoming Atmosphere. 113

Encouragement of Involvement. 113

Two-Way Communication 113

Parent and Guardian Education. 114

Home Visits 114

Academic Essential 10: Trauma-Informed Practices 115

Relevance of Instruction to Students 115

Predictability 116

Academic Expectations. 116

Independent Learning. 116

Behavior Supports. 117

Language-Based Teaching 117

Conclusion. 118

Next Steps *119*

Chapter 6

The Second Cornerstone of the Resilient School: Addressing Students' Social-Emotional Needs

. . . . 121

An Emphasis on Hope 123

An Institutional Culture Versus a Culture of Hope 124

The Teaching of Hope. 126

The Culture of Hope and the Seeds of Hope 127

The First Seed of Hope: A Sense of Optimism and Hope. 130

The Second Seed of Hope: A Sense of Place and Belonging. 134

The Third Seed of Hope: A Sense of Self-Regulation 139

The Fourth Seed of Hope: A Sense of Pride, Self-Esteem, and
Self-Confidence 144

The Fifth Seed of Hope: A Sense of Purpose. 147

Conclusion. 151

Next Steps *152*

Chapter 7

The Third Cornerstone of the Resilient School: Addressing Students' and Their Families' Human Needs

. . . . 155

The Emergence of Community Outreach. 157

Step 1: Identifying the Needs of Families. 162

Families Identify Their Needs. 163

Teachers and Staff Identify Their Students' Needs 164

Students Voice Their Needs 164

Step 2: Establishing the School as a Hub of Coordination. 165

Family Services and Supports. 169

Family Education 171

Community Development. 171

Wraparound Educational Programs. 171

Step 3: Setting Up the Community Outreach Center. 172

The Community Resource Center Coordinator 172

Center Facilities 174

Local Advisory Council or Board of Directors 175

Community Partners 176

Step 4: Monitoring the Community Outreach Center's Outcomes. 181

Vancouver Public Schools, Washington 182

Central Oregon 182

Step 5: Funding Community Outreach. 182

The Long-Term Impact of Community Outreach. 184

Conclusion 188

Next Steps *190*

Chapter 8
The Fourth Cornerstone of the Resilient School: Addressing Staff's Relational and
Professional Needs. 191

Supporting Staff With the Seeds of Hope. 192

Seed 1: A Sense of Optimism and Hope. 192

Seed 2: A Sense of Place and Belonging 194

Seed 3: A Sense of Self-Regulation. 196

Seed 4: A Sense of Pride, Self-Esteem, and Self-Confidence. 197

Seed 5: A Sense of Purpose 199

Fostering Staff Resilience in Difficult Times. 200

Support. 200

Self-Care as a Moral Responsibility. 201

Meeting Staff's Professional Needs 202

Policy Rollout Includes Teachers' Agency and Voice. 203

Structures Support Staff Job Satisfaction and Morale 204

Conclusion 208

Next Steps *210*

Epilogue
A Personal Note and a Vision for Resilient Schools 211
    Listening to Student Voices 214
    Meeting the Emotional Challenges of Students 214
    Becoming Trauma-Informed, Trauma-Sensitive Schools. 215
    Increasing Engagement and Personal Connections 215
    Teaching Hope and Finding a Vision for a Better Life 216
    Conclusion 216

Appendix. 217

References and Resources 225

Index. 259

About the Authors

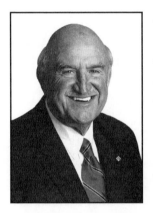

Robert D. Barr, PhD, is recognized as one of the leading experts in the United States on reaching and teaching students of poverty and minority students and helping high-poverty schools become high-performing ones. He is an educator, speaker, author, and emeritus analyst with the Boise State University Center for School Improvement and Policy Studies. Bob has keynoted hundreds of state, regional, national, and international conferences and has provided workshops for schools, school districts, and state departments of education in every area of the United States.

Escaping poverty and realizing the American dream are part of Bob's personal story. His grandparents were migrant workers, and the overriding values of his family were hard work, thrift, and the abiding belief that if you kept at it, life would get better. When Bob was in fifth grade, he cashed in his school banking account so the family could use the forty-eight dollars to buy a mule. Through hard work and sacrifice, his parents saved enough to buy an acre of land, then eight acres, and finally, their dream: a 150-acre ranch in the cedar breaks and rolling hills of Glen Rose, Texas. His parents found their American dream through sacrifice and hard work; Bob found his through education.

Bob has been selected for the National School Boards Association's prestigious Meet the Expert sessions at its national conferences twelve times and has received three national awards for distinguished achievement. He has been a guest on the PBS television show *Firing Line*, the ABC show *World News Tonight*, and the Fox News show *The O'Reilly Factor*, and has been quoted in *The New York Times*, *USA Today*, and *The Wall Street Journal*. In addition, he has provided expert testimony to the U.S. Congress and a number of state legislatures and often serves as an expert trial witness.

Bob is the author or coauthor of over a dozen books on education and has served as professor and director of teacher education at Indiana University, dean of the Oregon State University College of Education, and dean of the Boise State University College of Education.

Emily L. Gibson, EdD, has worked in rural and high-poverty schools since she began teaching in 1992. Her research interests include the education of children of poverty, equity and access to quality education, differentiated instruction, school improvement, writing instruction, and classroom and school community and culture. A fellow of the National Writing Project, Emily led K–12 professional development in writing instruction as a teacher consultant with the Redwood Writing Project from 1997 to 2013. In 2002, she started Blue Heron Middle School, a charter school learning center for students in grades 6–8 who were struggling to find success in more traditional middle school settings. Emily served as an instructional coach in high-poverty schools in California and Washington, and now works as a social-emotional learning specialist in high-poverty schools in Bend, Oregon. Since 2013, she has provided targeted professional development for high-poverty schools and districts in the Culture of Hope and staff resilience.

Raised primarily by a single mom with health issues, Emily grew up on welfare, Aid to Families with Dependent Children, and Medi-Cal, yet her childhood home was filled with laughter, creativity, and a passion for learning. But school was not a place where she felt belonging, hope, or safety. Instead, she experienced bullying and the social stigma that came with being a child on pubic assistance. She made it through high school with the help of her biology teacher, Jim Welsh, who called her *Dr. Gibson*, and her equine friends at a stable down the road, who taught her about hard work, responsibility, and love. During her high school years, she mucked stalls, carried feed, brushed horses, cleaned tack, and rode in the Pacific Coast rain. Working two jobs, she put herself through college and earned her first bachelor's degree in liberal studies elementary education from Humboldt State University (HSU).

After teaching in K–6 and K–8 schools for a decade, Emily returned to HSU to earn a second bachelor's degree in psychology and a master's degree in education with an emphasis on differentiation, brain-based instruction, and parent involvement. Seeking to learn more about school improvement, she studied at Boise State University, earning her doctorate in education in 2011, where her research focused on equity and access to quality education and school improvement.

Emily coauthored the study "Graduate School Learning Curves: McNair Scholars' Postbaccalaureate Transitions" with Scott Willison, which was published in the journal *Equity & Excellence in Education* in April 2011. In 2013, she coauthored the book *Building a Culture of Hope* with Robert Barr for Solution Tree Press. Emily and Bob have published numerous articles supporting the Culture of Hope since their book's publication in 2013.

To learn more about Bob and Emily's work, visit www.cultureofhope.com or visit www.facebook.com/cultureofhope to connect with them on Facebook.

To book Robert D. Barr or Emily L. Gibson for professional development, contact pd@SolutionTree.com.

Introduction

Poverty: Our Greatest Challenge

In 1964, President Lyndon B. Johnson declared "unconditional war on poverty in America." . . . Fast-forward 51 years: That same number (51) now comes to signify the percentage of public school students who live in poverty.
—Association for Supervision and Curriculum Development

The United States faces a great challenge in the poverty epidemic. While the issues of poverty may in many cases fail to gain significant traction in the halls of Congress, we teachers, leaders, and administrators cannot overlook the calamitous issues of poverty at the local level—at the level of our public schools and surrounding communities. As citizens and community members, what do we do about homelessness? How do we deal with the crushing costs of health care for the uninsured and the insured? How do we find sufficient resources to provide food for the hungry? What do we do about the overwhelming issues of drug and alcohol addiction? And of course, as educators, how can we provide high-quality education for our neediest students? Poverty is surely the single greatest challenge confronting our communities and public schools.

In 2013, the United States reached a new milestone, but not one to brag about: for the first time, a majority—51 percent—of K–12 students enrolled in public schools lived in poverty, as measured by qualification for the free and reduced-price lunch program (Association for Supervision and Curriculum Development [ASCD], 2015; Suitts, 2015). In one of the wealthiest countries on earth (Sauter & Stebbins, 2020), poverty is widespread and insidious, an economic cancer eating away at our strength and stability as a people. Poverty touches practically every community and every neighborhood. In areas of high poverty, families' needs all but swamp the county, city, state, and federal governments' abilities to respond. The hope for a better future represents a monstrous challenge facing every community—none is immune. A future without devastating destitution can only become a reality if communities across the United States mobilize and demand that the three branches of the federal government as well as local and state entities make a widespread concerted effort to address the sources and effects of poverty. To wage a successful new war on poverty will demand sweeping changes and will surely include public sectors beyond education. In the 21st-century political climate, equitably expanding opportunities to all citizens may be a far and fleeting dream, but it is worth fighting for. In fact, providing an equal, high-quality education for all students surely must be the great civil rights battle of our time.

No longer can schools focus simply on teaching academics, for poverty has engulfed schools with a set of new and complicated responsibilities for meeting students' social-emotional, mental health, and basic human needs of food, clothing, and resources. School districts almost everywhere have concluded that they cannot ignore the basic survival needs of students and families living in poverty if they are to achieve high levels of student learning. According to researcher Steve Suitts (2013):

> No longer can we consider the problems and needs of low income students simply a matter of fairness. . . . Their success or failure in the public schools will determine the entire body of human capital and educational potential that the [United States] will possess in the future. Without improving the educational support that the nation provides its low income students—students with the largest needs and usually with the least support—the trends of the last decade will be prologue for a nation not at risk, but a nation in decline. (p. 13)

In answer to this challenge, some schools have coupled local innovation and bold creativity with the best research from various fields to provide a new vision for public education in the United States. These schools are confronting poverty head-on and rallying entire communities to help families build new futures for themselves. These schools are emerging as poverty's first responders and helping transform the lives of our poorest students. These schools are not just focusing on students' academic needs; rather, they have embraced a *whole child* approach to schooling that addresses students' social-emotional needs as well as basic human needs. They are helping students succeed in school, stay in school, graduate, and go on to postsecondary training and education. They are helping students find pathways to a better life. We believe that these schools represent a new concept of schooling in the United States, one that can be applied to any school or district facing these issues throughout the world—the *resilient school*.

Within this watershed concept of public education, two fronts of activity have come together, coursing a mighty river of possibility: on one front, educators have been creating more effective ways to address students' real needs, while on the other front, researchers have been documenting emerging understandings about poverty's impacts on learning and effective responses. This has resulted in a vision—the resilient school—of how schools are becoming first responders to the outcomes of poverty, standing as the primary line of defense for children and families. When schools focus on addressing the effects of poverty head-on, they switch from a fixed, reactionary frame to a growth, prevention frame. In essence, they become *resilient* because they are able to bounce back and effectively respond to adversity. In fact, schools provide one of the few doors of opportunity available to students living in poverty, one of the few pathways students can travel to break out of poverty and find a better life. The path to a new American dream surely goes through our public schools.

In fact, a growing number of high-performing, high-poverty schools are already doing many things to alleviate the effects of poverty on students right now. This book attempts to capture the best of how high-poverty, high-performing schools are becoming resilient schools, providing a safety net for students and families, a pathway out of poverty, and hope for a better life.

> **" "**   Poverty really is the lack of possibility.
>
> ## —Mentor, A Little Creative Class, Troy, New York

Poverty: An Ever-Growing Epidemic

The collateral damage of poverty threatens to undermine and overwhelm communities. Children who grow up in persistent poverty are more likely to (Hoynes, 2012; Ratcliffe & McKernan, 2010):

- Have no preschool
- Perform worse in school
- Drop out of high school
- Have lower educational attainment
- Become a teen parent
- Be incarcerated
- Live in poverty as adults

- Be homeless
- Struggle with addiction
- Access social safety net services
- Be served by the child welfare system
- Have poor health
- Live shorter lives

According to Jonah Edelman, cofounder and chief executive officer of Stand for Children:

> *The impact of poverty on a child's academic achievement is significant and starts early. Young children growing up in poverty face challenges with cognitive and literary ability and [often] begin school both academically and socioeconomically behind their peers from higher-income backgrounds. (as cited in Taylor, 2017)*

These and other negative effects of poverty represent a plague of physical, mental, economic, and social difficulties.

A U.S. Census Bureau report shows 11.8 percent of people in the United States, or nearly thirty-nine million people, lived in poverty in 2018 (Semega, Kollar, Creamer, & Mohanty, 2019). For many, the American dream has become an American nightmare. Many Americans seem to have given up and accepted that their life in poverty is the status quo—an unchanging, permanent state extending into the future. They have accepted that they will live out their lives unemployed, underemployed, or unemployable and that they will pass on that legacy of poverty to their children. In so many communities, despair often overwhelms hope and optimism for the future.

However, this potential outcome does not have to be an inevitability. Research shows that it is possible to break the cycle of poverty and alleviate its effects on children—and that, although the challenge of helping students break out of poverty represents a long and difficult road, schools can effect such change—primarily through the teaching of executive function skills and reducing the effects of trauma for students (Babcock, 2014b). This provides great hope and agency for those who work in schools: we can make a difference with the cornerstones of the resilient school (see chapters 5–8, page 95–191). In our opinion, based on the work of multiple pioneering schools and districts we have witnessed in person as well as the schools and districts described in the research literature, schools can best begin to provide hope to students, staff, and communities dealing with poverty by focusing on the principle of *resilience*.

Field Note

Poverty is hating weekends because you only have breakfast or lunch at school. Poverty is having adults at home who do shift work and are unavailable to help with homework or help structure the evenings. Poverty is an emotional distraction that makes it hard to focus on everyday things. Poverty is always there like a toothache or a headache, pulsing in the background. Poverty is just the way things are. You get used to it. —Emily Gibson

Resilience: The Antidote to Despair

In our experience, any effort to develop students' *resilience*, or their ability to bounce back from challenges or adversities, and ensure such resilience is sustainable must have trauma research as a foundation. The reasons that hope, optimism, and engagement are such powerful tools against the effects of poverty lie in the nature of trauma, and the internal and environmental protective factors that lead to resilience.

As anyone who works in high-poverty schools can attest, students living in poverty can bring a wave of trauma and stress in through the classroom doors each day, enormously impacting their own and their peers' ability to participate in and learn in school (Burns, 2016). Research shows that trauma can lead to biological changes, eventually hardwiring the brain to react in fight-flight-freeze mode (Perry, 2002). This often damages students' learning and social relationships in school. Fortunately, while it was once thought that resilience was a fixed asset that students either had or didn't have, research now shows that resilience can be learned, and schools can provide protective factors that build resilience in learners (Henderson, 2013).

A great, innovative experiment is underway in communities around the United States, where schools and school districts are supplementing their efforts to effectively teach students impacted by poverty and meet their social-emotional needs by reaching outside their walls. We have visited some of these schools in person since 2013 to gather evidence of their work, including Boise School District in Idaho and Vancouver Public Schools in Washington, while others are documented in high-performing, high-poverty and community outreach school research (see chapter 7, page 155). These schools have gone far beyond previous efforts by becoming *community outreach schools*, which develop widespread partnerships with churches, agencies, nonprofits, businesses, and even professional clubs and organizations, all to address the overwhelming challenges of poverty. In these efforts, the school has emerged as the focal point for the coordination and delivery of services and supports.

The results of these experimentations have remarkably transformed the notion of schooling. Rather than viewing schools as purely the mechanism to convey academic information to students, community outreach schools model how education can make a better tomorrow possible by making the local school the centerpiece in building resilience and helping the poor find a pathway to a better life. And while the tendrils of poverty touch every aspect of communities, issues surrounding poverty cannot be effectively addressed *without* education. The challenge seems to center on how to bring opportunity and equality to vast numbers of schools serving the poor.

These schools, rather than reacting to the challenges of poverty, stress, and trauma with frustration, resistance, or blame, have taken action to ensure that students can and will learn. Resilience is the ability to rebound from adversity, becoming stronger in the process, and we describe these community outreach schools as *resilient schools*, for they are mobilizing entire communities to face the widespread issues accompanying poverty, becoming places where people are hopeful and optimistic and truly making a difference. Our definition of a resilient school is a school where, despite great odds, the following four characteristics are evident:

- Socioeconomic and ethnic or minority achievement gaps have been closed or significantly reduced

- Students succeed in school and graduate

- Students successfully transition to postsecondary education or jobs

- Teachers and school staff maintain these remarkable achievements over time

These schools are *factories of resilience* that replace despair with hope as they address the four major cornerstones of school resilience that we have found in schools we studied and in the research literature: (1) students' academic needs, (2) students' social-emotional needs, (3) students' and their families' human needs, and (4) staff's relational and professional needs. Many schools have started on the journey toward becoming a resilient school, implementing a few of the preceding elements, and are beginning to see results. Where these schools do exist, they are both transforming communities and serving as essential research and development centers for other struggling schools. For example, after Vancouver Public Schools (VPS) developed and implemented family-community resource centers in all Title I schools in the district, the Boise School District consulted with VPS and began to develop their own model of community outreach to fit with their community's needs. This exemplifies the replication of resilient schools. We believe that these remarkable resilient schools serve as brilliant lighthouses that can guide the improvement of other schools and communities and bring hope to a generation that has experienced very little reason to be optimistic about the future.

In the coming pages, we describe and explain the successes of resilient schools by pulling together a veritable avalanche of research from numerous fields—neurobiology, trauma, adverse childhood experiences (ACEs), staff attrition, secondary traumatic stress, community outreach schools, social-emotional learning (SEL), and more—to create a perspective never before available within the framework of trauma and resilience. We have used this research to identify the various components of a resilient school and to show how schools and communities can work together to help students have success in their education. Further, we show how schools and communities can build hope for students—hope that they can break out of the debilitating cycle of generational poverty.

> **❝ ❞** A simple shift in our thinking—that each child is our own child—could influence how we collectively work to better educate children in poverty.
>
> **—Association for Supervision and Curriculum Development**

Our Aim: A Look at the Chapters Ahead

In this book, our aim is twofold. First, we wish to provide our audience—stakeholders in schools and communities—with a broad understanding of poverty, its causes, and its effects on students, families, teachers, and indeed the wider community. Second, although the truths about poverty we present may be daunting, we wish to give our readers hope—hope that they can, in fact, effect change in students' and teachers' lives in communities of poverty, even in the absence of a more widespread legislative or political effort to do so. Thus, we have divided this book into two parts.

Part one, "Understanding Poverty," discusses topical and current research on poverty. Chapter 1 provides a summary of poverty in the United States, including research about the causes of poverty and proposed legislative or political solutions to the poverty epidemic. Chapter 2 examines the byproducts of poverty that impact teaching and learning in our schools. Specifically, this chapter focuses on how poverty and trauma can create academic deficiencies, increase absenteeism and family mobility, undermine social-emotional learning, and instill learned helplessness and an external locus of control in many students. Our deep examination of poverty concludes with chapter 3, which illuminates often-overlooked byproducts of poverty: the impacts of trauma and stress on staff who work in high-poverty and high-trauma schools, decreased job dissatisfaction, and low teacher retention. The appendix suggests several reports and resources on poverty, resilience, and trauma, which provide more thorough documentation for those who wish to dive deeper into these data.

In part two, "Introducing the Resilient School," we provide a model for resilient schools. This model builds off our prior work, *Building a Culture of Hope* (Barr & Gibson, 2013), which describes how schools can transform student engagement and learning by making four essential social-emotional assets (optimism, belonging, pride, and purpose) their core organizational framework. Chapter 4 summarizes the powerful research on resilience and then introduces the four cornerstones of a resilient school.

1. Addressing students' academic needs

2. Addressing students' social-emotional needs

3. Addressing students' and their families' human needs

4. Addressing staff's relational and professional needs

Chapters 5–8 then share the research and findings behind each of the four essential cornerstones. Last, the epilogue changes course a little and gives a final—and personal—view of how resilient schools can help students make the long and complicated transition out of and away from poverty for life. Each chapter also includes Next Steps focusing on what readers can do to reflect on the content and prepare for steps they may want to take in their own school or community contexts. Field Notes and pull quotes are included throughout to provide thoughtful insights and experiences from educators and schools already on the journey towards resilience.

By dividing the book into two parts, we have created a structure containing primarily a research and literature review in part one and a description of how to implement our recommendations for building a resilient school in part two. We have included the extensive review of poverty and its effects in part one of this book because we feel it is crucial that educators, educator leaders, and other stakeholders have an accurate and comprehensive understanding of the nature of poverty before helping students to overcome its effects. While we recommend reading the book in its entirety in order to more fully comprehend the issues facing students, their families, and staff, those wishing to dive straight into implementation and action can turn directly to part two (page 69) and begin from there. The latter part of the book is meant to help schools and districts identify where they are already serving their students, families, and communities well, and areas for continued focus and effort in their mobilization against poverty.

Our ultimate hope is that this book gives readers an overall understanding and blueprint of a resilient school and connects them to the abundant resources and supports that can help schools in their efforts toward resilience.

part one

UNDERSTANDING
POVERTY

Chapter 1

Poverty: On the Outskirts of Hope

Unfortunately, many Americans live on the outskirts of hope—some because of their poverty, and some because of their color, and all too many because of both. Our task is to help replace their despair with opportunity.

—Lyndon B. Johnson

Although understanding the daily reality of poverty in the United States can be overwhelming, we encourage educators and other stakeholders to do so, as this understanding provides the firm reference point needed to seriously address the complexities of poverty that students bring to their classrooms and schools. Also, we believe that a better understanding of poverty will give communities the data they need for building the grassroots political will to reduce U.S. poverty. Grit alone is not enough to develop students' resilience; thus, before getting to the model for resilient schools in part two (page 69), we first present this review of poverty and trauma in the United States. Our hope is that this information can help schools comprehend the complex, long, but doable journey required to help their students living in poverty succeed in school and in life.

In this chapter, we first provide a rationale for why educators—both teachers and leaders—must understand the comprehensive effects of poverty on their students and communities. We discuss how a true understanding of poverty involves examining both the *whys* and the *whats* of poverty, and how effective change takes a systemwide application. Next, we summarize the state of poverty in the United States, including some possible reasons and solutions for poverty's prevalence. This review should help explain the complex and long-term challenges that families and students face in trying to leave poverty behind. It will surely debunk some prevalent myths about the poor in the United States. Amid the pressing needs of each day, it can be easy to fail to see the real human side of poverty, which can leave educators vulnerable to the implicit biases about poverty and the poor in our society. And, while this chapter gives a rather short summary of this extremely complex and tragic issue, we suggest several reports in the appendix (page 217) that provide far more detail for interested readers. Finally, we close this chapter with a few suggested actions that promote a solution-minded focus on poverty and the needs of the poor in our communities.

The Need for Educators to Understand the Effects of Poverty

People can view poverty through either the lens of the masses or the lens of individuals. Those who work in schools typically use the lens of individuals—the students, the families, and the everyday stories. This lens is important because it is relational and ties educators directly to those they serve. However, this lens can also serve to insulate practitioners from the brutal truths in their neighborhoods, towns, cities, and nation, and it can allow practitioners to slip into the implicit biases surrounding poverty and the poor that exist in their culture. It can cultivate a mythology of poverty that adds a crushing layer of stereotypes about the poor onto the tangible difficulties of poverty. For example, a student's parent or guardian who is unemployed and not providing clean clothes, on an individual level, may seem like the problem, instead of the outside forces that make employment, housing, and even laundry so very difficult for families. Paul Gorski (2013), founder of the Equity Literacy Institute, shares the following guidance on how educators can avoid biases toward students who live in poverty:

> We can start by standing up to our own biases about families in poverty, even if it means taking the oddly unpopular view that poor people are not poor because of their deficiencies, that something bigger than that is amiss. Then we can do everything humanly possible in our spheres of influence to align our teaching and relationship-building and family outreach efforts with our good intentions. We can listen. (p. 156)

Those who work in policy or research typically use the lens of the whole, the data, or the construct. This cognitive and intellectual lens is important for viewing the context of the persistent problems of poverty, but it isolates these practitioners from the human reality that thirty-nine million people live out daily (Semega, Kollar, Creamer, & Mohanty, 2019). However, this lens of the masses can help those working at the individual level gain perspective on the enormity of the problem and how difficult it is to break free from poverty. Ultimately, it is necessary to see poverty through both lenses.

In order to bring together these two lenses—(1) the individual, relational, personal lens and (2) the cognitive, rational, data-driven lens—we hope to describe as fully as possible the pathology of persistent poverty in part one of our book. This pathology is not pretty. It will likely take you out of your comfort zone and may challenge some of your beliefs or perceptions. But it is important, because for over half our public school students, it is a matter of life and death. Equally important, we as educators and community members can do something to make a difference in students' lives. We can build resilience. There is great hope.

Many of the recommendations for improving schools that we find in books on poverty and education we consider to be superficial responses and interventions for alleviating poverty's impacts in schools, as they do not necessarily result from a deep understanding of the complexity of helping students escape lifelong poverty. Rather, they tend to come from a reactive, deficit-based perspective instead of a proactive, hope-based perspective.

A review of the large number of books on poverty and education sitting on our bookshelves reveals that many authors acknowledge poverty as a challenge in U.S. schools, but only a few provide a careful examination of the *whys* and *whats* of poverty. Some current books on poverty and education take poverty as a given and focus almost exclusively on effective strategies for addressing the challenges of students impacted by poverty. For example, Eric Jensen (2019) focuses on poverty for a few pages before pivoting directly to his focus on "rich teaching." Elaine Weiss and Paul Reville (2019) devote approximately ten pages out of nearly three hundred to explaining poverty and the impact of poverty on students. Other books address poverty in a more comprehensive manner. William Parrett and Kathleen Budge (2012) include a strong chapter (chapter 3: "Poverty and Our Moral Responsibility") that deals with the nature and the myths of poverty, as well as ways to deal with the myths. Further, in their 2018 book *Disrupting Poverty: Five Powerful Classroom Practices*, Budge and Parrett included a short chapter titled "A Poverty Primer," which includes the following topics:

- What is poverty?
- Poverty and race and gender
- Explanations for poverty
- Effects on lives and learning
- Myths about welfare

We recommend Gorski's 2013 book *Reaching and Teaching Students in Poverty: Strategies for Erasing the Opportunity Gap* as one of the few deep examinations of poverty in the literature.

When educators have a more thorough understanding of poverty's effects on children's minds, bodies, and spirits, we hope they may better recognize that applying a few superficial classroom strategies for engagement and learning, while possibly creating a more positive environment or allowing a teacher and class to get through a lesson, will not likely make much difference in the long run, regardless of the strategies' documented effectiveness. Instead, helping students break the cycle of poverty demands concerted school-, classroom-, and communitywide responses involving education at all levels—preK–14 and maybe beyond. It is our hope that the content of the next three chapters provides a more thorough understanding of the effects of poverty on students and staff in high-poverty, high-trauma schools.

> 66 99   The United States is one of the world's richest, most powerful and technologically
>   innovative countries; but neither its wealth nor its power nor its technology is
>   being harnessed to address the situation in which 40 million people continue to
>   live in poverty.
>
> —Philip Alston

The State of Poverty in the United States

In 2017, researcher Philip Alston noted that forty million people in the United States lived in poverty. Either these people were born into poverty or they landed in poverty due to circumstances largely beyond their control: physical or mental disability, divorce, family breakdown, illness or catastrophic health crisis, old age, unlivable wages, job discrimination, or job elimination due to automation (Alston, 2017).

Researchers and social scientists describe three main types of poverty: (1) *generational poverty*, which results from families' remaining poor across generations; (2) *situational poverty*, which is caused by unemployment, illness, or catastrophe; and (3) *place-based poverty*, which results from a loss of population, economic sources, or civic engagement (Public Schools First, 2016). Generational poverty is by far the most difficult form of poverty to escape. Up until the 1980s or 1990s, for generation after generation, workers in the United States truly believed that with sheer effort, determination, and hard work, they could obtain a better life. Yet dramatic changes in the world of work have combined to accelerate the rapid disappearance of family-wage job opportunities for the undereducated. The loss of low-skill, good-wage, labor-based work has led to increases in situational poverty, which, as the decades have passed, has morphed into generational poverty. In the 21st century, the vast majority of jobs that pay above the median wage ($38,000 per year) require education and training beyond high school (U.S. Bureau of Labor Statistics, 2019).

> 66 99   They used to say that to find greater opportunity, you had to "go West, young man,
>   go West." . . . Now the great frontier is not the West, it is education. That is where
>   the opportunity lies for my kids.
>
> —Retired autoworker, Detroit, Michigan

Too often, the poor are stereotyped as lazy wasters, losers, and scammers and a drain on the economy, while the wealthy are portrayed as industrious, entrepreneurial, and patriotic drivers of economic success (Durante & Fiske, 2017; Gorski, 2008, 2012, 2013). These negative stereotypes of the poor "appear deeply entrenched, despite the fact that people who live in poverty are as diverse in their norms, beliefs, and behaviors as people who live in any other socioeconomic stratum in the United

States" (ASCD, 2015, p. 22). In 2015, ASCD hosted a symposium on poverty and education, bringing together researchers and practitioners to discuss poverty. The symposium participants published a report, summarizing their discussions and conclusions. According to this report (ASCD, 2015):

> *Poverty spans geographical and ethnic boundaries, from urban cities to rural towns. It spans communities that have battled poverty for decades to communities where poverty has arrived recently, unexpectedly, and in a rush. [The majority] of our nation's [public] schoolchildren live in poverty, threatening to become the "new normal" of the public educational experience. (p. 22)*

Sadly, those who live in poverty continue to receive criticism for "not getting a job" or "not working hard enough." Others often assume that people who live in poverty wouldn't be poor if they only worked harder, were not so lazy, or were smarter about money (Gorski, 2013).

The reality is that most children who live in poverty have parents or other adult family members who worked at least part of the year (Child Trends Databank, 2018). About half of low-income children live with at least one parent employed full-time, year-round (Korball & Jian, 2018; National Center for Children in Poverty, 2017). Most poor adults (eighteen to sixty-five years of age) are working, are looking for work, or are too disabled or ill to work; in 2016, 70 percent of children living in poverty lived with an adult who worked during the past year (Stevens, 2018). The notion that poverty is a condition created by laziness or a refusal to work hard is surely part of the great American myth of upward mobility in the United States (Jacobs, 2018).

In this section, we provide the most accurate picture of poverty that we can, using data and statistics from U.S. and international sources to counter pervasive myths. We discuss the following questions.

- Who are the poor in our society?
- What are the challenges they face?
- What are the reasons for the continuing poverty epidemic?

Field Note

You have to understand, in Morganfield, Kentucky, we are dealing with "country poverty," which is very different than "city poverty." We don't have all of the usual safety net programs that urban areas do. We lack the transportation system available to the poor in cities, and our students and families are spread over a larger geographic area, which makes access to community resources very tough. Our area once boomed with a vibrant coal industry and many factories, and it had a large military base during World War II. Now there is only one coal company employing workers, and parts of the former military base are filled with poor families living in old dilapidated barracks, house trailers, and sometimes camping trailers . . . some live on dirt floors. And at no fault of their own, good, dependable workers are now unemployed, living hand to mouth, and have little hope of finding the type of employment that pays equivalent to what they had become accustomed to.

We now have a poverty rate in Morganfield where 77 percent of our kids live in high-poverty areas, and that includes 13 percent living in deep poverty, which means these families earn less than thirteen thousand dollars' annual income. Our labor participation rate is low but there are just so few opportunities for a job, let alone a good job. And in spite of promises in the last presidential election about improving jobs in the coal industry, we have yet to see the influx. So our community and school have come together; we have rolled up our sleeves and started to brainstorm ways we can help our youth. We believe that vibrant schools help make a vibrant community and vice versa. —Ryan Scott, former principal, Morganfield Elementary School, Kentucky

Who Are the Poor?

In 2017, one in eight people in the United States, or about forty million people, were classified as poor, and nearly half of those people (18.5 million) lived in deep poverty (also known as extreme poverty; Alston, 2017). *Deep poverty* is defined as a household with total cash income below 50 percent of the poverty threshold, or living on less than two dollars a day per person (Alston, 2017; Center for Poverty Research, 2018). Deep poverty tends to be a chronic condition that persists generationally. People who live in deep poverty lack access to the basic human services of sanitation, shelter, education, and health care. They cannot find work, they have reached their five-year limit on federal assistance programs, they do not qualify for any other programs, and they may live in remote areas, disconnected from safety nets and job markets. All this tragedy exists in one of the wealthiest countries in the world (Alston, 2017; Deaton, 2018; Nadasen, 2017).

Three groups make up much of the poor in the United States.

1. **Women, children, and minorities:** Disproportionately, families in poverty are single parents or guardians (mostly women) with children (Hoynes, Page, & Stevens, 2006). The poor are also disproportionately minority, meaning that greater percentages of minority populations are poor, though whites are the numerical majority of the poor in the United States. One of the hardest-hit minority populations is that of Native Americans; Indigenous peoples living on reservations have a staggering 39 percent poverty rate. Widespread deep poverty exists in nearly all

indigenous communities and reservations in the United States. Destitute conditions, poor health, and shockingly high suicide rates make the United States' indigenous communities akin to the poorest regions of the world (Alston, 2017; Green & Waldman, 2018). Immigrants, whether authorized or not, are overwhelmingly poor, as are their children, with immigrant poverty rates typically twice those of native-born residents. Perhaps the most devastating poverty statistics are those for children. The United States now has the highest child poverty rate in the developed world, with thirteen million children living in poverty (Nadasen, 2017). In the United States, babies have a 42 percent chance of being born into poverty, and over half of all children and youth attending public schools in the United States live in poverty (ASCD, 2015; National Center for Children in Poverty, 2017). Overwhelmingly, children who live in *persistent poverty*, defined as spending half or more of their childhood in poverty, are likely to remain persistently poor as adults (Ratcliffe & Kalish, 2017).

2. **The hidden suburban poor:** The poor live in every type of neighborhood and community, but medium-sized suburban communities are seeing the greatest increase in poverty—places like Vancouver, Washington; Bend, Oregon; Columbus, Ohio; and Boise, Idaho. In the Boise School District, the number of Title I schools has grown from two in 1990 to sixteen in 2015. The poverty rate in a Vancouver, Washington, school district's thirteen Title I schools skyrocketed from 25 percent to 53 percent in twenty years (Broader, Bolder Approach, n.d.). These communities represent *pockets of poverty*, concentrated areas that have a poverty rate of 40 percent to 80 percent. But poverty in these localized communities is often hidden away such that more affluent people are unaware of the staggering numbers or the plight of the poor living in their midst (Sauter, Stebbins, & Frohlich, 2017). In communities across the United States, thousands of elementary schools have poverty levels over 90 percent.

3. **The poorly or minimally educated:** Education is a strong predictor of poverty status, such that the lower a person's education level, the more likely that person is to live in poverty (Hoynes et al., 2006). In fact, education is the primary factor in determining whether a person lives in poverty or achieves a middle-class—or better—life in the United States. Receiving poor or minimal education is a characteristic of poverty in the United States.

What Are the Challenges of Poverty?

Regardless of their gender, their ethnicity, where they live, or their education level, people living in poverty face a nearly impossible set of challenges in meeting life's basic necessities, securing stable housing, solving health care needs, finding jobs that pay above-subsistence wages, and accessing a good education for their children. In this section, we attempt to describe the realities of the challenges faced by the poor in the United States. We will discuss the insecure or fragile housing and homelessness, inadequate health care, jobs at sub-living wages, and low-quality schools that those in poverty experience on a daily basis.

Insecure or Fragile Housing and Homelessness

Local communities and school districts have great numbers of families struggling to find adequate, stable housing. For every hundred extremely low-income families seeking housing, only thirty-seven rental units exist, representing a 60 percent decrease in available housing since 2010 (GAP Report, 2017).

As poverty rates in local communities increase, family mobility increases as families unable to pay their rents are forced to move and search for places to live again and again. Some classrooms in high-poverty schools across the United States experience a 100 percent student-turnover rate from September to June due to family housing turnover (National Low Income Housing Coalition, 2019; Sarkar, Barnes, & Noffke, 2018). And, increases in a school's student mobility and absenteeism rates strongly correlate with decreases in student achievement—it is difficult to help students learn when they are not consistently in school (see chapter 2 in National Research Council and Institute of Medicine, 2010; Smith, Fien, & Paine, 2008; Sparks, 2016b).

Field Note

When one of our teachers passed a beat-up old station wagon parked on an industrial cul-de-sac near our school for several days, she finally stopped to see what was going on. What she found was a teenager who had dropped out of school living in the car with a terminally ill mother. They were totally abandoned and without hope. They had no place to go, no one to help. And they were broke and hungry. It only took us about three phone calls, and we had the mother in a hospital and the son in temporary housing and enrolled in our little alternative school. It was a heartbreaking situation, but we were able to make a real difference in their lives. —Principal, Tulsa, Oklahoma

Inadequate Health Care

The United States is one of the world's wealthiest countries, yet health care expenditures per capita are double the average in other developed nations (Alston, 2017). Despite this spending, the United States' infant mortality rate (6.1 per 1,000 births in 2010) is the highest among developed nations, and Americans on average live shorter lives than people in other wealthy democracies (Economist, 2019;

MacDorman, Mathews, Mohangoo, & Zeitlin, 2014). This health gap continues to grow between the United States and other comparable countries (Alston, 2017; Sarkar et al., 2018).

Field Note

> Healthy food is often difficult to access for those living in *food deserts*, defined as places that lack a real grocery store. Many poor neighborhoods have only convenience stores, which rarely sell fruits or vegetables, and the transportation costs to get to a grocery store may be insurmountable. Prepackaged, shelf-stable foods that require minimal preparation or microwave preparation are lower in nutrition, higher in sugar and salt, and usually the only available food for poor children who feed themselves while adults are working two or three minimum-wage jobs. —Emily Gibson

Jobs at Sub-Living Wages

Counter to the myth that the poor are jobless, 70 percent of children living in poverty have parents, guardians, or caregivers who are employed during the year (Child Trends Databank, 2018; Korball & Jian, 2018; National Center for Children in Poverty, 2017). Wage stagnation and the disappearance of middle-income jobs are important factors in the poverty epidemic. Remarkably, a mother or father working a full-time, minimum-wage, year-round job is below the poverty threshold for a family of three, and often has to rely on food stamps to get by (Nadasen, 2017).

Low-Quality Schools

For families raising children in low-income communities, accessing high-quality public schools is a challenge. Public schools located in high-poverty areas are typically the least financially supported schools in a community and often face a shortage of qualified staff (Camera, 2018).

In many school districts that serve the largest populations of poor students, per-pupil funding is about one thousand dollars less in state and local funding when compared to low-poverty schools. This results in fewer resources that can be leveraged for student learning, such as high-quality teachers, diverse and motivating course offerings, early education programs, and nonacademic staff such as counselors and specialists (Camera, 2018). This funding gap would be bad enough if the student populations were equivalent, but when you also consider that students in high poverty schools have greater needs for supports and resources, it becomes clear that when high-poverty schools receive less funding, it serves to solidify the wealth gap by sentencing students to inadequate public education (Morgan & Amerikaner, 2018). Some states are working to erase these inequities, such as Utah, where high-poverty schools actually receive 21 percent more per pupil than low-poverty schools (Morgan

& Amerikaner, 2018). However, the per-pupil funding gap remains a serious barrier to accessing the education needed to break free from poverty.

K–12 public schools are the second-largest national infrastructure sector, topped only by highways (Litvinov, 2019). Yet school facilities have no dedicated federal funding, and local funding sources must cover 80 percent of school construction costs. As a result, schools in lower-income communities are more likely to go without needed construction and repairs. Educators and students in communities of poverty that lack sufficient local funding are frequently left to study and work in deteriorating school buildings with inconsistent heat, leaky roofs, moldy ceiling tiles, asbestos, radon, aging pipes, or water fountains with lead, among other things (Litvinov, 2019).

The housing, health care, income, and education challenges faced by families living in poverty affect not only schools but also the larger society. They all contribute to a dramatic splitting of the U.S. population into those with education and those without, those with money and those without, those with hope and those without.

Despite all the United States' past efforts as a nation to eliminate poverty—including the safety net programs of Roosevelt's New Deal, and Johnson's War on Poverty—why does poverty continue so persistently? In the next section, we posit some explanations.

What Are the Reasons for the Continuing Poverty Epidemic?

Despite robust growth in the U.S. economy since the 1990s, U.S. poverty rates have changed very little over that time. What is the source of all this poverty? Primarily, stagnant wage growth and ever-growing income inequality are at the root of persistent poverty. As wage growth stalled in the 1980s, and workers benefited less and less from their increased productivity, the level of income inequality—or the divide between the haves and have-nots—increased. Like a slippery slope, the more wealth that is accumulated in the hands of the few, the less wealth is obtained by the hands of the many (Hoynes et al., 2006; Mishel, Gould, & Bivens, 2015).

In this section, we discuss six major factors that perpetuate poverty: stagnant wage growth; income inequality; the lack of good-wage, low-skill jobs for those with little to no education; society's shifting social safety net; inequities in access to quality education; and the broken criminal justice system.

❝❞ Wage stagnation for the vast majority was not created by abstract economic trends. Rather, wages were suppressed by policy choices made on behalf of those with the most income, wealth, and power. In the past few decades, the American economy generated lots of income and wealth that would have allowed substantial living standards gains for every family.

—Lawrence Mishel, Elise Gould, and Josh Bivens

Stagnant Wage Growth

A lack of wage growth is a key factor in the widening income inequality in the United States. Across all measures, low-wage and middle-wage earners make the same as or less than they made in the late 1970s (DeSilver, 2018; Mishel et al., 2015). The federal minimum wage has stagnated at $7.25 per hour since 2009, though in 2020 would have been $15.00–$20.00 per hour if it had kept pace with inflation (Mishel et al., 2015).

From 2018 to 2019, states, cities, and even some corporations made real gains by enacting living-wage policies, but the battle is far from over. Despite rising wages in some states, cities, and corporations, people in much of the United States work for wages far below the subsistence level, with more and more families living paycheck to paycheck (Bach, 2019; Mui, 2016). Costs of basic needs—food, housing, health care, and fuel—have risen, and rents have gone up faster than incomes in nearly every urban area. Almost half of all families report being unable to pay an unexpected bill of four hundred dollars, such as for obtaining an auto repair, receiving health care, or flying out of state to attend a funeral (DeSilver, 2018; Fight for $15, n.d.; Lieb, 2018; Mishel et al., 2015; Mui, 2016; Sarkar et al., 2018). Millions of working Americans are only one missed paycheck away from poverty (Bach, 2019; Mui, 2016).

Field Note

One of our families loaded up their twenty-year-old automobile and drove down to Oklahoma to attend a grandmother's funeral. They were to be gone only a long weekend. Unfortunately, their car broke down somewhere along the way, and it was three months before they were able to repair the car and get back home to Wyoming. —Principal, Lander, Wyoming

Income Inequality

Income inequality has largely contributed to increased poverty rates. Today, there are two Americas, separate and unequal, one existing alongside the other. The rich keep getting richer, and the poor keep getting poorer. More and more wealth has accumulated at the very top of the economic pyramid. The very rich are now billionaires rather than millionaires, and researchers describe our government not as a democracy but as an oligarchy, where the wealthy elite, rather than the vast citizenry, control governmental decisions (Gilens & Page, 2014).

Those living in poverty have fewer and fewer opportunities to break out of poverty and obtain middle-class status. And while most Americans still believe that all citizens should have equal opportunity to improve their lives, it is all but impossible for millions of Americans to rise above the poverty level (Azerrad, 2016; Hoynes et al., 2006). The deck is stacked against them. The great income inequality in the United States continues to maintain the status quo of the haves and have-nots, and sentence families to poverty.

In addition to stagnant wage growth and income inequality, four factors further contribute to the overwhelming growth of poverty, especially among children: (1) inadequate jobs for blue-collar workers with little to no education, (2) a shifting social safety net, (3) inequities in access to quality education, and (4) a broken criminal justice system.

> **66 99** Americans love the myth of [class mobility] despite evidence that it is widely exaggerated. The United States has less class mobility than many European nations, but Americans think that we enjoy more. In the United States, the quickest and easiest way to make it to the 1 percent of wealth holders and remain in that world is to be born into it.

> —Helaine Olen

Inadequate Good-Wage, Low-Skill Jobs for Blue-Collar Workers With Little to No Education

The world of work has undergone dramatic transformation. Technology has swept across the world of work, eliminating many good-paying, low-skill or low-education jobs while also increasing the skill set necessary to get a job with a good salary and benefits. For example, jobs in automotive manufacturing that paid family-living wages have been replaced by a skilled technology worker who programs and services the robots that now do the manufacturing (Dautovic, 2019). By some estimates, up to 70 percent of the available living-wage jobs in the U.S. economy—jobs that can adequately provide for a family's needs—require education beyond high school, and 40 percent of all new living-wage jobs require an associate's degree (Carnevale, Smith, & Strohl, 2013). Even as unemployment rates have decreased to a new low from 2017 to 2019, most of the growth represents low-skill and low-wage positions (Brown, 2019) with low benefits, little opportunity for advancement, and inconsistent schedules that make life impossible for families with kids.

U.S. suburbs are populated with blue-collar workers who once used their muscles and sweat to make a living, with little advanced education or vocational training required. Thus, the loss of low-skill jobs is raising poverty in many of these suburban areas. Automation and new technologies such as driverless cars, 3-D printers, and robot-staffed factories and warehouses will continue to reduce the demand for low-skilled labor. Due to this rising joblessness, "the U.S. poverty population is becoming a more deprived and destitute class, one that's disconnected from the economy and unable to meet basic needs" (Varner, Mattingly, & Grusky, 2017, p. 4).

Families living in our poorest communities—those left behind as corporations have shuttered factories, shut down coal mines, closed fisheries, and sent lumber mills overseas—may find it difficult to change with the times (Lopez, 2018b). The social and economic changes in the workplace have erased old ways of getting by and left families without feasible ways to support themselves or the financial ability to relocate. Through these changes, some families come to believe that no matter how hard they try or how hard they work, their life does not seem to improve. They learn helplessness and hopelessness. Inevitably, many simply give up and stop trying, accepting their life in poverty as an unchanging future.

Field Note

After twenty years, just like that, my GM plant has shut down [in 2018]. I don't have a plan B. I bought a home ten years ago, and it's worth nothing now. Who would want to move here? How am I going to find another job around here? Everyone worked for GM. —General Motors worker, Ohio

A Shifting Social Safety Net

The concept of a *social safety net* designed to support the unemployed, the poor, the aged, and the people unable to work first appeared as federal policy during the Great Depression of the 1930s, when millions of Americans were suddenly out of work and confronted with poverty and destitution. Then in 1964, President Johnson's War on Poverty legislation launched programs and policies to quickly connect people with jobs and career paths. At the time, the country's industrial, production-based economy required unskilled labor. The United States needed people who could work hard with their hands and muscles. Thus, the programs could quickly and realistically place individuals into jobs and consequently prevent poverty. The social safety net helped people temporarily struggling due to job loss or illness, gave the elderly more financial support, and provided people access to disability and medical coverage. In the decades since the War on Poverty began, despite worsening income inequality and increased unemployment, the United States substantially reduced poverty, thanks to the social safety net (Edelman, 2014).

While poverty declined as a result of Johnson's War on Poverty, that progress stagnated in the 1980s, when industrial jobs started to disappear as companies downsized, moved to other countries for cheaper labor, were reduced due to improved environmental regulations, or transitioned to robots. For example, during the 1990s in the Los Angeles area, General Motors, Hughes Aircraft Company, Litton Industries, Northrop Grumman, Rocketdyne, Lockheed Martin, and Price Pfister all scaled back or closed, leaving thousands of families unemployed or underemployed (Lopez, 2018b). Workers who had made twelve dollars or more an hour were suddenly scrabbling to find jobs earning a minimum wage and struggling to hold on to their homes. Many of the poorest towns and neighborhoods in the greater Los Angeles area continue to struggle decades later, as the housing costs have continued to rise while job opportunities that would enable workers to support their families have not materialized (Lopez, 2018b).

Over time, as the political climate in the United States has shifted, the safety net concept has given way, with fewer and fewer programs supporting the working poor. Today's poor—working families, immigrant families, single parents, and the homeless—are often demonized and even criminalized. This fragile safety net continues to be a factor as poverty, especially childhood poverty, grows (Sarkar et al., 2018).

Field Note

After the insurance company where I worked downsized me out the door in 2016, I spent three years without finding a single full-time job. All that was available were jobs as "temps" that paid the minimum-wage rate and of course offered no benefits. One major retailer offered me a job as a "temporary temp," which meant that I had no established hours but was on call. After a year of that, I had hopes of moving up to a permanent temp job with an established schedule. Then sometime later, I might qualify for a full-time job at a salary above minimum wage. After three years of this struggle, I had used up all of my savings and was desperate. I finally packed up and started looking for jobs out of state.
—Unemployed worker, Des Moines, Iowa

Inequities in Access to Quality Education

The perpetuity of poverty is compounded by ongoing inequities in access to high-quality education due to segregation and school funding. Schools in the United States are segregated along socioeconomic lines as well as racial lines, and often, these two lines align; many of the poorest schools also have a majority of students from ethnic or racial minorities. As discussed in an earlier section, school districts with high-minority, high-poverty student populations often receive less funding for student services and less funding for school facilities, which impacts student access to quality instruction in safe, well-maintained buildings (Camera, 2018; Morgan & Amerikaner, 2018). Thus, the issues of school funding further enhance the effects of segregation:

> For most public school systems in America, the majority of funding is based upon the collection of local property taxes, so the ability of a child to receive a high-quality, whole child education often depends upon [a] zip code [or neighborhood]. (ASCD, 2015, p. 10)

As a result, public schools located in high-poverty areas are typically the least financially supported schools within a community, and teachers in these high-poverty schools face greater challenges in working with students impacted by poverty. Many high-poverty schools often struggle to fill posted job opportunities with qualified applicants. This means the students who need the most support end up having the fewest resources, and the schools with the least funding end up being unable to recruit and retain quality staff or to maintain and repair buildings (ASCD, 2015; Suitts, 2013). Inequities in access to quality education continue to be an important factor of generational poverty in the United States, especially given the crucial role education plays in helping students break out of poverty.

A Broken Criminal Justice System

Since the 1970s, the enormous increase in incarcerations in the United States has been intertwined with poverty, the war on drugs, racial justice, and inequities in the criminal justice system (Alston, 2017; Sentencing Project, 2018). The U.S. criminal justice system, the largest in the world, has, over time, evolved into one that disproportionately impacts poor and minority populations (Sentencing Project, 2018).

An overwhelming 95 percent of growth in the incarcerated population since 2000 is due to an increase in nonconvicted defendants who cannot make bail and thus must wait for trial *in* jail (Sarkar et al., 2018). When a defendant spends pretrial time in jail in lieu of making bail, the costs and responsibilities of life continue:

> Jobs are lost, rent and car payments are not made, and parents cannot care for their children or keep the lights on in the home. Sometimes this can result in loss of custody of children. Pretrial incarceration can lead to a loss of access to public benefits, including Social Security and Medicaid. (Sarkar et al., 2018, p. 67)

An inability to make bail sinks poor defendants and their families into deeper and deeper poverty, regardless of guilt or innocence (Alston, 2017).

Additionally, the criminal justice system seeks to profit off these predominantly poor and minority inmates. The United States has more people in prison than any other country in the world, and prison costs have mushroomed to ten times greater than the costs in 1976 (Sarkar et al., 2018; Sentencing Project, 2018). Prison management, in an age of privatizing correctional institutions, is a huge growth industry in the United States. As more and more prisons become privatized, more and more owners profit from the hardship of others, and the existence of those profits translate into ever-increasing prison populations.

An often-quoted figure related to our huge prison population is that, sadly, 80 percent of people in prison are school dropouts and 75 percent are illiterate (Lynch, 2014; Sainato, 2017). This speaks to the critical importance of education, and how failure in school is often linked to continued failure into adulthood. Knowing that access to quality education is impeded in many high-poverty, high-minority schools, the disproportionate percentage of poor and minority populations in jails and prisons begins to seem like the only logical outcome. This is the *school-to-prison pipeline* (Elias, 2013; Saady, 2018).

The United States' burden of poverty is enormous, especially for those living in our poorest communities and those trying to help. Perhaps the heaviest burden of poverty rests on children who grow up knowing no other life than a life of want. In the final section of this chapter, we consider some possible actions that we, as educators, administrators, community members, and educational stakeholders, can take to start turning the tide against poverty for the sake of students and their families.

The Role of Hope in Ending Poverty

The scourge of poverty may seem insurmountable, given the weight of statistics and history. The deck appears to be truly stacked against anyone born into poverty in the United States. However, hope can be found in what we, as educators, are able to do in our schools, and there are solutions that can be implemented to eliminate the stacked deck of poverty. Enacting these solutions will require great political will from people of all walks of life, redirection of monies, and the efforts of many.

The Children's Defense Fund's (2015) report *Ending Child Poverty Now* presents a groundbreaking proposal for ending poverty. In this report, a nine-point plan (see figure 1.1) shows how, by reinforcing, strengthening, and building on existing policies and programs, the United States can reduce the number of children living in poverty by 60 percent (6.6 million children), bringing its child poverty rate of over 20 percent more in line with that of other developed nations like Switzerland and Germany, both at 9.4 percent (Children's Defense Fund, 2015). Many of the factors of child poverty are reduced with this plan, either directly or indirectly: housing security (housing vouchers), adequate food (SNAP benefits), living wages (through increased minimum wage and subsidized jobs), and increased income (through tax credits and childcare credits). Additionally, some of the effects of poverty are expected to lessen as families have more income (increased access to health care and decreased involvement in criminal justice system, for example). Ensuring a strong social safety net will greatly help people who are suffering from unemployment or health crises and support those who desire education to improve their employment prospects (Allard, 2018).

While we may not all agree on the role of budget increases to solve all the problems that schools face, it is important to note that research on increased funding for families living in poverty shows that it does, in fact, seem to make considerable positive differences, including reduced family stress (which reduces household trauma),

1.   Increase housing voucher program so all eligible families (below 150 percent of fed-eral poverty rate and not already receiving housing assistance) can have adequate housing. This reduces child poverty by 20.8 percent.

2.   Increase each eligible family's Supplemental Nutrition Assistance Program (SNAP) benefits by 30 percent so all children have food security. This reduces child poverty by 16 percent.

3.   Make the Child Tax Credit fully refundable so that the lowest income families are able to receive the entire $2,000 refund per child. This increases incentive to work, and benefits poorest families the most. This reduces child poverty by 12 percent.

4.   Increase the availability of publicly funded (or subsidized) jobs for teens and adults in families with children, so all who work have adequate funds for living. These govern-ment funds increase wages provided by employers, or pay workers while they receive job training. This reduces child poverty by 11 percent.

5.   Increase the value of the earned income tax credit, which would increase the amount families receive, and increase the number of eligible families. This reduces child pov-erty by 9 percent.

6.   Raise the minimum wage to $10.10 or higher so more workers have a living wage. While the inflation-adjusted minimum wage should be around $18, lifting the wage to $10.10 (in 2015) would reduce child poverty by 4 percent.

7.   Expand access of childcare subsidies to families earning up to 150 percent of the poverty level. This helps ensure the working poor have adequate, safe childcare and reduces child poverty by 3 percent.

8.   Make the child and dependent care tax credit fully refundable for all families, regard-less of income, and increase its value so the lowest-income families benefit more. This reduces child poverty by 1 percent.

9.   Require a full pass-through and disregard of child support for families that receive Temporary Assistance for Needy Families (TANF) so families are not penalized for child support. This reduces child poverty by less than 1 percent.

Source: Adapted from Children's Defense Fund, 2015.

Figure 1.1: The Children's Defense Fund's nine-point plan.

increased health, and improved attendance (see the following Field Note). It also makes the most economic sense in the long term, as child poverty has huge economic costs for the United States:

> Year after year the lost productivity and extra health and criminal justice costs associated with [poverty] add up to roughly half a trillion dollars, or 3.8 percent of our nation's gross domestic product. What we can never measure though are the countless innovations and discoveries and contributions that did not occur for our nation because children's potentials were stunted by poverty. (Edelman, 2014)

In truth, allowing poverty to continue at current levels costs far, far more than it would cost to eliminate poverty (Blow, 2015). A 60 percent reduction of child poverty could be achieved immediately by implementing the nine-point plan outline above, at a cost of $77.2 billion, or 2 percent of the national budget (Children's Defense Fund, 2015). However, continuing to keep 14.7 million children in poverty costs the United States an estimated $500 billion each year in lost productivity, health costs, and criminal justice costs attributed to adults who grew up in poverty (Children's Defense Fund, 2015). Reducing child poverty would be a net savings of over $400 billion!

Field Note

A comprehensive review and analysis of twenty different studies that examined the outcomes of various social safety net programs considered the effects of increased family income (through food stamps, health insurance, tax benefits, and other safety net programs) on students' success in school (Barnum, 2018). In this review, the author found that increased income for low-income families was directly associated with increased student achievement, higher graduation rates in high school, and increased likelihood of college enrollment (Barnum, 2018). Remarkably, the increases in family income in these studies were small—as little as three thousand dollars annually—or applied only to existing state and federal programs. This meta-analysis concludes that social safety net programs work, helping families and helping students succeed in school (Barnum, 2018).

If Americans truly believe in the hope of upward mobility—in the hope of a better life through effort and sacrifice—then political solutions to poverty will eventually come to pass. However, those of us who work in schools need not wait for these solutions. In fact, we can't wait, because our students today depend on our efforts. We believe that it is possible to build a better nation, with all of our efforts in our schools and communities. This is our greatest hope.

<blockquote>
" " Growing up poor adversely affects children's health, as well as their intellectual and social development. It lowers earnings in adulthood, and reduces future tax revenues for the government while increasing government social spending. The annual cost of child poverty comes to around $1 trillion, but every dollar spent in reducing child poverty is estimated to yield $7 in the future. This exceeds the return on most private investments.

—Steven Pressman
</blockquote>

Conclusion

We currently live in an America where many children and adults can die of hunger or from a lack of health care—where they live their lives in deprivation amid great economic wealth. At this time, our schools and communities are the first responders to the scourge of poverty. While poverty is a massive and complex issue and surely demands responses from the government at all levels, the state of education research and practice in the United States provides a detailed understanding of how we can effectively teach all students, especially those of poverty. Schools can do much to prepare students for lives beyond poverty. They can become resilient schools where students impacted by poverty can learn the academic, social-emotional, and executive function skills needed to access a better life. In U.S. classrooms, there is hope for a life beyond poverty.

Before exploring these solutions in part two (page 69), we find it helpful, if not critical, to understand the impacts of poverty on teaching and on learning. This helps us, as educators and administrators, to work for proactive and preventative actions, rather than reactive. The next chapter examines several negative byproducts of poverty for students, including absenteeism, adverse childhood experiences, and learned helplessness.

Next Steps

Please complete the following Next Steps, to integrate your experiences within your own schools and communities with the information presented in this chapter.

1. In your community, what are some of the largest contributors to poverty, and what is the historical background for each of these contributors? (For example, did a factory close down or an industry die off? Is there a Native American reservation nearby? Is it a rural area with reduced resources and services?)

2. Where have all the jobs in your community gone? Are they coming back, or are new job sectors coming in?

3. Estimate how many students in your classroom, school, or district are impacted by different factors of poverty (low wages, lack of good paying jobs, housing, health care, criminal justice system, inadequate access to education or training for adults, and so on).

4. How many families in your classroom, school, or district would benefit from each item in the nine-point plan? Would voters in your community support the nine-point plan?

5. What are two to four of your biggest ah-has or takeaways from this chapter, framing the reality of poverty in the United States? What did you already know? What surprised you?

Chapter 2

An Invisible Barrier: The Impacts of Poverty on Teaching and Learning

Not everything that is faced can be changed, but nothing can be changed until it is faced.

—James Baldwin

Although poverty affects millions of different people from many different circumstances, it tends to manifest itself in predictable ways in the classroom. Thus, it is imperative that educators, in particular, have a thorough understanding of the impacts of poverty within the classroom itself, so they are able to counter these impacts, act proactively instead of reactively, and provide understanding, compassion, and hope for the future to children and their families.

As mentioned in the introduction (page 1), students living in poverty first became the majority of students attending U.S. public schools in 2013, and that status has maintained since then (ASCD, 2015; Suitts, 2015). The growing number of students who live in poverty poses a great challenge for public education. In many communities, often called *pockets of poverty*, the number of poor students attending public schools has increased until the needs of these students and their families have all but overwhelmed classrooms, schools, and community services.

Students living in poverty face a wide range of barriers to learning, growth, and development; hunger, mental stress, inadequate housing, limited health care, and trauma are just a few real challenges, or *corrosive cruelties*, of poverty that students and staff experience daily (Blow, 2015). These challenges disrupt students' learning and impact achievement for all. As described in the previous chapter (page 11), the antidote to all this struggle and strife is complex, involving government agencies at all levels as well as new and dramatic responses from schools (these responses are discussed in more detail in part two, page 69). All these actions focus on addressing families' human needs to help them find stability and resilience (Blow, 2015; National Education Association, 2016).

This chapter's examination of poverty and trauma's negative impacts on learning is not intended to overplay or dramatize the fact that many students living in economically impoverished, violent, or deteriorating communities exhibit resilience and are able to flourish in their lives. These students have assets, characteristics, and adults in their lives that help them have resilience, even in the face of great challenges. Later chapters cover in full how to support the development and maintenance of student resilience (see part two, page 69). The purpose of this chapter is to delve into some specific challenges that students of poverty experience in our schools and classrooms to better understand the impact poverty wields in our schools. We will discuss:

- Students' lack of academic preparation for school
- Absenteeism, illness, and interrupted learning
- Learning loss over summers and holidays
- Adverse childhood experiences and behavior challenges
- Learned helplessness

Finally, we will discuss the "quicksand" of poverty and how easily, without interventions, all these factors can build on each other and keep students trapped in the cycle of poverty. It is here that we explain the hope of education, the hope of educators, to be able to change students' life trajectories and offer students a rope to pull on as they climb out of poverty.

Lack of Academic Preparation

Many students living in poverty arrive at school far behind academically—up to four months behind peers from more affluent families—with limited academic vocabularies and little or no reading readiness or school readiness (Cohen, 2003; Mader, 2017). Less than half (48 percent) of children living in poverty are ready for school at age five, compared to 75 percent of children living in moderate- to high-income households. Preschool attendance, parenting behaviors, parental education, maternal mental health, prenatal exposure to tobacco, and low birth weight also contribute to school readiness (Isaacs, 2012). Despite increasing efforts at preschool interventions since the late 1990s, low-income children continue to enter school behind more affluent peers (Mader, 2017). Without intense and continuing intervention, these students will most likely fail to learn effectively and fall even further behind. If students do not learn to read well and quickly, they struggle with their schoolwork and their homework. When they experience difficulties in carrying out school assignments, they often become embarrassed and dread the teacher calling on them. They may not want to go to school, leading their absences to slowly increase. This may in turn make them fall even further behind.

Ultimately, students who do not master reading at an early age have a high probability of dropping out of school (Birdsong, 2016; National Education Association, 2016). Without at least a high school education, these students are likely to stay trapped in poverty—a poverty that will pass to each succeeding generation. The antidote to academic failure is for schools to give students additional learning opportunities and support so they gain lacking skills before they begin to struggle (National Education Association, 2016).

Students living in poverty experience these school difficulties for varied and complex reasons. For example, many low-income families' homes have few of the accepted supports that help students successfully prepare for school. Too often, their homes contain few books, printed materials, and writing and drawing materials. Educators know that surrounding young students with a rich print environment and reading to them on a daily basis is essential for making them reading ready (Logan, Justice, Yumus, & Chaparro-Moreno, 2019). Parents and guardians in impoverished communities may not recognize the importance of reading to their children, they themselves may have literacy issues that make reading difficult at best, or they may speak a language other than English and worry that reading in their primary language will somehow interfere with their child's learning of English. Without the support of early literacy activities, students of poverty may arrive at school far behind their more affluent peers, not only unprepared to learn to read but also far from ready to *learn*.

Unfortunately, the lack of home supports may even cause students to fail to complete homework assignments and arrive the next day or the next week less prepared than other students. Over time, if schools do not develop effective programs for working with families, providing parent or guardian education, and having comprehensive enrichment for struggling students, the gap between poor and affluent students only increases (Barr & Parrett, 2008; Epstein, 2011).

In addition, the documented digital divide between affluent and impoverished families results in students from low-income families arriving at school with far fewer digital skills than their more affluent peers (Barr & Parrett, 2008). Further, studies have documented significant language and vocabulary differences between poor and affluent families in their types of conversations, types of language used, and structure of responses. Affluent families use approximately 2,300 words per hour in their home, while blue-collar families use 1,200 words per hour and low-income families use 600 words per hour (Bracey, 2002; Hart & Risley, 1995). The content of conversations can be strikingly different as well, with children in higher-income families hearing more words of praise (six encouragements for every discouragement) than children in low-income households (two encouragements for every discouragement; Hart & Risley, 1995). If this research accurately reflects family vocabularies, it is little wonder that students living in poverty arrive at school academically challenged, without the background knowledge, vocabulary, schema, or even self-confidence necessary for formal learning (Sprenger, 2013).

Low-income parents and guardians may also have had little or inadequate schooling themselves and may feel uncomfortable or embarrassed when talking with teachers or working with schools. As a result, they may fail to interact or connect with their children's teachers. Many of these parents and guardians may have had negative school experiences and may be very distrusting of schools, which can manifest as reluctance to attend school functions and report card conferences or to support what their children are learning in more traditional ways. In interviews with low-income parents and guardians over the years, we have heard them explain that they are reluctant to meet with teachers because they have nothing acceptable to wear or that they are embarrassed by their lack of English skills. Ultimately, a combination of these factors often makes students of poverty unprepared for reading, academics, and other aspects of schooling or school interactions.

> " In today's knowledge-based economy, moving out of poverty is far more complex. With more competition for unskilled work and a minimum wage that has not kept up with inflation, attaining economic independence requires more education, planning, and interpersonal skills—precisely the areas in which low-income individuals are disadvantaged to begin with.
>
> —Kristina Birdsong

Absenteeism, Illness, and Interrupted Education

As described in chapter 1 (page 11), families in poor neighborhoods inevitably deal with low-wage jobs and unemployment because good-paying jobs for people with little or no education are extremely limited. Available jobs are often part-time, temporary, or both; minimum wage; and without health benefits. Though the adults in poor families are working, they may earn an insufficient income to provide for basic human needs like housing, clothing, and food. As a result, children and youth living in poverty tend to suffer from poor nutrition and a lack of health care, which invariably leads to illnesses that keep them away from school. Even students who do come to school may arrive hungry, sleepy, and inattentive, making learning quite difficult if not impossible.

The conditions of poor families often lead to high absence rates in high-poverty schools. Poverty-level students tend to miss many more days of school than more affluent peers (U.S. Department of Education, 2019). In many districts, a large number of students may suffer from chronic absence issues, often missing as many as twenty to thirty days each school year. Because students who are behind academically must have additional instructional time in order to catch up, missing as much as a month of instruction a year can have a disastrous effect on students' academic progress.

Having many students with alarming absenteeism rates has motivated a growing number of schools and districts to mount a wide variety of programs so they can help these students attend school more regularly. These efforts include everything from providing families with alarm clocks and bicycles to holding classroom attendance competitions. Schools and districts have also begun to make more ambitious efforts to address families' fundamental needs. They have established community outreach programs with food banks, clothing closets, health checkups, and extensive parent-education programs. All these services focus on students' staying in school, attending school regularly, and learning successfully.

Field Note

As part of a full-court press to increase attendance at a high-poverty elementary school, teachers designed a "High-Five for Attendance" button using the school's mascot. Each week, on Friday, any students who had been at school every day of the week wore the pin. They gleefully approached every adult on campus to get their high-five for attendance. While it may not have increased attendance for chronically absent students, it did celebrate attendance and gave needed recognition and attention to those who were making improvements!
—Emily Gibson

A problem related to absences is family mobility and homelessness. Unfortunately, with escalating housing costs in most areas of the United States, along with shortages of affordable housing, more and more families find themselves unable to pay their monthly rent and are forced to move again and again, double or triple up in a house with other families, or fall into homelessness (GAP Report, 2017; Janosko, 2019; National Alliance to End Homelessness, 2018). As the families repeatedly change residences, their children find themselves moving from school to school, having their education constantly disrupted. Mobility negatively affects academics and social relationships—students lose an average of three months of mathematics and reading instruction each time they move (National Research Council and Institute of Medicine, 2010; Smith et al., 2008; Sparks, 2016b). By the time students have changed schools three times, some start distancing themselves from academics and social activities since they know that soon they and their family will be on the move again (Rumberger, 2015). And the negative academic outcomes of mobility are not simply isolated to the students who are changing schools. A study in Chicago public schools found that students who moved four times by sixth grade were a year behind peers academically, and that nonmobile students who lived in schools disrupted by high mobility were, in fifth grade, a year behind peers in non-mobility impacted schools (Sparks, 2016b).

Homelessness is a major issue for families and for teenagers who are without family support. With too few low-income housing opportunities and homeless shelters with long waiting lists, both families and teenagers must rely on the kindness of friends for lodging or else move out onto the streets. This serves to increase their mobility. An estimated sixty thousand families, and as many as forty-one thousand unaccompanied minors, are homeless on any given night in the United States (National Alliance to End Homelessness, 2018; National Conference of State Legislatures, 2019). Homelessness has a negative impact on student learning. Students who have been homeless are more likely to have higher mobility rates even after their families are no longer homeless (Sparks, 2016b). According to the Department of Education, students experiencing homelessness and housing insecurity often have significantly lagging academic, social, and socio-emotional skills. Students who experience homelessness and high mobility are more likely to have lower academic achievement and increased risk of leaving school before graduation (U.S. Department of Education, 2016; for greater details on academic consequences of homelessness, see Firth, 2014).

More and more schools are facing the great challenge to help families find affordable housing and remain within one school's attendance zone. Increasingly, schools in high-poverty areas are attempting to coordinate with local housing authorities, churches, and nonprofits to better address the housing needs of their students and their families.

Learning Loss Over School Breaks

For some time, researchers and scholars have agreed that students living in poverty experience serious learning loss during the summer months (Kuhfeld, 2018b; Quinn & Polikoff, 2017; Weiss & Reville, 2019). Summer learning loss along socioeconomic lines can be described as a faucet of resources that gets turned down to a trickle for low-income students (Entwisle, Alexander, & Olson, 2000). During the school year, all students benefit from the school's resource faucet, but during the summer, this resource faucet largely turns off for all students. For students with financial and parental resource streams at home, their learning continues to be reinforced during school vacations. But students living in poverty or low-income homes often have smaller or nonexistent resource streams at home, and their access to brain-building activities and experiences during vacations can be minimal. Students of poverty spend much of their summers doing activities that are passive or not particularly mentally stimulating: watching TV, playing video games, or taking care of siblings inside the house while family adults are at work. More resourced students may spend their summers reading, going to the library, visiting parks or zoos, playing intellectually demanding computer games, going on family vacations, attending summer camps, and generally experiencing a wide variety of stimulating and engaging activities that help maintain their academic levels.

" " America doesn't have a school problem. It has a summer vacation problem.

—Malcolm Gladwell

Many students, including those who live in poverty, often return to school after summer break with a serious loss of the prior year's academic gains, which causes teachers to need to review and reteach the previous year's content and skills for the first month or two (Bracey, 2002; Kuhfeld, 2018a; Quinn & Polikoff, 2017). As a result of research on learning loss, more and more schools and districts are providing summer- and school-break enrichment for students. However, intensive, school-based summer programs do not often live up to the expectations or promise of boosting achievement, due to their costs and the difficulty of attracting students and skilled staff. Instead, schools are working with public libraries, local colleges and universities, and even health providers to sponsor successful enrichment activities that help students maintain their academic achievements. Programs that blend academic activities with recreational, hands-on, or exploratory activities, such as a STEAM camp or an arts academy, are ideal, because they tap into students' enthusiasm and engagement. Research indicates that maintaining learning gains over breaks from school does not need to be complicated or expensive; it just needs to be consistent and well thought out, such as the READS for Summer Learning program. READS sends eight books to students over the summer, with pre- and post-reading activities to do and a mailer to send back after each book. Research on the READS program shows a positive impact on students' reading comprehension (Quinn & Polikoff, 2017).

Adverse Childhood Experiences and Behavior Challenges

Since the early 2000s, classrooms and schools have increasingly faced challenging problems and behaviors associated with childhood trauma and adverse childhood experiences that threaten an orderly, systematic approach to teaching and learning. Though not all stress is harmful—and, in fact, some stressors are necessary for living—it is important that educators help students learn to cope with stress in healthy, mindful ways. The reality of life in the United States is that many students face significant adversity on a daily basis, which is extremely detrimental to their healthy development as well as the health of our society (Center on the Developing Child, n.d.).

Studies of adverse childhood experiences have made large contributions to the research available on the effects of trauma since the original study emerged in the late 1990s (see, for example, Bellis et al., 2018; Felitti et al., 1998; Hughes et al., 2017). These studies show that a strong connection exists between the number of traumatic experiences a person has before age eighteen and the likelihood that the person will develop risky behaviors or chronic health conditions, have low life potential, have children who are exposed to more ACEs, and die early. Rather than detailing the enormity of this research, we direct readers to ACES Too High (https://acestoohigh. com) and the Centers for Disease Control and Prevention's (n.d.) ACEs webpage (www.cdc.gov/violenceprevention/acestudy/index.html) for more information.

Though no demographic category is immune to ACEs, students living in poverty are more likely to experience high levels of trauma and ACEs than more economically advantaged peers (Brendtro, Brokenleg, & Van Bockern, 2019; Child Trends, 2019; Hughes & Tucker, 2018). In fact, living in poverty is related to, or found alongside of, many traumas listed in the ACEs survey (National Council of Juvenile and Family Court Judges, 2006), like homelessness and incarceration of a parent, as well as adverse experiences not listed in the original study (Felitti et al., 1998), such as living on a reservation, being an immigrant or refugee, or walking to school through streets rife with drugs, gangs, and violence (Hughes & Tucker, 2018). Youth living in poverty are six times more likely to experience significant levels of adversity than high-income peers, with 25 percent of children living in poverty reporting three or more ACEs by adolescence (Center for Promise, 2017; Child Trends, 2019).

Sadly, many young people in low-income communities experience cycles of adversity and trauma that block their social mobility, educational progress, and development. It is important to recognize that minority children are disproportionately poor and that "children of color and children living below the federal poverty line are much more likely to experience myriad adversities in their homes and throughout their communities" (Center for Promise, 2017). Schools with minority and poor populations will likely have far more students with ACEs exposure, along with the accompanying detrimental effects to learning and school culture.

Poverty frequently causes changes in family members' relationships, roles, and routines that greatly affect children and cause them great stress. Breakdowns in these areas—which require children to adjust to changing relationships as different people move in or out of their lives, changing roles for themselves as they must care for younger siblings or ill adults, changing roles for their significant adults, changing schools, and changing routines—can create overwhelming stress for young people (Frankel, 2001).

> **❝ ❞** Damaging levels of stress in childhood may result not only from dramatic or
> traumatic life events like divorce, death or disability but also from a prolonged
> and unrelieved pile-up of minor every-day stressors like conflicts with siblings,
> being teased or bullied, being pressured around school performance or being
> too hurried and overprogrammed. Damaging stress is like an alarm bell going
> off constantly in a child's ears, telling him that there is danger but never telling
> him what to do about it, nor giving him a chance to turn off the alarm.
>
> **—Mark Frankel**

Some threats, fears, and other stressors that children experience can be chronic, occurring day after day, such as walking home from school through a dangerous neighborhood or witnessing domestic violence at home. Other threats can be acute or crisis generated, such as having an accident, experiencing a natural disaster, or witnessing a single violent event (Konnikova, 2016; Patterson & Kelleher, 2005). Chronic adversity is especially debilitating because it repeatedly and cumulatively drains available resources, and it requires adaptation over months and years, which can result in brain structure changes (Konnikova, 2016). Most public-school students who experience trauma, regardless of demographics, are experiencing chronic adversity, rather than acute or crisis types of trauma. The ripple effects of this chronic trauma are evident in classrooms across the United States (Autio, 2019; Patterson & Kelleher, 2005).

Students impacted by trauma and adverse experiences may exhibit a wide range of behaviors that are detrimental to learning and cause difficulties with developing healthy relationships. These students may struggle with self-regulation, which can lead to impulsivity and aggression. They may overreact to events and misinterpret them as threatening or aggressive, or they may refuse to respond to adults in the school through behaving defiantly, acting out, or becoming passive. Some students suffering from trauma may simply withdraw from their surroundings. When triggered by some perceived threat, be it physical, emotional, environmental, or social (the brain does not differentiate among threats and responds the same way to all), people respond with some form of *fight*, *flight*, or *freeze* (Hammond, 2015). Figure 2.1 (page 40) defines what these responses may look like in the classroom.

Traumatized students may be very wary of adults in school and unable to trust them. Forced interaction with the adults and the school expectations may lead to aggression, confrontation, or both. Relationships with other students may also be fraught with conflict and misunderstanding, as a student's impulsivity, aggressive posturing, and negative worldview may lead peers to avoid, withdraw from, or even ostracize the student impacted by trauma.

Fight:
Acting out, behaving aggressively, acting silly, exhibiting defiance, being hyperactive, arguing, screaming or yelling

Flight:
Withdrawing, fleeing the classroom, skipping class, daydreaming, seeming to sleep, avoiding others, hiding or wandering, becoming disengaged

Freeze:
Exhibiting numbness, refusing to answer, refusing to get needs met, giving a blank look, feeling unable to move or act, hiding

Source: Souers, 2016, p. 29.

Figure 2.1: What fight, flight, and freeze look like in the classroom.

When it comes to learning, traumatized students may have trouble understanding the concept of cause-and-effect in their lives and fail to recognize their own ability to affect what happens. They may struggle with academic and social tasks requiring them to take the perspective of another person, and they may have difficulty regulating their emotions. Effective schools work to address these complex trauma-related issues by developing a schoolwide response, often called a *trauma-sensitive* response. You'll gain specific strategies for positively working with students impacted by trauma in chapters 5 (page 95) and 6 (page 121). We also encourage you to read *The Trauma-Sensitive Classroom: Building Resilience With Compassionate Teaching* (Jennings, 2018b) and visit the Trauma and Learning Policy Initiative website (https://traumasensitiveschools.org/about-tlpi) to find a vast trove of free resources and current research on trauma-sensitive schools (Cole et al., 2005).

Learned Helplessness

Of all the negative outcomes, stressors, and traumas associated with poverty, easily the most debilitating is *learned helplessness*, a feeling of despair that can overwhelm families and students (Beaumont, 2009; Jensen, 2009, 2019; Rothstein, 2008; Rotter, 1975). With learned helplessness, families and students come to believe that they have little power to alter their futures and that their lives are governed by external forces completely beyond their control. Psychologists refer to this as experiencing an *external locus of control* (Beaumont, 2009; Rothstein, 2008). Students who arrive at school with a sense of learned helplessness and an external locus of control assume there is little they can do to succeed in school. Too many students living in poverty believe that they cannot learn, and consequently, they do not even try to learn. This feeling of helplessness fosters an attitude of surrender, of simply giving up. It is the antithesis of achievement, leading invariably to failure and defeat (Jensen, 2019).

Field Note

While working with the Longview, Washington, school district in 2019, a middle-school principal shared a story with me that illustrates the power of staff and a community to overcome learned helplessness and an external locus of control. The principal talked about a student, Hank (name changed), who exuded an *I don't care about anything* attitude. He rarely did any work, was disruptive in class, and struggled to come to school every day. He had little support at home and lived in generational poverty. It was increasingly hard for his teachers to find a way to even like this prickly, defensive student. After being escorted out of his English class for the third time in as many days, Hank sat in the principal's office, absently thumbing a regional magazine with a photo of an indoor climbing wall on the cover.

"Hey, have you ever done that?" the principal asked.

"No. But it looks interesting."

The principal pounced on this spark. "Oh? What do you think about it?" he asked.

In the conversation that ensued, Hank revealed that he felt he had never really accomplished anything, and thought he might not ever. The principal set up a plan with Hank: If he went a whole week with zero problems in class, and 100 percent attendance, the principal would take Hank to the local rock-climbing gym for a lesson. By the skin of his teeth, Hank met the goal, and after school on a Friday Hank's parent took him to the gym. The prinicipal described how Hank almost didn't make it to the top of the wall. He stopped once, came down, and got a pep talk from the trainer and the principal: "You can do it. It may not be easy—things worth doing are rarely easy. Don't give up on yourself. Show yourself you can do this!" After some water and a snack, he went back to it, and made it to the top.

By Monday, Hank's teachers and a number of students had seen the photos from his accomplishment, and he received many high-fives that day. But what happened afterward is where the hope lies, because one day doesn't change a lifetime of self-defeating patterns. Hank asked the principal if they could go again. The gym teacher and another of Hank's teachers signed up to be on Hank's team, so he had an adult to meet him there each week he successfully met school expectations. Soon, community members were wondering how they

> could sponsor students at the gym. Firefighters, counselors, and others signed up for shifts, and soon they had ten students participating in the rock-climbing gym motivation program. What started out as a last-gasp incentive to try and get a student to care about school grew into a larger effort of hope for students many had all but given up on . . . students who had given up hope on them-selves. —Emily Gibson

Life in poverty, especially generational poverty, almost inevitably fosters deep-seated feelings of despair and hopelessness as families struggle daily with immediate needs, such as obtaining food for everyone and having warm clothes for the kids during the winter. Even when adults in families of poverty have a job, or obtain a new job, the wage is rarely sufficient to pay for housing and food, let alone provide any extra for emergencies. They may work three jobs and still not scrape together enough dollars to pay rent. The families may then get evicted and struggle with find-ing another place to stay, moving again and again, or living in an old beat-up car that is almost out of gas. They may have to decide whether to put food on the table or pay the electricity bill. They may worry about finding and paying for a doctor for a sick child, or losing a job or being laid off—and these are just some of the struggles that affect families in poverty day in and day out, year after year.

Living with stress and anxiety in simply trying to get through another day or week delivers a debilitating blow to people's optimism. It makes it nearly impossible to believe that life will be better someday, let alone muster the energy to take action. The adults in families living at or below the poverty line may wonder, "Why keep trying?" They may sink into a debilitating emotional depression or turn to alcohol or drugs to escape the unrelenting stress and pressures that they face each day. They may come to believe that nothing they do ever improves their lot in life. They may see little or no possible avenue to a better life for themselves or their kids. Too often, they give up, concluding that forces far beyond their control are dominating them and have doomed them to a life of want. Many are unable to envision any other possibilities or choices.

In *Teaching With Poverty in Mind*, Eric Jensen (2009) describes the deep-seated negative effects of poverty on children in this way:

> *Young children are especially vulnerable to the negative effects of change, dis-ruption, and uncertainty. Developing children need reliable caregivers who offer high predictability, or their brains will typically develop adverse adaptive responses. Chronic socioeconomic deprivation can create environments that undermine the development of self and the capacity for self-determination and self-efficacy. (pp. 8–9)*

Eventually, generation after generation comes to believe that anything positive gained in life is just due to luck or chance.

Field Note

I've heard people joke that the state lotto or lottery is the poor person's retirement plan: "Play the scratchers every day, and someday, you might win and your life will change." When you are trapped in poverty, with no visible way out, it seems that you can't get ahead by working, because work doesn't even pay enough for basic needs. But, hey, if you win the lottery, you're set for life! This is a classic example of an external locus of control. Rather than seeking ways to use one's agency to influence the trajectory of one's life, learned helplessness and an external locus of control keeps people trapped in "waiting for their ship to come in." And without executive function skills needed to make a plan for the future and act on it, winning the lottery may seem like the only way out. —Emily Gibson

Students living in our poorest communities too often absorb this learned helplessness and bring it to school (Hammond, 2015). They may arrive at school with a deep belief that they cannot learn. This learned helplessness stymies the efforts of classroom teachers to reach and teach these students. To combat this helplessness and despair, schools need to address a range of students' social-emotional needs. They must surround students with a Culture of Hope (Barr & Gibson, 2013) by focusing school and classroom culture around the social-emotional assets of optimism, belonging, self-regulation, pride, and purpose. The students of poverty bring a tangle of stress and trauma to school that school staff must address; however, the greatest challenge is to help them overcome that sense of helplessness and come to believe that they can learn and succeed in school and life (National Education Association, 2016). The school must overcome helplessness and bring all its students hope for a better life.

The Role of Executive Function Skills in Ending Poverty

In the United States, poverty can be incredibly *sticky*; this means that, like with quicksand, the longer one is in poverty, the more difficult it becomes to break free from it (Babcock, 2014b). This stickiness makes it likely that children born into poverty will stay in poverty for life (Boghani, 2017), continually impaired with the "corrosive cruelties of childhood poverty" (Blow, 2015). Students who experience poverty at any point in their childhoods are more likely to be poor as young adults, and those who spend half their childhoods in poverty are far more likely to drop out

> 66 99   Getting out of poverty has always been tough, but it has become even harder over the past generation. The increasing costs of housing, health care, and child care, coupled with stagnant low-end wages and rising education requirements, have made today's pathway out of poverty a journey that fewer than one in four people complete.
>
> —Elisabeth Babcock

of high school than never-poor peers (Edelman, 2014). According to Public Schools First (2016), nearly half of all children born into poverty remain persistently poor as adults (and, nearly half make it out!).

Finding a pathway out of poverty is a journey that takes many years, significant education, and tremendous effort and focus. This complex pathway requires strong *executive function skills*—the skills of impulse control, emotional regulation, attention management, task prioritization, and working memory—skills that often lag in children who have grown up in poverty without interventions and internal or environmental protective factors (Birdsong, 2016). The detrimental outcomes of a life in poverty—learned helplessness, low self-worth, an external locus of control, and a fatalistic view of life—disrupt executive functions.

The development of executive function skills is undermined by ACEs, by the inherent trauma and stresses of poverty: "Chronic exposure to childhood stress—including abuse, neglect and household dysfunction—can hinder brain development and cause physical and mental-health problems. Not temporarily, but for life" (Lopez, 2018a). This chronic stress leads to increased anxiety, impaired memory, and worsened mood control, which can impair a child's ability to handle other stressors, pay attention, follow rules and directions, and learn (Boghani, 2017).

The limbic system, which trauma and immediate needs or stressors activate, overruns the prefrontal cortex responsible for executive function (Babcock, 2014b). In the classroom, this translates into disruptive behaviors, such as blurting out questions, failing to follow directions, "acting before asking permission, and forgetting what to do next" (Jensen, 2009, p. 12). This is why educators may describe students living in poverty as impulsive, disrespectful, and inconsiderate in school when, actually, these students often don't have the ability to regulate themselves because they have not learned these skills (Brendtro et al., 2019). Students who have lagging executive function skills often struggle with an avalanche of negative outcomes, including poor school performance, poor social-emotional development, more criminal incidents, teen pregnancies, low levels of postsecondary education or training, lower earnings, and failure to form independent households as young adults (Babcock, 2014b). In general, they are more likely to drop out of high school and suffer the ills and troubles that plague young adults in poverty in the United States.

> **❝ ❞** Moving out of poverty is no longer a short process of following a simple roadmap to a good job. It has become a lengthy, complex navigational challenge requiring individuals to rely on strong executive function skills (impulse control, working memory, and mental flexibility) in order to effectively manage life's competing demands and optimize their decisions over many years.

—Elisabeth Babcock

The social safety net that helped millions of people stay out of poverty during the War on Poverty now just barely keeps people afloat, instead of helping them move into stable jobs and homes where they can take care of themselves and their families. Available jobs for workers with lagging executive function skills and job skills are predominantly service-industry jobs with low wages, low benefits, and no room for growth. Gone is the era when a willingness to work hard was enough to provide for a family. Many of today's living-wage jobs require knowledge and education. The catch is that, to obtain knowledge and education, "low-income families must navigate complicated challenges for years because there are no short-term career paths to the family-sustaining jobs of today" (Babcock, 2014b, p. 3).

Accessing the postsecondary education and training needed to get good jobs takes two things that the poor typically have in short supply: (1) money—education costs have skyrocketed at the same time postsecondary education has become as necessary as a high school diploma was in the 1960s and 1970s (Loschert, 2017)—and (2) time. This brings us back to the lag in executive function skills common in people who grow up in poverty. To strive for the long-term goals of training, education, and a good job, people need to be able to plan, adjust plans, and sustain focus over time, which are all executive function skills. For the poor, one misstep in the journey out of poverty can derail those plans for years, decades, or a lifetime. And for the poor, a misstep can be as simple as losing transportation, not paying a parking ticket, or having a prolonged hospital stay—anything that, without resources and resilience, can trap them in the cycle of debt, criminal justice, job loss, and housing insecurity. People stuck in poverty need help to get out—a rope, if you will—and they need to pull on that rope until they are fully free from the quicksand of poverty in the United States. That *rope* represents relationships, resources, and reasons to stick out the difficult journey. It represents resilience, and it represents what we, as educators, can provide in public schools.

Thus, executive function skills are the most important skills that students living in poverty can gain in public schools. Without them, students are most likely doomed to a life of cyclic failure, which they will likely pass down to their children. Luckily, our public schools are exceptionally well equipped to teach executive function skills within the context of the academic and social-emotional learning that is already occurring. For example, Common Core standards are embedded with executive function skills, like citing textual evidence, backing up arguments with reasons, trying alternate solutions to problems, and problem-solving with peers (National Governors Association Center for Best Practices & Council of Chief State School Officers, 2010a, 2010b). This teaching is where our greatest hope lies.

Conclusion

Our schools face numerous hurdles from poverty's influence on students' lives, and responding to needs represents the greatest challenge facing schools today—a challenge that a growing number of schools—resilient schools—are successfully meeting. We addressed five of these hurdles in this chapter.

1. Lack of academic preparation. Students from impoverished backgrounds often arrive at school less prepared for learning than their more affluent peers, and without extra time and resources, they are unlikely to catch up.

2. Absenteeism, illness, and interrupted education. Children living in poverty are more likely to be homeless or housing insecure at some point during childhood, are likely to have higher rates of mobility and higher absences related to illness, housing, and adult job loss or searches. Homelessness, mobility, and high absence rates negatively impact learning.

3. Learning loss over school breaks. The reasons low-income children are more likely to enter school poorly prepared are the same reasons that school breaks lead to learning loss: the financial and parental resource streams too often are unable to provide stimulating and engaging activities that continue learning during vacations.

4. Adverse childhood experiences and behavior challenges. The traumas of poverty, including abuse, witnessing violence, food insecurity, and homelessness, cause real impacts on children's brain development. Without appropriate interventions, these changes can lead to learning and behavior challenges in school and life.

5. Learned helplessness and an external locus of control. The conditions of living in poverty, especially generational poverty, can cause a feeling of learned helplessness and an external locus of control, or the belief that one cannot change things for the better because other forces are controlling you. It is, in essence, a lack of a sense of personal agency. In classrooms, it can manifest in children as an unwillingness to try, and in giving up as soon as things seem difficult.

Finally, we considered the quicksand of poverty and how easy it is for poverty's negative effects on students and families to sustain themselves over time.

The good news is that resilient schools are showing how these negative effects of poverty can be responded to effectively in our public schools and classrooms. Though we, as educators, administrators, and stakeholders in public schools, may not be able to eliminate poverty in our current communities, we can start the change now, one child at a time, by providing hope, and a rope of resilience in the form of relationships, resources, and reasons to climb out of poverty. It takes great effort, and a reimagining of the worlds we create within our school and classroom walls. We hope that the content of this chapter helps build more will and determination to make this possible.

While this chapter has concentrated on the impacts of poverty on children and learning, we cannot ignore an additional stakeholder group affected by poverty—the staff members who work and teach in high-poverty schools. The next chapter will delve into the detrimental effects of poverty on the adults who work in schools—an often overlooked but tremendous factor in student success.

Next Steps

Please complete the following Next Steps, to integrate your experiences within your own schools and communities with the information presented in this chapter.

1. How have executive function skills played a role in your own success in life? Which executive function skills do you see your students struggling with the most?

2. Do you see learned helplessness or an external locus of control playing a role in your students' choices and approaches to learning?

3. What types of actions has your school or district taken to remediate, or even begin to prevent, students who arrive at school without readiness to learn?

4. What are your school or district's mobility, homeless, and absence rates? Find out what your school and district are doing to address these factors, and see how you can contribute to the conversation.

5. If you haven't done so, consider taking the original ACEs survey (available at https://acestoohigh.com/got-your-ace-score) for your own information. Are there ACEs that your students experience, which are not on the original study's list? What would an ACEs survey for *your* community look like?

6. How much review do you plan for, at the beginning of a new school year? Have you noticed that some students require more review than others? What is happening in your community to increase the resource stream for students during vacations?

Chapter 3

An Unanticipated Challenge: The Detrimental Impacts of Poverty on School Staff

It's important to keep good teachers in the profession and to keep good teachers motivated, because education is a job that relies very much on the intrinsic motivation of the teacher to want to do their job and perform their duties.

—Patrick Neuman

Just as teachers' attitudes, expectations, and instructional skills can have a tremendous influence on student learning and behavior, students' behavior, assets, and response to instruction can have a great influence on teachers' job satisfaction and morale. In high-poverty, high-trauma schools, the effort it takes to reach and teach students affected by the traumas of poverty can have a tremendous—often negative—impact on teachers, administrators, and other school staff. In this chapter, we shift attention from the needs of students to the needs of teachers and other school staff who work in not just high-poverty schools but any school that has students experiencing trauma and ACEs—what we call *high-poverty, high-trauma schools.*

Over time, teachers working in high-poverty communities may experience *secondary traumatic stress,* vicariously facing the same types of stress that their students experience in their homes and neighborhoods. The traumatic stress experienced in some schools can be enough to effectively cripple teachers, if not the entire staff. When school staffs suffer from detrimental aspects of working at a high-poverty, high-trauma school, they may experience higher rates of staff absenteeism, increased teacher attrition, and a range of personal health issues. This may, in fact, contribute to growing difficulty in recruiting strong, skilled individuals into the teaching profession. We must drag the relationship between poverty and school staff's health and well-being out of the shadows of misunderstanding and into the spotlight of concern so we can take action. Unless school staff recognize and address these effects of poverty on school personnel, the socioeconomic achievement gap will likely continue, and students will not receive the high-quality education that they need and deserve.

This chapter explores two detrimental impacts of poverty on school staff: (1) the increasingly high turnover and attrition rates of educators across the United States and (2) the effects of secondary traumatic stress. Similar to the previous chapter, which focused on students and poverty, this chapter focuses on staff and poverty, sharing the sobering realities as well as a great measure of hope, because there *are* ways to combat the effects of poverty on staff and ensure staff resilience. Chapter 8 (page 191) on staff resilience as a cornerstone of the resilient school goes into much greater detail about how school leaders and staff members can effectively combat and prevent the secondary traumatic stress found in high-poverty, high-trauma schools, with an emphasis on the relational and professional needs of staff.

Staff Turnover and Attrition

Teacher recruitment is a concern in every state. In fact, a 2018 Gallup poll finds that 61 percent of superintendents rank teacher recruitment, teacher engagement, and retention of quality teachers as significant challenges (Hodges, 2018). K–12 teachers are more likely to leave their profession than individuals in nursing, architecture, engineering, law, and higher education (Senechal et al., 2016). Disengaged, disaffected, and demoralized teachers often emotionally distance themselves from students and colleagues and hold lower expectations for student work and behavior. This, coupled with increasing rates of staff absenteeism, serves to undermine school climates, disrupt daily routines, and lower the quality and continuity of learning.

Sadly, these negative impacts of teacher dissatisfaction, withdrawal, and attrition more frequently and more intensely impact communities with the most needs, further exacerbating achievement gaps and existing inequities (Senechal et al., 2016). The bottom line is this: our high-poverty schools, serving populations most in need of support, must hire and retain high-quality, dedicated, powerful educators and staff.

Students reap tremendous benefits when staff turnover is low because it provides them with consistency and stability, which those experiencing the traumas of poverty and discrimination need (Podolsky, Kini, Bishop, & Darling-Hammond, 2016). Students feel a great sense of safety when they know who works in their school, who will teach them in fourth grade or in biology class, or who taught their older siblings or even their parents.

Field Note

When speaking in Johnson County School District in Kentucky in 2015, I asked the superintendent how on earth the district attracted teachers to come to this high-poverty area to live and teach.

He smiled and said, "Hang on, I will show you."

When he took the podium to introduce me, he asked for all the teachers who grew up in the area to stand. Just a mob of teachers stood up and cheered.

He turned to me and said, "Dr. Barr, you may wonder where we get our outstanding teachers. Well, now you know: we raise them!"

Later, a number of teachers told me the same story. From the time they were in the first grade, kids grew up hearing that Johnson County was the gold standard for public education and that, if they were fortunate, someday they might get to teach for Johnson County. —Bob Barr

Unfortunately, teacher attrition disproportionately impacts high-poverty schools. U.S. averages for new teacher attrition by the fifth year of service hover between 15 and 20 percent, meaning at the beginning of their fifth year of service, 80 to 85 percent of new teachers are still on the job (Podolsky et al., 2016). Sadly, the attrition number is even higher for Title I, reservation, urban, and rural schools, which already have shortages of qualified teachers (Carver-Thomas & Darling-Hammond, 2017). In these schools, which tend to hire more alternatively credentialed teachers, the attrition for new teachers at the beginning of their fifth year ranges from 30 to 50 percent (Podolsky et al., 2016). In the United States, approximately 8–10 percent of all teachers either leave teaching or switch schools each year, and rates in high-poverty and high-minority schools can be upwards of 20 percent, meaning one-fifth of the schools' staff may change every year (Podolsky et al., 2016). For comparison, the attrition rates for Singapore, Finland, and Ontario, Canada, hover at 3 to 4 percent (Sutcher et al., 2016). The resulting staffing churn in all schools, but especially in high-poverty, high-trauma schools, undermines student achievement as a function of teachers' inexperience, underpreparation, and overall instability (Sutcher, Darling-Hammond, & Carver-Thomas, 2016). Additionally, school cultures suffer from fractured collegial relationships, decreased engagement, and a deterioration of institutional knowledge over time (Sutcher, et al., 2016). It is very difficult to create hope and optimism in this environment, no matter how skilled the school leaders, but it is possible.

Field Note

When I visited a high-poverty middle school in Washington State in 2019, the principal described his efforts to turn the school around. Not only was his school the largest middle school in the district, but it was also the oldest building and the one most in need of renovation or replacement. The feeder elementary schools were all Title I schools, with great ethnic, racial, and language diversity and an overwhelming majority of low-income students. In attempting to change the school culture and implement positive behavioral interventions and supports (PBIS) and restorative discipline practices, he faced resistance to the changes, which undermined the efforts of the administration and the core group of teachers who supported the changes. For the past three years, he had hired new teachers to fill vacancies, only to fill the same positions the following year when those new hires or other staff left. He said, "It is a challenging school, with students who have a lot of needs. This isn't for everybody. But the high turnover makes it near impossible to move beyond square one, no matter how hard we work. And the teachers who have been with me since the first year are tired of waiting for the improvements to take hold."

The school culture suffered from the turnover, as did morale. According to this principal, "The worst part of it is that these students *can* learn. When presented with engaging, active lessons, led by teachers who care and have high expectations, they excel. Much of the staff resistance comes from teachers who don't want to change what they do. They want the students they used to have twenty years ago, and they seem to think that harsh, punitive discipline will make the students we have now behave like the students they had then."

Despite these challenges, this principal remains a beacon of hope, optimism, and courage for students and staff, and it is clear his efforts are making inroads. I look forward to continuing to check in on a yearly basis to see the results of his Culture of Hope. —Emily Gibson

Numerous studies have found higher rates of teacher absenteeism in high-poverty and high-minority schools than in low-poverty schools (for example, Bruno, 2002; Clotfelter, Ladd, & Vigdor, 2009; Miller, Murnane, & Willett, 2007), while two more recent studies have found no significant difference in teacher absenteeism rates between high- and low-poverty schools (Joseph, Waymack, & Zielaski, 2014; Sparks, 2016a). But none of these studies disputes the negative effect teacher absences have on student achievement. In general, more than one out of four teachers is *chronically absent*, with eighteen or more total absences (counting professional development, sick leave, and personal days, but not counting extended absences of ten or more days). This leaves students' learning in the hands of substitutes who may or may not have the experience and skills to lead quality learning experiences (Sparks, 2016a). Unfortunately, students' engagement, connection with the school, and sense of belonging suffer as days with substitutes increase, regardless of the purposes of the absences. Hard-to-staff schools do whatever it takes to keep classrooms staffed, including relying on a rotating staff of substitutes, especially in the difficult-to-fill positions of science, mathematics, English language development, and special education. They also hire emergency-credentialed or temporary-credentialed teachers, increase class sizes, use short-term substitutes, pull staff from other "less important" assignments, and give teachers assignments outside their areas of expertise. Each summer, in response to the yearly churn of staff, hard-to-staff schools often must hire a disproportionate number of inexperienced teachers, who then typically leave at higher rates than other teachers, continuing the churn. These stopgap measures are understandable in the moment, but over time, they undermine the quality of education that our most vulnerable students receive by concentrating the least-experienced, least-prepared teachers in our most challenged classrooms (Carver-Thomas & Darling-Hammond, 2017; National Commission on Teaching and America's Future, 2016; Podolsky et al., 2016; Sutcher et al., 2016).

When you consider the difficulties of teaching in high-poverty schools—the challenges of funding, facilities, and school culture—and the further instability of turnover and attrition, it is easy to see how those schools that most need to retain teachers are the least likely to do so. In the United States, the monetary cost of yearly turnover is approximately twenty thousand dollars per lost teacher, or about eight billion dollars each year to hire, train, and provide mentoring and professional development for new hires, many who are likely to leave within five years. Decreasing teacher turnover reaps benefits beyond saving teacher replacement costs when districts can avoid spending money on remediating poorly educated students (Carver-Thomas & Darling-Hammond, 2017; Senechal et al., 2016; Sutcher et al., 2016).

The following sections explore three additional aspects of staff turnover and attrition: (1) factors related to the teacher shortage, (2) teacher job satisfaction and morale, and (3) high morale as a form of optimism. These three issues help to show the complexity of staff turnover and attrition as well as offer a ray of hope.

> **" "** We are shutting down the pathways, aspirations, and the potential of millions of children and driving great teachers from the schools that need them the most, or from the profession altogether.

—National Commission on Teaching and America's Future

Factors Related to the Teacher Shortage

Factors related to the shortage of available teachers include increased student enrollment, class size–reduction legislation that requires more teachers, reinstatement of positions and programs that were cut in response to the 2007–2009 recession, high teacher turnover, and fewer graduates from teacher education programs (down 35 percent since 2010). Of all these factors, teacher turnover is most in our control. Teachers' most frequently cited reasons for leaving the profession or changing schools or districts are dissatisfaction with testing and accountability pressures, a lack of administrative support, dissatisfaction with teaching as a career, and unsatisfactory working conditions (Carver-Thomas & Darling-Hammond, 2017; Senechal et al., 2016; Sutcher et al., 2016).

Many promising teachers work in schools where extrinsic factors (factors outside of a teacher's sphere of influence) represent significant challenges. Large class sizes, increasingly disrupted learning environments, limited budgets and resources, and inadequate salaries can make even the most dedicated teacher question his or her choice of career. Educators can find it nearly impossible to keep connected to the purpose that led them to the profession when curriculum is highly prescribed or "teacher-proof," when mandates and policies do not make sense in a given community's context, and when teachers are asked to do more and more reporting as proof of what they are doing. Those who leave sometimes consider teaching a dead-end street, but not because of salaries, working conditions, or daily demands (Tomlinson, 2018). Rather, the lack of passion, creativity, or innovation required makes it a dead-end street, especially in those districts still focused on increasing test scores at the cost of both student and teacher engagement.

Regardless of reasons for leaving, the resulting catastrophic drain of teachers in the first decades of the 21st century represents a loss of knowledge, expertise, and institutional memory. It represents a devastating deterioration of the profession, especially given the passion and commitment so many new teachers bring to their classrooms—they become teachers to make a difference, and too many leave convinced they can't make a difference.

❝ ❞ I believe that teaching is all about cultivating and nurturing relationships. It doesn't matter how great our lessons are, how skilled we are at delivering those lessons, if our students don't understand how much we care about them.

—Alhassan Susso

Teacher Job Satisfaction and Morale

Reducing teacher turnover requires addressing job dissatisfaction and low morale, two distinct yet related constructs or threads. One unifying characteristic among those drawn to the education profession is that they feel a *calling* to the job—a deep desire to help and have a positive impact on individuals and the world as a whole. In other words, they feel a moral duty or an ethical responsibility to help students learn and find their purpose and passion (Senechal et al., 2016). We call this the *relational* or *emotional* aspect of teaching. Another common characteristic among educators is a strong intellectual curiosity and creativity. This may look like a love of a subject, a desire to create incredible lessons, or an insatiable thirst for learning more effective ways to teach. This we call the *intellectual* or *cognitive* aspect of the teaching profession. Both the relational or emotional and intellectual or cognitive aspects need to be fulfilled for educators and their students to experience success and satisfaction.

1. **Intellectual or cognitive aspects of teaching:** These aspects of the teaching profession frame an educator's expectations of what being a

teacher entails. An educator's expectations of what he or she will do in and out of class need to match well with the actual work environment in order to foster job satisfaction.

2. **Relational or emotional aspects of teaching:** These aspects of the teaching profession frame an educator's expectations of the personal and professional relationships connected to his or her job. How well these expectations match the educator's actual lived relationships within the profession helps determine his or her job satisfaction.

Teacher job satisfaction can be explained as the *fit* between individuals' ideal vision of the profession and the actual representation of the profession found in their school's particular context or professional culture (Evans, 1997). In theory, educators' current satisfaction with the teaching profession is directly related to their ability to fulfill their roles and responsibilities and to enjoy and nurture the quality and type of relationships they hope for with students and staff. A *good fit* is one in which an individual's current ideal and the school context are close. This makes one satisfied and fulfilled in one's job, regardless of day-to-day ups and downs. As one teacher in the *Understanding Teacher Morale* study explains it, "I love my job. I love what I do. . . . Even when there are days when I hate my job, I still love my job" (Senechal et al., 2016, p. 38).

This concept of *fit* resonates with the necessity to have personnel reach schoolwide agreement on beliefs about students and the goals of the school. The better the fit, the better a school takes on the quality of a surrogate family and builds caring relationships, which causes both students and teachers to think of their school as "my school."

Field Note

At the beginning of No Child Left Behind (NCLB) policy implementations in the late 1990s, I taught fifth grade alongside a gifted, creative educator who taught first grade at our K–5 elementary school. He came to our school after a decade teaching in Central America, and he was one of our best and brightest educators. He was also one of the first of our staff to get censured by the "curriculum police."

As he explained to me one day after school, all the first-grade classes had read a story about a gingerbread man. In the afternoon, he worked with his students on some extensions to deepen their understanding and engagement, which included making gingerbread people and writing and then performing a class story about their gingerbread people. He posted photos from the enrichment on his class webpage. The next day, someone from the district came to speak with him, admonishing him for spending time on nonapproved and nonadopted curriculum activities. He relayed the district curriculum representative's words:

"If you were following the curriculum and doing all the activities required, you would not have had time to make cookies with your class." He felt that his judgment as a professional was not valued and his creativity was stifled, so he returned to Central America the next year. What a loss to the district and school, and especially to the students. —Emily Gibson

High Morale as a Form of Optimism

Morale is closely associated with a teacher's decision to stay or leave a particular position or school (Senechal et al., 2016). High teacher morale can be viewed as a form of optimism. When teachers have high morale, it means they envision a good fit, or the ability to fulfill their expected roles and responsibilities and relationships in the future. Some refer to this as being compatible with the school culture and "patterns of behavioral regularities" (Sarason, 1971, p. 27). Low morale is the opposite, the feeling a job will be a poor fit in the future.

As an example, a new teacher may feel overwhelmed and currently have low job satisfaction because he is struggling to learn the ropes and he cannot yet fulfill his expected roles and responsibilities. However, that teacher may have high morale, believing he *will* be able to fulfill those duties in the future as he gains more skills and abilities. Or perhaps a teacher has high job satisfaction, enjoying strong collegial relationships and feeling like her students are really learning. Looking ahead, however, that teacher sees some policies coming along—perhaps a rote, scripted writing curriculum with little room for creativity or enrichment—that will drastically challenge the teacher's ability to fulfill her ideal professional roles and responsibilities. This could result in low morale for this educator because she perceives a future conflict. If her morale and job satisfaction fall low enough, she may attempt to find a different teaching context or, if that is not possible, leave the profession altogether (Evans, 1997; Senechal et al., 2016).

Field Note

During the 1980s, my wife worked for ten years in a small elementary school in Albany, Oregon. At the time the small town was going through a transition from a timber industry, blue-collar town to more of a blue-collar unemployed town. Sunrise Elementary School was in a high-poverty section of Albany, and most thought of it as one of the most challenging schools in the district. When my wife first arrived at the school and met the other teachers, she was asked with laughter, "Well, what did you do to get sent here?" There was an assumption among the school staff that the district administration used placement at Sunrise Elementary as a form of punishment for "uppity" teachers. My wife discovered that the school was actually staffed with a large number of highly talented, dedicated teachers who believed that, together, they made the school the best assignment in town. The teachers, all teaching veterans with low-income

students, had banded together into a strong group of men and women dedicated to working together, playing together, and ensuring their students were
successful in school. They had high morale and high job satisfaction. They were
able to meet their relational and professional needs together, in this school.
—Bob Barr

Interestingly, teachers with low morale are not necessarily poorly engaged. Instead,
they often have high expectations of themselves and work hard, but they do not
feel like they have a good fit with their context or with the profession as a whole.
Those who have low job satisfaction and low morale are more likely to become disengaged because they have little hope for improving their lot. Without appropriate
intervention and development of resilience, they are also more at risk of leaving the
profession (Senechal et al., 2016). In the next section, we will explore how secondary
traumatic stress reduces the resilience of staff and increases the likelihood of staff
dissatisfaction.

Field Note

Too often, we see high-poverty schools that become the training ground for
new administrators who then transfer to other schools once they have shown
their worth. Too often, we see the churn of teacher turnover when new, creative,
passionate teachers take their first jobs in whichever school is hiring only to find
that the reality of the context does not match their expectations, so they transfer
at the first opportunity. These and other scenarios help create struggling schools
with high turnover, where even the most passionate and knowledgeable principal
cannot shift the school culture because every year is year one all over again, like
some horrific version of the film *Groundhog Day*. Instead, the administration's
efforts focus on teaching new staff the school's expectations and discipline,
grading, and teaching methods; managing continuing staff's frustrations at not
moving forward; and handling students who feel let down and like they don't
matter because staff keep leaving or because their class is taught by a cycle of
long-term subs. Sadly, these schools earn a reputation for being the place where
"bad" kids go and where "bad" teachers end their careers. Such a reputation
can last long after a school has transformed. —Emily Gibson

Staff Exposure to Trauma

Any discussion of staff retention must touch on school staff's increasing exposure
to trauma, both secondary and primary. *Primary trauma* is the experience of actual
trauma, and is discussed in a later section in this chapter on disrupted learning (see
page 63). *Secondary trauma* (also called *secondary traumatic stress, compassion fatigue,*
or *vicarious trauma*) is "the emotional duress that results when an individual hears
about the firsthand trauma experiences of another" (National Child Traumatic Stress

Network, n.d.). For our purposes, we use the term *secondary trauma* throughout this section. It can occur when an educator hears students talking about traumatic life experiences, or reads their writing about traumatic events (Finley, 2017). The effects of secondary trauma can mirror some effects of post-traumatic stress disorder (PTSD), including anxiety, depression, avoidant behaviors, and panic attacks (Chawla, 2014).

About half of K–12 students have been exposed to one or more traumatic events (ACEs), and hearing the stories of these events can weigh emotionally on adults who work in schools (Data Resource Center for Child and Adolescent Health, 2012). The increase of students exposed to trauma in our schools has meant the addition of social-emotional lessons in classrooms, and educators adapting to helping students under the influence of trauma by taking on more responsibility for students' emotional well-being. This can increase teachers' exposure to students' traumatic experiences. Without supportive professional development to understand this emerging role, educators run the risk of secondary trauma. In this section, we examine the increasing prevalence of secondary traumatic stress among school personnel and consider the traumatic effects of disrupted learning environments.

> **❝❞** Humans tend to adapt to chronic stress in order to be able to survive and thrive in challenging contexts. But these adaptive behaviors can impede success in the classroom context.
>
> **—Patricia Jennings**

Secondary Traumatic Stress

Educators frequently cite working conditions as a reason for leaving the teaching profession, and exposure to secondary trauma is an often-overlooked working condition of schools. The day-to-day reality of teaching in high-poverty schools, no matter where they are located, is filled with the impacts of trauma. In urban, suburban, semirural, rural, and reservation schools, poverty is increasing, and with it the disruptions to teaching and learning and the toll on school climate, which all people who work in schools feel (Autio, 2019).

The effects of trauma on students' learning and brain development are well documented (see chapter 2, page 31; Babcock, 2014b; Boghani, 2017; Lopez, 2018a; Perry, 2002). But while the effects of working with clients who have experienced trauma is well documented for other caring professionals (that is, firefighters, law enforcement officers, trauma doctors and nurses, child welfare workers, therapists, and case managers), the impacts on school personnel is less explored (Gunn, 2018a; Lander, 2018). One study (Hydon et al., 2015) found high levels of secondary trauma among staff who work in reservation schools and high-poverty communities impacted by trauma from natural disasters. The prevalence of poverty and trauma in our public schools nationwide indicates that schools need to consider the effects of trauma on staff, especially if staff attrition, turnover, and absenteeism rates are on the rise.

Field Note

> While talking about classroom trauma, a Washington State middle-school principal shared the following story.

A teacher called for help with a verbally and physically out-of-control student. The student, in a highly escalated state, had threatened to punch the teacher, the student's fist stopping mere millimeters from the teacher's face. After the student was removed from the classroom, the teacher turned back to teaching the algebra lesson to the rest of the students. However, the principal insisted she take a break. He called for an assistant principal to take over the teacher's class for the rest of the class period and then the rest of the day, while the teacher processed and recovered from the event. Only later that week, after the student and teacher were able to successfully repair, did the student return to the classroom. The principal shared that, all too often, teachers go back to their classrooms before dealing with the real effects of primary trauma because it is just expected of them to move on and carry on. But he explained that the effects of trauma linger on too long if they aren't dealt with initially. —Emily Gibson

Chronic stress from working in underresourced schools, with traumatized students, or in chaotic environments can take a toll on staff's physical and mental health, leading to weakened immune systems and illnesses. Teachers may feel on edge, hypervigilant about potential problems or confrontations with students, or numb and distant from their lives and who they are outside school (Dorado & Zakrzewski, 2013). Staff and administrators often do not realize their symptoms point to secondary exposure to trauma (Lander, 2018).

66 99 We live in a world in which we need to share responsibility. It's easy to say "It's not my child, not my community, not my world, not my problem." Then there are those who see the need and respond. I consider those people my heroes.

—Fred Rogers

Educators are at risk of secondary trauma because they, like other helping professionals, tend to run *toward* problems, with empathy, as a normal part of their job. Many of these problems have no quick fixes. Those who care for people who have been traumatized will, by virtue of caring, be inclined to absorb trauma and will likely experience symptoms of trauma at some point during their career (Costa, 2012).

The good news is that school leaders can provide tremendous support and truly mitigate the effects of secondary traumatic stress for staff members. In this section, we will discuss both individual and collective signs of compassion fatigue and secondary traumatic stress, as well as how leaders can monitor and respond to secondary traumatic stress when the signs are evident.

Field Note

After three years working at a high-poverty school, on the front lines with K–6 elementary school students impacted by trauma in their neighborhoods and homes, I found myself waking up every morning just before the deadline to call in for a substitute. The weight of so many concerns lay over me like a lead blanket—the students in conflict with each other or with me, the girl I suspected was being molested, the family evicted from their home, the child who had been out for a month due to chronic head lice, the angry parent who claimed I made racist statements to her son. I would tell myself, "You could call for a sub. You don't have to go in." And then I would run through the plan for the day—envisioning how it would go with a substitute, the students I wanted to connect with, the writing conferences students were counting on, and the field trip we were organizing—and I would feel enough motivation and hope to convince myself to go in. This repeated for months, until I finally checked in with a therapist to work on my chronic stress and anxiety and was able to return to my optimistic, hopeful, mentally engaged self.

What I learned from this experience was the importance of not going it alone. My colleagues and I often joked that we made as many decisions, and were under similar stress, as air traffic controllers and emergency room staff. Sometimes as educators we feel we have to have all the answers, and that to ask for help or lean on one another is a sign of weakness. In fact, we are stronger when we share the realities of our profession, and the more open we are about our struggles, the less of a burden they become. —Emily Gibson

Individual Signs of Compassion Fatigue and Secondary Traumatic Stress

The individual symptoms of secondary trauma are similar to those associated with firsthand trauma. All school personnel need to have awareness of these symptoms because trauma can impact anyone—even the most seasoned and balanced professional—and people can often recognize symptoms of traumatic stress in their colleagues before they notice it in themselves. Table 3.1 is a matrix of cognitive, behavioral, emotional, and physical symptoms that may indicate someone is struggling with the effects of secondary traumatic stress (Administration for Children and Families, n.d.; Finley, 2017; Gunn, 2018b; Lander, 2018).

Table 3.1: Symptoms of Secondary Traumatic Stress

Cognitive	Emotional
Decreased concentration or focus	Guilt
Apathy or cynicism	Anger or aggression
Rigid thinking	Numbness
Perfectionism	Sadness
Preoccupation with trauma	Helplessness
Mental fixation on students	Irritation
Loss of creativity	Anxiety
Poor boundaries	Denial
Behavioral	**Physical**
Withdrawal or isolation	Increased heart rate
Avoidance of communicating	Difficulty breathing
Sleep disturbance or insomnia	Muscle and joint pain
Appetite change	Impaired immune system
Hypervigilance	Increased severity of medical concerns
Elevated startle response	Poor self-care
Substance use or abuse	Chronic exhaustion

Source: Adapted from Administration for Children and Families, n.d.; Finley, 2017; Gunn, 2018b; Lander, 2018.

Collective Signs of Compassion Fatigue and Secondary Traumatic Stress

The effects of trauma and chronic stress can also be felt within an entire school's community and culture. Over time, ongoing exposure to trauma can negatively affect a school organization's functioning and its ability to meet student needs (Administration for Children and Families, n.d.). Like an organism, the integrated system of a school begins to break down under chronic stress. A school's culture and sense of community can start to disintegrate, and things that once seemed easy or had solid routines can become derailed. People make choices that don't consider others' needs or viewpoints, and the cohesive whole becomes fragmented, territory lines are drawn, and trust erodes (Dorado & Zakrzewski, 2013).

Field Note

In a high-poverty, high-trauma school in central California, I witnessed staff stepping into the role of leadership to fill a void. At the height of pressure from being a low-performing school under NCLB, the principal was almost solely focused on raising test scores, and expected herculean efforts from staff while providing little of the relational supports that people need in order to invest deeply. Several teacher-leaders met with the principal to get permission to lead staff activities to boost positive feelings, including a message board where people could leave notes for other staff to acknowledge them, monthly potlucks, and

> coffee cards for randomly drawn teachers in attendance at staff meetings. While these efforts did not turn the school climate around overnight, they served as a pressure relief that helped staff members make it to the end of the school year and provided a model for the principal of what could be done. —Emily Gibson

Staff and school leaders should be alert to these common signs of collective secondary traumatic stress within an organization (Administration for Children and Families, n.d.; Gunn, 2018a).

- Chronic absenteeism (10 percent or more missed school days)
- Increased friction among teacher teams
- Aggressive staff behaviors
- Colleagues feeling overwhelmed or unable to finish their work
- Negativity toward school leadership
- Impaired judgment or decision making
- Lower quality of work or productivity
- Resistance to change
- Higher staff turnover
- Increased gossip and lack of trust among staff groups
- General apathy toward the school's mission and its success

As leaders recognize the signs of secondary traumatic stress within their school, they can help everyone recognize what is happening and take steps to mitigate the effects and rebuild self-regulation and resilience in staff. Instead of descending into self-criticism or meanness, or feeling lazy or inadequate, staff can realize they are facing incredible expectations and situations, and the antidote is to take care of themselves and each other with compassion and empathy. In addition to the following section, chapter 8 (page 191) provides more in-depth strategies and resources for combating staff's secondary traumatic stress.

Response to Secondary Traumatic Stress

School leaders who lead the schools that most need consistent staffing must monitor and respond to signs of secondary traumatic stress in order to address the related concerns of reduced staff morale and high staff turnover. See figure 3.1 for specific resources school leaders may find helpful in this regard. Focusing on staff's relational, or social-emotional, needs can help combat the impacts of secondary trauma, incredible workloads, and often-overwhelming student needs. Further, addressing staff's professional needs can help build staff morale, job satisfaction, and engagement. Later, chapter 8 (page 191) develops the relational and professional areas of need as a cornerstone of the resilient school model.

Professional Quality of Life: This scale allows individuals to measure their compassion satisfaction, burnout, and secondary traumatic stress. Scores are compiled and users learn if they have had high, medium, or low levels of compassion satisfaction, burnout, and secondary traumatic stress over the previous thirty days. It is available at https://bit.ly/33EuZbn (Stamm, 2009, 2010)

 Resilience Self-Reflection Survey: This survey provides individuals with the opportunity to reflect on ways to increase or maintain resilience. It is available at https://bit.ly/2xfCwkO (Weis, 2017).

 Burnout Self-Test: This test allows individuals to monitor their feelings about their job and work experiences for signs of burnout. It is available at https://bit.ly/3ad5znR (Mind Tools Content Team, n.d.).

Figure 3.1: Tools for measuring secondary traumatic stress.

Disrupted Learning Environments—A Primary Trauma

In some of our most traumatized communities, teachers are actually facing primary trauma as a result of living and working in traumatic environments. School staff are not trained on how to respond to extreme or traumatic environments, where they have chairs thrown at them or get seriously injured. However, teachers are expected to return to those environments every day and continue to teach, as opposed to soldiers with PTSD, who are removed from the battlefield and not allowed to return (Chawla, 2014). These high-trauma school environments have become so common they now have a specific name: *disrupted learning environments.*

The Oregon Education Association conducted an extensive study of disrupted learning environments, defined as places where "student behavior significantly interferes with instruction and/or school staff members' ability to maintain a stable classroom or ensure student safety" (Autio, 2019, p. 6). In this study, educators from throughout Oregon describe the disruptive student behavior as including verbal abuse, physical abuse, the "weaponizing" of items in the classroom, and the destruction of property (Autio, 2019).

The Oregon Education Association study cites multiple factors for the rise in disrupted learning environments in Oregon's schools. These include chronic school underfunding; increased class sizes; decreased staffing for student support; lack of resources to meet student needs; decreased whole-child education opportunities like recess, physical education, playtime, and the arts; lack of staff training; and lack of clarity in new discipline policies meant to reduce suspensions, expulsions, and punitive responses (Autio, 2019).

In the study's poll of Oregon educators, a third said they were scared for students' safety at school, a quarter said they feared for their own safety, and half said their classroom or their child's classroom had experienced at least one *room clear*—when students are moved out of their learning environment to protect them from a student who has lost control and become a potential threat to peers or adults—that year. An astonishing 91 percent said their school lacked adequate resources to provide safe, welcoming, and inclusive classrooms (Autio, 2019). A similar study of disrupted learning occurred in Connecticut (Connecticut Education Association, 2019), and in our work with schools across the county, we continue to hear of the increasing rates of classroom disruption as a result of out-of-control student behavior. We believe these disrupted learning environments have been commonplace in inner-city schools for decades—Herbert Kohl's (1967) *Thirty-Six Children* and Jonathan Kozol's (2005) *The Shame of the Nation* fuel this consideration—and they are only now garnering more mainstream attention because they have become more commonplace, occurring not only in high-poverty, high-minority schools but also in suburban, white, middle-class schools.

Field Note

 In a kindergarten art class, I conducted a room clear when a student began throwing pencils and pens at other students (weaponizing items). Normally, I could talk with him and help him regulate, but for whatever reason he was not able to hear me. I quietly called the office for assistance and evacuated the class into the hallway, where I instructed them to look at the art on the walls. After the student was escorted out to get what he needed, I gathered the students together and explained, "I asked you to come into the hallway because we had a friend who was really struggling and I wanted you to be safe. I want you to know that I will always do what I can to keep you safe. He is gone now, and if you are ready, we can go back in to do art." I then let students talk about their feelings before we went back to work. I find that it is critical to talk with students about what happened, to let them process whatever feelings they have about what happened, before expecting them to go back to learning. This process also allows me to deal with my own feelings about the incident, which is a big part of dealing with the trauma we experience in our jobs. —Emily Gibson

" " For the past three years, I have experienced severe, violent and disruptive behaviors on an hourly basis. Behaviors range from constant interruptions to instructional time (yelling in the room, leaving the classroom, turning over furniture, dumping supplies and materials off of shelves and desks, ripping instructional materials off of the walls) to verbal abuse (threatening or obscene language) to physical contact (being hit, jumped on, scratched, or grabbed). All of these actions impact my ability to teach, but more importantly they impact every other child's ability to experience school as a safe, supportive environment. Classmates begin to normalize the disruptive behaviors of their peers, they learn to dodge chairs, protect their schoolwork, move away from threatening behavior. Not only are the needs of the disruptive student unmet—but the situation has caused the trauma to ripple out to classmates.

—First-Grade Teacher, East Portland, Oregon

In a disruptive learning environment, the disruptive students' social, emotional, and academic needs go unmet; the disruptive behaviors traumatize the students' peers and causes them to lose their learning time; and the disruptive behaviors become normalized over time. The teacher, charged with keeping students safe and reaching and teaching all learners, is traumatized as well, and often unable to process the trauma before moving on to the next lesson. At times, disruptive students are brought back into the classroom environment before the student, teacher, or classmates have repaired the damage done. The impact of disrupted learning environments reverberates out from the classroom to the entire school. All school staff can experience trauma, leading to higher absenteeism and turnover. Disrupted learning environments also impact the community surrounding the school, which may weaken the community-school partnerships that high-poverty schools rely on to meet students' needs.

Three recommendations for addressing disrupted learning environments resulted from the Oregon Education Association's study: (1) "increase onsite student supports with a focus on mental health"; (2) "reduce class sizes and caseloads"; and (3) "fully fund targeted professional development and ongoing supports for consistent, high-quality implementation" (Autio, 2019, pp. 12, 14, 16). However, these recommendations all relate to external decision makers, outside staff members' locus of control. As discussed earlier in this chapter, leaders can support staff resilience by taking actions from within one's sphere of influence. Thus, school leaders and staff must take steps to make protocols for disrupted learning very clear, so all know what to expect and how to proceed.

In some schools we've observed or worked in, a teacher exposed to primary trauma is provided the option to have their classroom covered until they are able to return—administrators or specialists are called in. In other schools, students who have traumatically disrupted the learning environment do not return to class until the teacher and student have been able to repair and reconnect—an administrator may cover the class while the teacher ducks out into the hall for a quick conference, or the student may work in another classroom until the teacher is ready to reconnect.

The most important aspect of these protocols seems to be ensuring that all staff know what to expect and how to proceed, because this knowledge is power, and power is a great antidote to stress.

Conclusion

In this chapter, we have presented the impacts of poverty on teaching and learning as evidenced by staff. The ongoing teacher and administrator shortages across the United States are connected to the working conditions in schools and individual school staff members' level of job satisfaction. A school's morale and culture also have connections to how staff respond to working conditions. As a result, recognizing when individuals or the collective staff are exhibiting signs of secondary traumatic stress is crucial if school and team leaders are to alleviate secondary traumatic stress's effects on staff and on student learning. When educators and administrators have awareness of the prevalence of trauma exposure in their schools, they are better able to mitigate or prevent trauma's effects on staff morale and job satisfaction.

The antidote to the traumas and adversities of poverty is resilience—student resilience and staff resilience. In the next part of this book, we share the research on resilience and introduce our framework of resilience: the resilient school.

Next Steps

Please complete the following Next Steps, to integrate your experiences within your own schools and communities with the information presented in this chapter.

1. Have you noticed any indications that members of your school staff may be experiencing secondary traumatic stress (for example, outbursts of anger or emotion, or extensive absences)? Have you and your colleagues discussed the issue of secondary stress among the school staff? Have you had professional development relating to this issue? Consider discussing these questions and how you may respond to them during a group staff discussion or professional training day.

2. Do you and your colleagues on the school staff have scheduled experiences designed to alleviate stress? Do you have a before-school workout team at a local recreation center? A before- or after-school yoga session? Do you have a group of runners who regularly meet and exercise together? These are all effective antidotes to stress.

3. Do you feel like a strong team member of your school staff? Sometimes secondary stress causes teachers to pull away and isolate themselves. Are there ways you can think of to develop a strong team spirit of support among your school colleagues? If you have not done so, your school staff might consider organizing as a professional learning community (PLC) as a way to strengthen the team morale of the instructional staff (see DuFour, DuFour, Eaker, Many, & Mattos, 2016).

4. Use local mental health providers to provide professional development around the issue of stress and secondary traumatic stress, or organize a book group to read and discuss a publication on the topic.

5. Consider staff get-togethers, weekend parties, or other school celebrations as a way to have fun and alleviate pressure.

6. Education has become more and more politicized over the years, with issues such as working conditions, class size, and availability of adequate mental-health professionals for staff and students among several hot-button issues. Sometimes the only effective way to deal with school stress is to mobilize politically to help the school boards, legislators, and the larger community better understand the nature and the needs of public education today. Consider organizing such an effort in your school or district. Data can be unusually powerful when presented in arguments for better funding for schools, and teacher and administrative organizations can work together to present their ideas and lay out a pathway to better education. The Oregon Education Association's (n.d.) disrupted learning report can be a catalyst for such presentations.

part two

INTRODUCING *the* RESILIENT SCHOOL

Chapter 4

The Research: Studying Resilient Students and Resilient Schools

School was my haven, my solace, the alternate universe I stepped into most days with relief. School counteracted the trauma of the rest of my life.

—Nan Henderson

Like trees that resist the buffeting winds of storms, many students are able to defy the overwhelming pressures of poverty, stress, and trauma. In spite of the odds embedded in their experiences, these students are confident, optimistic, and fueled with motivation, effort, and creativity; they embody hope amid the hopelessness of poverty and trauma. We describe these students as *resilient*—when bent, they spring back instead of breaking. *Resilience* can be defined as the ability to bounce back from adversity, to cope successfully with challenges, and to turn the stresses of life into opportunities (Benard, 1993; Frankel, 2001). Resilience is multidimensional, and it is research based. According to the Center on the Developing Child (n.d.), understanding more about what makes some students "do well despite adverse early experiences" is vital because "it can inform more effective policies and programs that help more children reach their full potential" in school and beyond. Individual characteristics, personalities or natures, and environmental components can all play a role in an individual's resilience.

Supportive relationships, adaptive skill building, and positive experiences are also ingredients of resilience. The level of social support in someone's family and neighborhood can act as a strong buffer against adverse experiences, essentially filling a reserve of resilience that the person can draw from during hard times (Center for Promise, 2017). Further, an individual's capacity for resilience is elastic over time—it expands or contracts, given input from within and without the individual (Patterson

& Kelleher, 2005). The more one uses resilience, the stronger one gets, providing more fuel for the future, and providing motivation for us as educators: we can teach resilience and help students grow their capacity for it. Resilience is a set of cognitive skills and capabilities that people can learn at any age, just like mathematics, science, or writing (Hansen, 2017; Jensen, 2019). Regular physical exercise, stress-reduction practices, and programs that actively build executive function and self-regulation skills are ways to improve healthy responses to adversity (namely, strengthen resilience or the ability to recover from adversity). They are also ways to increase academic success. And, adults who strengthen their own resilience in turn improve the resilience of the children around them (Center on the Developing Child, n.d.; Healy, 2014; Konnikova, 2016).

> **" "** One way to understand the development of resilience is to visualize a balance scale or seesaw. Protective experiences and coping skills on one side counterbalance significant adversity on the other.
>
> **—Center on the Developing Child**

When we as educators focus on student resilience, we shift from a deficit model (what students are missing), to a strengths model (what students have within themselves) (Patterson & Kelleher, 2005). In this chapter, we will present the results of our extensive literature review on resilient students and resilient schools. We begin by presenting the research on resilience in young people (children and youth), and then discuss key protective factors of resilience—both internal and external. Then, we consider the research on poverty and resilience and its impact on education. Next, we present research on whole-school models of education and identify several factors that a school framework must have or build in order to be truly effective in the fight against poverty. Finally, we bring it all together by presenting our framework for the resilient school.

Field Note

Friends of the Children is a nonprofit program founded by Duncan Campbell (2016) that mentors students throughout their years of public schooling and beyond. These students are those who are least likely to find success in schools, but a whopping 83 percent of participants graduate from high school or earn a GED, 93 percent avoid the juvenile justice system (despite 50 percent having incarcerated parents), and 98 percent avoid teen parenting (though 83 percent were born to teen parents). Mentors are paid living wages with benefits, receive extensive training and support, and often stay with the program for twelve years. This program fosters resilience in children by providing a caring, present, positive adult who spends quality time mentoring each child. Mentors are there in good times and bad, providing a consistent presence who sees and believes in each child. Friends of the Children is a solution for breaking the cycle of poverty and the intergenerational repetition of low educational attainment, teen parenting, and criminality. As a volunteer, I was able to see a new chapter start in central Oregon in 2018, and witness the birth of hope in twenty-eight students' lives. —Emily Gibson

Research on Resilience in Youth

Interactions between biology and environment can build and reinforce youths' resilience, or their ability to cope with threats to healthy development (Center on the Developing Child, n.d.). Early efforts at the Northwest Regional Educational Laboratory helped synthesize research on resilient youth and the Laboratory, along with other researchers, showed that resilient children and youth are more likely to have the following characteristics (Benard, 1991).

- Increased social competency

- Better problem-solving skills

- More personal autonomy

- Better self-esteem

- A higher sense of purpose and future

Identification of these characteristics of resilience was as important as Northwest Regional Education Laboratory's impressive research documenting that schools were successfully teaching these characteristics, because we can now better predict which students might or might not be resilient, an important factor since we know we can teach resilience (Benard, 1993; Henderson & Milstein, 2003). Schools and classroom teachers can target and cultivate the characteristics of resilience listed above as instructional goals to help students become more confident, more successful academically, and more resilient. This means that while teachers and schools utilize all the identified strategies that help students learn effectively, they can also work to teach students powerful skills and attitudes that will help them become more effective learners. Taken together, teaching students how to learn and teaching students how to be resilient represent a powerful, two-pronged approach to teaching and learning.

Key Protective Factors for Resilience in Youth

Some people come to resilience naturally, and others need help in developing resilience. In either case, students become more resilient when internal and environmental protective factors exist and are strengthened. These *protective factors*—or elements of background, personality, and environment—have the capacity to buffer, ameliorate, and mitigate the effects of risk and stress (Frankel, 2001; Garmezy, 1991; Henderson, 2013; Konnikova, 2016). According to researcher Bonnie Benard (1993):

> The ability to separate oneself from a dysfunctional family environment—to detach enough from parental distress to maintain outside pursuits and satisfactions—[is] the major characteristic of resilient children growing up in families with alcoholism and mental illness (Berlin & Davis, 1989).

Demographics do not equal destiny. Protective factors are more powerful predictors of students' future success than stressful life events that require resilience.

Outside of families and neighborhoods, schools and teachers are among the most common sources for helping students develop the protective factors that will help them go on to do well in both their schoolwork and their adult lives (Henderson, 2013). One-third to one-half of children impacted by adversity go on to become well-adjusted adolescents, and a majority of maladjusted adolescents overcome the effects of adversity as adults in their thirties (Benard, 1993; Rutter, 1985; Werner & Smith, 1992). This must not be overlooked. Just because students are living in poverty and beset by all sorts of stress, trauma, and adversity does not mean they are beyond help. Quite the opposite—school personnel need to constantly remind themselves that they can make, and are currently making, huge differences in the lives of their students. The fact that so many children impacted by trauma and poverty go on to live successful lives is where we, as educators, find hope. Reflecting back to the *quicksand of poverty* presented in chapter 2 (page 31), the rope of resilience in the form of relationships, resources, and reasons to keep trying are directly related to protective factors. Students who are able to circumnavigate stress and trauma *without* school-based interventions likely have internal and environmental protective factors in their lives, and can avoid the quicksand of poverty more easily. Students with fewer protective factors in their lives will likely require the protective factors provided by schools and the adults who work in them, if they are to step around the quicksand of poverty and attain success beyond pubic school.

When staff have awareness of protective factors and commit to strengthening those factors, it turns schools into powerful resilience-building organizations. This awareness, and the ensuing actions, can also strengthen the resilience of educators who may feel powerless in the face of the adversities and stresses in students' lives (Henderson, 2013). In this section, we will consider three protective factors for resilience: (1) internal protective factors of resilience, (2) external or environmental protective factors of resilience, and (3) the self-righting capacity of learners to build resilience.

> **" "** Much attention has been focused recently on "at-risk" children, especially those who face poverty, neglect, abuse, physical handicaps, war, or the mental illnesses, alcoholism, or criminality of their parents. Amazingly, while researchers have found that these children do develop more problems than the general population, they have also learned that a great percentage of the children become healthy, competent young adults.

> —Bonnie Benard

Internal Protective Factors of Resilience

Of the two types of protective factors, internal factors are of specific importance because they are tied to self-efficacy and an internal locus of control. Internal protective factors are inherent to the individual—they are characteristics that build resilience from the inside out. The good news is you only need a few, and they can be learned and strengthened over time.

Many sources have identified internal protective factors, attributes, and characteristics in different ways, and we found it helpful to consolidate these into one list, organizing them under the National Dropout Prevention Center's (n.d.b) five attributes of resilience (see figure 4.1). When students possess these five attributes—(1) relationships, (2) independence, (3) competence, (4) creativity, and (5) optimism, often learned in what the Search Institute (2016) calls *developmental relationships* (consistent relationships with caring adults)—they are more able to protect themselves from traumas and stressors, both chronic and temporary.

1. Relationships

Care: Is able to care for others, to express care, and to be kind

Connection: Has a sense of belonging in one or more areas of life (family, club, peers, school, or community) and provides a sense of belonging to others

Compassion and empathy: Shows feelings, understanding, and empathy for others experiencing difficult times or sorrows

Social competence: Communicates well with others in a variety of social situations; responds appropriately to others; is friendly and engaging; forms positive relationships with peers and adults

Trust: Is able to trust and rely on others in healthy ways

Altruism and helpfulness: Engages in service or helpfulness to others; gives time and energy to a cause

---

Figure 4.1: Internal protective factors of resilience.

continued →

2. Independence

Autonomy: Is capable of making decisions and acting on them independently; can distance self from unhealthy people and situations

Responsibility: Acts in consistently conscientious, trustworthy, and reliable ways; has proven responsibility and reliability; has self-discipline

Internal locus of control: Exhibits regular sense of control of self, having the agency and ability to influence events; takes initiative; is a self-starter; has an internal moral compass—knows right from wrong or has a conscience

Positive identity: Believes in own worth and value as an individual or as part of a family, culture, or group; uses positive self-talk

Perception: Is insightful about self, others, and situations; often sees below the surface; recognizes own feelings and needs

Self-regulation: Has and uses self-regulation, patience, and impulse control skills

3. Competence

Expertise and mastery: Is an expert in one or more areas; has deep knowledge or outstanding ability and proven success; derives personal pride from mastery of skills

Confidence: Believes in own abilities, judgment, resources, and ideas; backs self up

Persistence: Continues on in the face of adversity; is unlikely to give up or quit

Self-efficacy: Influences others with own thoughts and behavior; believes in own capabilities; advocates for self

Critical thinking: Is able to think critically, explain thinking, and reason with facts

Humbleness: Is able to ask for help when needed, yet is assertive about getting what is needed; acknowledges others' competence without defensiveness

4. Creativity

Problem solving: Develops solutions to problems; meets problems head-on and views problems as opportunities

Resourcefulness: Is full of initiative; is solution oriented, especially in difficult situations

Imagination: Thinks outside the box; develops new or original ideas

Flexibility: Is able to adjust as circumstances change or new information is discovered; bends when necessary to cope with situations

Personal expression: Expresses self through artistic endeavors or by using imagination and creative thinking or other processes

Ability to learn: Has a capacity for and connection to learning and enjoys learning for learning's sake

5. Optimism

Hopefulness: Has hopes and dreams for the future; thinks of good things that can happen; has learned optimism instead of learned hopelessness

Purposefulness and motivation: Has goals and aspirations; is driven to get things done

Self-motivation: Is motivated from within; has initiative and purpose to actions; sets goals and strives to attain them; has interests or enthusiasms that inspire action

Faithfulness and anchors: Has religious or spiritual anchors, which serve as a source of sustenance; has personal faith in something greater than self

Humor: Has a sense of humor; uses humor to defuse situations; can laugh at self or difficult situations

Source: Adapted from Benard, 1993; Cherry, 2019a; Frankel, 2001; Healy, 2014; Henderson, 2012; Konnikova, 2016; National Dropout Prevention Center, n.d.b; Tileston & Darling, 2008.

*Visit **go.SolutionTree.com/schoolimprovement** for a free reproducible version of this figure.*

Knowing the internal, individual protective factors can enormously help anyone who works with children. While taken on its own, the complete list might be too unwieldy to use as a set of school or classroom goals, we recommend teachers, specialists, counselors, and administrators be aware of the factors and seek to recognize them in students' behavior. Some schools have used the five attribute categories as guiding character themes, and students select specific attributes to focus on each month or for the whole year. Professional staff can use this list of characteristics as a checklist when working with individual students and discussing strengths to build from. The list can remind staff of the concept of resilience when they see students exhibiting particular characteristics. The list can also help focus instructional efforts on very specific attributes. Helping a student develop or improve even just a few of these characteristics can have powerfully positive results because it gives the student a handful of strengths that can become lifelines for resilience (Henderson, 2013). However staff decide to use the list of internal protective factors, the goal is to ensure that students recognize their own strengths in each of the five categories and develop new strengths over time.

Field Note

Educators can use the list of internal protective factors to more effectively *mirror* student strengths, or strengthen, acknowledge, and emphasize the factors that students do have. All students have strengths, no matter how troubled or lost they may seem on the surface, and it is up to us educators to dig in deep—to mine students for their nuggets of gold—so we can then show them their capabilities. Students need to know what they are doing well and what strengths they already have.

When educators can reflect these strengths back to students, it has a powerful impact for youth who rarely, if ever, hear they have strengths. When staff are such "environmental mirrors" (Henderson, 2013), they become incredibly powerful environmental protective factors—those of caring, kind, present adults. Research has well documented how often the "single most common factor for children who develop resilience is at least one stable and committed relationship with a supportive parent, caregiver, or other adult" (Center on the Developing Child, n.d.). These relationships buffer children from developmental disruption (Center on the Developing Child, n.d.). —Emily Gibson

External or Environmental Protective Factors of Resilience

In addition to internal protective factors, external—or environmental—protective factors can bolster students' resilience. These protective factors are embedded in an individual's life, such as within the home, neighborhood, school, and peer group. To a great extent, staff can develop these factors in schools, by which staff can support resilience in students. Thus, they represent a treasure trove of hope for educators searching for ways to dramatically impact students' lives.

Research on resilience supports the idea that schools can be safe havens where students, especially struggling students in high-poverty schools, find academic and social success. This research has identified key elements of school climate—external protective factors—that, when emphasized and improved on in high-poverty schools, can lead to higher student achievement, higher morale among students and teachers, more reflective practice among teachers, fewer dropouts, reduced violence, better community relations, and increased institutional pride (Bryant & Kelley, 2006; Henderson, 2013). In essence, they provide an atmosphere of care and trust that supports growing resilience for our most traumatized and troubled students.

One environmental protective factor of note is providing opportunities for students to contribute to their community. Being needed and being depended upon builds resilience.

> The challenge for our schools is to engage children by providing them opportunities to participate in meaningful activities and roles. There are many ways to infuse participation into the school day. Some examples include: giving students more opportunities to respond to questions; asking their opinions on issues; asking questions that encourage critical, reflective thinking; making learning more hands-on; involving students in curriculum planning; using participatory evaluation strategies; and employing approaches like cooperative learning, peer helping, cross-age mentoring, and community service. Such strategies bond young people to their school community and can promote all the traits of resiliency—social competence, problem solving, autonomy, and a sense of a bright future. (Benard, 1993)

Another positive outcome of implementing the above ideas is to boost executive function skills, which are critical for successfully navigating a pathway out of poverty.

Similar to the internal protective factors, various resources have represented the key environmental protective factors in numerous ways. We have combined a number of these resources (Benard, 1993; Center on the Developing Child, n.d.; Healy, 2014; Henderson, 2013; Konnikova, 2016) into one list that school personnel can use to evaluate existing practices and identify ways to strengthen and build environmental protective factors within the school (see figure 4.2, page 80).

When it comes to providing external supports for students, a whole-school approach is essential. This means that all the school's staff must have unified beliefs and behaviors regarding the essential messages, or essential mirrors, that they convey to students day after day. Teachers and other school personnel must provide a

- Provide care and support; teach students how to ask for help.

- Set and communicate positive, high expectations.

- Provide opportunities for meaningful student participation, voice, and choice.

- Facilitate supportive, positive adult-student and student-student relationships.

- Establish and reinforce clear and consistent boundaries, expectations, and rules.

- Teach life skills, like skills for coping with the inevitability of change and the uncertainty of life.

- Teach mindfulness skills and self-regulation or self-care strategies.

- Help students learn their strengths and needs.

- Specifically teach optimism and hope.

- Project the view that bumps in the road are minor setbacks, not insurmountable obstacles.

- Provide a school environment that is clean, organized, and structured.

- Create opportunities to utilize sources of strength (faith, spirituality, culture, and community).

Figure 4.2: External or environmental protective factors of resilience.

*Visit **go.SolutionTree.com/schoolimprovement** for a free reproducible version of this figure.*

welcoming community where they surround students with a common voice of positive support and they assist students in overcoming feelings of disconnection and building skills that will help them be successful at school and in life (Cole, Eisner, Gregory, & Ristuccia, 2013). All caring adults in a school are potential agents of protective factors. They can notice and reinforce students' internal protective factors, they can help students recognize and grow these traits, and they can create classroom and school cultures that are infused with the environmental protective factors of regular structures, routines, civility, and care (Henderson, 2013).

❝❞ School has become a vital refuge for a growing number of children, serving as a "protective shield to help children withstand the multiple vicissitudes that they can expect of a stressful world" (Garmezy, 1991).

—**Bonnie Benard**

Field Note

Growing up in poverty with a parent dealing with significant mental and physical health issues, my brother and I were often left to our own devices. When I learned about the internal and environmental protective factors, I shared them with my brother, and we reflected on how we made it out of poverty—what were our protective factors that kept us from making disastrous choices?

One big internal factor of resilience for both of us was a sense of agency or an internal locus of control. We both developed a strong inner sense that we could do things. Our creativity, curiosity, and willingness to try things and fail served us well in turning our initial clumsy attempts into strengths of self-confidence.

A big external factor of our resilience was the numerous positive connections we had with adults in our community. We grew up in a small town, where everyone knew everyone. When our mom was sidelined with her own struggles, we were able to find jobs as teenagers and transition into the world of work and belonging in our community. —Emily Gibson

The Self-Righting Capacity of Learners to Build Resilience

The innate self-righting capacity of the human spirit is often mentioned in resilience literature (see, for example, Benard, 1993; Henderson, 2013). It is through fostering the external protective factors, which, in turn, strengthen students' internal protective factors, that schools can help students "right themselves." Educators, leaders, and staff members can use the previously presented list of environmental protective factors (figure 4.2) to assess, through surveys or focus groups of stakeholders, how well a school is supporting student resilience (Henderson, 2012). In schools where environmental protective factors are in force (see Benard, 1993; Frankel, 2001; Garbarino, Dubrow, Kostelny, & Pardo, 1992), students experiencing adversity, trauma, and stress show impressive gains, including:

- Real academic growth and progress
- Lower levels of disruptive behaviors
- Healthy social adjustment
- Increased attendance
- Greater engagement

In addition to the research on resilience in youth, we considered the research on poverty and resilience in education. Research on each of these topics gave us the foundation for a new understanding of an effective high-poverty school; it provided the opportunity to define a *resilient school*. Both topics, in our eyes, would be integral to any comprehensive plan we could create to foster resilient schools. The next section will thus outline the research on poverty and resilience in education and describe how this research helped form the basis of our resilient school model. These threads of research come together in a tapestry of resilience that ultimately supports not only students but also staff and families.

Field Note

Children learn to make choices from the adults in their lives. When their parents or guardians are unable to make choices that improve their own circumstances, when they have learned helplessness or a fatalistic view of life, or when they are just so overwhelmingly tired and worn-out that they can't make decisions, children will likely follow suit—that is, unless other adults model, provide support, and expect better for children. This is where all the adults in schools come in. If parents or guardians are not able to pass on these skills to their children, the schools can provide that foundation and transfer those needed, lagging executive function skills of planning, dreaming, accessing resources, and learning. —Emily Gibson

Research on Poverty and Resilience in Education

Since the 1990s, a growing number of schools scattered across the United States have gradually but seriously been learning how to address the needs of students and families impacted by poverty. During that time, many high-poverty schools have made incredible improvements. As a result of educators' grassroots efforts to close achievement gaps, researchers (for example, Carter, 2000; Chenoweth, 2007, 2009; Education Trust, 2005; Stringfield & Teddlie, 1988) have been able to identify and study high-poverty, high-performing schools, a concept that people had previously assumed to be an oxymoron. Over time, this growing body of high-quality research from different fields of study, including sociology, psychology, education, history, and economics, began to coalesce knowledge around public education's role in responding to the issues of poverty and learning (see Barr & Parrett, 2007; Budge & Parrett, 2018).

This foundation of essential knowledge grew, describing the nature of effective schools for those impacted by poverty. As these isolated research efforts continued, these pioneers began to question some early conclusions and replicate others. Occasionally, articles, books, and reports would appear that collected, synthesized, and analyzed research from many individual efforts. This research focused on school culture, trauma and childhood adversity, effective schools, community outreach programs, and school staff needs. And with each new piece of research, a new aspect of the gestalt of an effective school emerged. It is this growing conception of a schoolwide effort, plus the analysis and synthesis of these new insights, that has enabled researchers to give educational practitioners strong, reliable knowledge that will guide their school practices with more predictable outcomes. In 2020, this research on poverty and education makes it possible to provide better, more effective schooling for students living in poverty.

All this research can coalesce into a network of resilience, a blueprint for a resilient school. When implemented in schools, this network has the capacity to reduce poverty's impact on learning and human development by stabilizing families, continuously reinvigorating school staff, and supporting low-income students—now the majority in our public schools—to find success in school and beyond. This research promises that schools can provide a pathway to a better life for students impacted by traumas and ACEs and help them break out of the endless cycle of generational poverty that entraps so many people.

The concept of the resilient school brings together the efforts of a broad spectrum of research since the 1990s. It combines research on developmental risk factors and assets; trauma and stress neuroscience; high-poverty, high-performing schools; childhood trauma and adversity; social-emotional needs of the whole child; the needs of families; and school staff attrition, job satisfaction, and morale. In the following sections, we will briefly touch on notable research from each of these topics and identify key qualities for any framework that will truly make a difference in the fight against poverty.

" " Educators cannot eradicate poverty, remove neighborhood gangs, stop cultural violence, heal parental addictions, or prevent the myriad of other types of stress, risk, and trauma that many students face daily. Yet my teachers . . . did much to foster my resilience without even knowing that they were doing it.

—Nan Henderson

Developmental Risk Factors and Assets

In 1997, the Search Institute shared forty developmental assets essential for positive youth development that resulted from their extensive research in youth development, resilience, and prevention of problems during adolescence and young adulthood (Benson, 1997). Half of the assets relate to internal protective factors, such as commitment to learning and positive identity, and half relate to external or environmental protective factors, such as support and empowerment. (Visit www.search-institute.org /our-research/development-assets/developmental-assets-framework/ for the full list of all forty assets.) Since the original identification of the developmental assets, the Search Institute has surveyed over six million youth as part of its positive youth development research. This continued research led to further refinement and deepening of the important role these assets play in positive life outcomes. The forty developmental assets can be viewed as milestones and learning gained by successful youth, within the context of the environment and community. Stakeholders in high-poverty communities can use surveys—developed by the Search Institute—to focus on assets youth need and opportunities for youth to gain needed assets.

In the mid-1980s, researchers at the Centers for Disease Control and Prevention (2018) began collecting data from nineteen other federal agencies to identify the risky behavior of teenagers (see Barr & Parrett, 2008). These efforts resulted in a definitive list of risk factors that tend to put youth at greater risk for school failure, including alcohol use, drug use, sex, suicide, unsafe behaviors, tobacco use, and poor nutrition (see Centers for Disease Control and Prevention, 2018; Eaton et al., 2006). Taken together, the research into assets and risk factors supports the research on resilience and the internal and external protective factors. The Search Institute's work emphasizes what communities can do to inoculate youth against the risk factors identified by the CDC research.

Trauma and Stress Neuroscience

Neuroscience has also provided essential contributions in the understanding of poverty and education. Neurobiologists at the Child Trauma Academy, including Bruce Perry (2002), have been researching the effects of trauma and stress on the developing brain. Cultural class and social threats are processed the same way as physical threats, and any threat triggers protective factors in the brain which impede learning. Perry (2002), Eric Jensen (2009, 2013, 2019), Zaretta Hammond (2015), and others have helped popularize and expand the connection between the brain, poverty, culture, and learning.

High-Poverty, High-Performing Schools

At the same time, researchers focused on schools. Dozens of high-quality research studies, some complex and long-range (for example, the Louisiana School Effectiveness Study that lasted ten years and involved hundreds of studies; see Barr & Parrett, 2007), began coming together to form a bold new concept: the high-poverty, high-performing school. Effective school studies likewise grew and fit neatly together with studies on effective high-poverty schools. Research on high-poverty, high-performing schools was replicated again and again in state and national studies until an accepted understanding of the essential elements of an effective high-poverty school emerged (see Barr & Parrett, 2007; Budge & Parrett, 2018; Parrett & Budge, 2012). The Education Trust in Washington, DC, served as a major collection and dissemination hub for the research, identification, and celebration of these remarkable schools (see https://edtrust.org).

Childhood Trauma and Adversity

An avalanche of psychology, brain, neuropsychology, biology, and social work research combined insights into the impact of stress, adversity, and trauma on human behavior and learning. At the same time, health research led to the discovery of adverse childhood experiences and the effects of trauma in the home and community. In combination, these studies helped connect the dots between student behavior and stress responses. Brain development and trauma research combined to provide effective strategies for identifying and addressing these challenges in schools and classrooms. (For more information, see the Trauma and Learning Policy Initiative website [https://traumasensitiveschools.org]; the ACES Too High website [https://acestoohigh.com]; and Sporleder & Forbes, 2016.)

Social-Emotional Needs of the Whole Child

Amid the research on high-poverty, high-performing schools, ASCD (2007) established its Commission on the Whole Child. This commission's landmark report helped turn the attention of researchers and educators away from curriculum, instruction, and school strategies to focus squarely on students' social-emotional needs, including the learned helplessness associated with students impacted by poverty (Barr & Gibson, 2013). ASCD (n.d.) has continued to focus on the whole child in the ensuing years, building an intentional movement to address the needs of students—academic, social-emotional, and resource needs (see www.ascd.org /whole-child.aspx).

Needs of Families

Researchers have long considered the relationship between family needs and success in school. In the landmark work *Within Our Reach: Breaking the Cycle of Disadvantage*, authors Lisbeth and Daniel Schorr (1989) raise the idea of disrupting the cycle of disadvantage through the integration of social services and the local school. Later, Lisbeth Schorr (1992) challenged participants at a Northwest Regional Educational Laboratory forum to explore integrating education and human services. Also during this time, sociologist Joy Dryfoos (1998) synthesized research and proposed for the first time the *full-service school*, where local schools would coordinate human services in order to keep students impacted by poverty in school and learning effectively. More recently, a synthesis of twenty studies on the connections between poverty, the needs of low-income families, and education revealed the positive relationship between social safety net programs and student success (Barnum, 2018).

School Staff Attrition, Job Satisfaction, and Morale

Research seeking answers to the high staff attrition and turnover rates, especially in high-poverty and high-minority schools, emphasizes the need to address and support educators' professional needs for training, autonomy, voice, creativity, and success, and their social-emotional needs for relationships, collaboration, connection, pride, and efficacy (Bosso, 2017; Evans, 1997; Senechal et al., 2016). This research helps clarify the debilitating stress of working in high-poverty schools and begins to identify how teachers, administrators, and specialists working in these schools can gather strength and resilience and become more effective.

With this research on poverty and resilience in education forming the basis of our resilient schools model, we next turned our efforts to the framework. The next section details the considerations our framework had to meet in order for it to effectively build resilience in children, families, and schools and help fight the effects of poverty.

A Whole-School Model: The Search for an Effective Framework

The history of education during the last three decades has been a story of an ever-growing research base coupled with more and more studies of effective schools. As scholars and organizations have analyzed these two streams of development together, they have developed a number of effective frameworks, often integrating early conceptions with new areas of research. These early concepts of full-service schools, effective schools, community outreach schools, trauma-sensitive schools, whole-child schools, effective schools, and even high-poverty, high-performing schools each proved extremely useful and helped to integrate what was known to researchers at the time.

Each of these earlier models tended to focus on one major area of improvement. Early efforts like the effective school model and the high-poverty, high-performing model focused primarily on instructional strategies, curriculum, and instruction; others, like the whole-child model, focused initially on the social-emotional needs of students and later combined these with the students' academic needs. More recent efforts, like the community school model, focused primarily on the interrelationship between the school and the community and the human needs of students and their families. While all of these efforts at conceptualizing the effective school for high-poverty communities are powerful and have proved extremely useful in school improvement efforts, each of them tends to focus on certain areas of research and development to the exclusion of others. None offers a comprehensive model that includes and integrates all of the available educational knowledge bases. In 2020, it seems possible to collect all of the available research from the many diverse fields that we have reviewed into a single comprehensive framework that might be used as a blueprint for developing and improving an effective high poverty school—a resilient school. We believe that the resilient school framework provides just such a comprehensive framework for improving schools.

In the following section, we will review the essential elements of an effective high-poverty school These elements include educating the whole child, addressing learners' academic needs as well as social-emotional needs, utilizing a schoolwide framework, becoming trauma-sensitive schools, and leading to relational and professional support for staff working in high-poverty, high-trauma communities, all under the umbrella of hope and optimism.

The Framework Must Educate the Whole Child

Since ASCD's first Commission on the Whole Child (ASCD, 2007), the importance of *whole-child* strategies and efforts for developing and maintaining student engagement and learning through both academic and social-emotional channels has gained in relevance and importance (Jensen, 2019; Darling-Hammond & Cook-Harvey, 2018; Liew & McTigue, 2010). Early interest in educating the whole child led to an essential conclusion: to successfully educate students of poverty, schools must effectively address their cognitive, physical, and social-emotional needs (ASCD, 2007; Aspen Institute, 2018; Darling-Hammond & Cook-Harvey, 2018; Liew & McTigue, 2010). At the Aspen Institute, two hundred researchers, scientists, and practitioners converged to discuss whole child education and review the body of literature on whole child education. Their consensus was that the literature and evidence "confirms that supporting students' social, emotional, and academic development benefits all children and relates positively to the traditional measures we care about: attendance, grades, test scores, graduation rates, college and career success, engaged citizenship, and overall well-being" (Aspen Institute, 2018, p. 2). An interesting outcome of the Aspen Institute's work was the understanding that whole-child education benefits all learners, but it *disproportionately benefits* those who come from low-income neighborhoods (Aspen Institute, 2018, p. 2).

The Framework Must Address Social-Emotional Needs

Research on social-emotional needs documents that schools must surround students with a schoolwide atmosphere of optimism, high expectations, and trust in order to help students impacted by poverty overcome their negative experiences (Aspen Institute, 2018; Barr & Parrett, 2007). To effectively address the effects of poverty, a school's entire staff must share a set of positive values and goals so that all students experience consistent, optimistic messages in every corner of the school (Barr & Gibson, 2013).

The Framework Must Be School- or Districtwide

While understandings about how to best address poor and minority students' academic needs will continue to mature and grow, for the most part researchers have achieved a remarkably consistent and strong consensus that schools should take a school- and districtwide systematic approach to teaching low-income students. We know that what works with students impacted by poverty and the stress and trauma associated with poverty is a complex, demanding, concerted schoolwide effort. The importance of a schoolwide systematic approach has emerged in high-poverty, high-performing school research; school culture research; research on students' social-emotional needs; and resilience research. The specific features of a whole-school systematic approach to school improvement appear in almost every study conducted on poverty, education, and academic learning (Aspen Institute, 2018; Barr & Parrett, 2007; Budge & Parrett, 2018; Chenoweth, 2010; DuFour, DuFour, Eaker, & Karhanek, 2010; DuFour et al., 2016; DuFour & Marzano, 2011; Lezotte & Snyder, 2011; Parrett & Budge, 2012). In 2018, educators assembled at the Aspen Institute reviewed and analyzed over two hundred research reports and came to a clear conclusion: any successful effort to educate children and youth impacted by poverty must involve an agreed-on schoolwide framework that integrates three essential elements of success—(1) cognitive skills and competencies, (2) social and interpersonal skills and competencies, and (3) emotional skills and competencies (Aspen Institute, 2018). These elements are essential because "learning has many dimensions, and they are inextricably linked" (Aspen Institute, 2018, p. 15). The Aspen Institute's (2018) final report, *From a Nation at Risk to a Nation at Hope*, concludes that when a whole school employs a single framework of success, it is clearly observed that "children and youth are engaged, have a sense of ownership, and find purpose in their learning" (p. 22).

In their book *Broader, Bolder, Better: How Schools and Communities Help Students Overcome the Disadvantages of Poverty*, authors Elaine Weiss and Paul Reville (2019) build a strong argument that focusing on a single school requires far too much work for a modest payoff. They argue that to maximize success, entire school districts should support a single system of educational reform. They use New York, Boston, and Vancouver, Washington, as examples of places where districtwide reform efforts have focused on the development of community outreach schools. (Note: the authors have worked extensively in the Vancouver, Washington, school district and share more about this district's efforts and leadership in development of community outreach schools in chapter 7, page 155.) The importance of a single reform system is well documented and powerful, and a single reform system is exactly what a resilient school needs.

The Framework Must Produce a Trauma-Sensitive School

A 2019 report from Harvard's Trauma and Learning Policy Initiative emphasizes that to overcome the effects of trauma and other adversities associated with poverty:

- A schoolwide welcoming and supportive community is essential
- No one teacher can do it alone
- Students must feel safe and connected everywhere in the building

The researchers at the Harvard center describe a school that has these qualities as a *trauma-sensitive school*. In this whole-school model, staff have a schoolwide understanding of the widespread adversity in students' lives and how this adversity affects learning, behavior, and relationships (Cole et al., 2013). This understanding leads to the knowledge that a whole-school response is necessary and that all staff members must work together to support their students. As with the other areas of research, the emphasis is on a whole-school framework for success.

The Framework Must Lead to Relational and Professional Support for Staff Working in High-Poverty, High-Trauma Communities

Though rarely discussed in depth in the literature on high-poverty, high-performing schools, the relational and professional needs of the adults who work in schools must be addressed for a school or district to be resilient. Securing and safeguarding the consistent, stable staff needed to create resilient environments depends on ensuring that staff have what they need to engage fully with students, curriculum, and families without burning out. An additional, rarely mentioned aspect of staff resilience is the secondary traumatic stress that can be experienced by staff working in high-poverty, high-trauma communities. The real needs of staff in this area is noticeably absent from the literature on trauma-sensitive schools (for example, Cole et al., 2013), and we, the authors, believe that this must become a higher priority for schools in order to stem the tide of teacher attrition that disproportionately impacts low-income and minority students (Podolsky et al., 2016).

The Framework Must Lead to a School Filled With Hope and Optimism

A growing body of research and practice emphasizes the importance of surrounding students with hope, optimism, high expectations, and positive reinforcement in overcoming the hopelessness of poverty (Jensen, 2009; Seligman, 2007; Sharot, 2011). In our 2013 work *Building a Culture of Hope: Enriching Schools With Optimism and Opportunity*, we describe such a school as having a Culture of Hope (Barr & Gibson, 2013). Underlying all the research-based strategies for improving student learning described thus far is the truth that students will respond to an atmosphere of hope and optimism in a positive manner, rising to high expectations and fueling their dreams with hope.

The Framework of the Resilient School

In our observations of schools and our review of the literature, it appeared to us that we could pull these various research conclusions and experiences together into a meaningful whole. We wanted to provide a conceptual organizer, a capstone of what we know about teaching, learning, and the needs of students living in poverty. Our concept of the resilient school seems to do just that, capturing the concept of a transformed school that serves students impacted by poverty in a value-added way, going beyond the concepts of full-service schools, community outreach schools, trauma-sensitive schools, whole-child schools, effective schools, and even high-poverty, high-performing schools. In our experience, no other established model incorporates the vast and varied research bases in quite the same way, nor organizes thinking in as effective a way as our resilient school model.

In this book, we attempt to share our vision of the resilient school as a blueprint for school improvement. A blueprint for a house will have all the expected elements—a roof, walls, entryways, and windows—but the contractor decides the details. Such is this blueprint of the resilient school, a representation of what is possible. Each school and each community can thus determine exactly how to use this blueprint to develop its response to poverty in its given context.

The resilient school provides a schoolwide framework, a whole-child emphasis, and four essential cornerstones of success, each serving to bolster student resilience (see figure 4.3).

1. Addressing students' academic needs

2. Addressing students' social-emotional needs

3. Addressing students' and their families' human needs

4. Addressing staff's professional and relational needs

Figure 4.3: The framework of the resilient school

Within the framework of the resilient school, a further expansion of the concept the Culture of Hope also occurs. Rather than focusing solely on student's social-emotional needs, the Culture of Hope now relates directly to all of the school shareholders: students, parents, and school staff. In fact, the Culture of Hope permeates the four cornerstones of the resilient school. Through the community outreach of resilient schools, it is now possible to see the impact that a Culture of Hope has on students' families and, in fact, on the community as a whole. Optimism and hope can have a transforming effect on staff, families, and their students. It opens up a new horizon of possibilities, and replaces futility and despair with hope for a better life. A Culture of Hope must permeate the school, it must also extend like a lighthouse of optimism throughout the community. Thus, the Culture of Hope is woven throughout the four cornerstones of the resilient school; the two concepts are inseparable.

Over the next four chapters, we will present, in detail, each of the four cornerstones of a resilient school. Our aim is to bring hope to educators by providing a blueprint for actions they can take to begin creating resilient schools and fostering resilient students within the context of their communities and student populations. When schools combine their energies in this way, they have the capacity to become truly resilient schools. When a school district rallies a community to join in the massive job of providing for children and youth, incredible things happen: "It is absolutely possible to radically transform America's schools into powerful institutions that offer children, their families and entire communities true hope for a better future" (Quinn, 2011, p. ix). For families living on the "outskirts of hope" (Johnson, 1964), resilient schools bring them into hope for improved circumstances in their current lives and better future lives. The stakes are high—but there is hope!

Conclusion

In this chapter, we have reviewed the expansive body of research supporting the concept of *resilience*. This research documents the unique factors associated with resilience and the incredibly hopeful fact that those factors can be taught. As educators, we now know that we can actually teach students to become more resilient through reinforcing their internal protective factors and creating school communities that provide the external protective factors associated with resilience. And, we can strengthen and support students' natural self-righting capacity, which enables them to overcome the debilitating effects of poverty. In these ways, we can help students learn how to bounce back from trauma and adversity in their lives.

As so often happens in the world of research, as new insights and information become available and the various new pieces of knowledge merge with existing knowledge and practice, new patterns can emerge. As we examined the interrelationships between personal resilience, the social-emotional needs of youth, research on the whole child, the effects of trauma and childhood adversity, and the ever-growing research on effective high-poverty schools, a new gestalt seemed to click into place. This new gestalt describes the most effective approach to supporting and fostering resilience and helping students succeed in school as an approach that surrounds students with a whole-school culture of optimism, caring, respect, and high expectations—surrounding students with a Culture of Hope. We, the authors, call this new gestalt of research the *resilient school*.

Building a resilient school is a "process of becoming." Our description of a resilient school in the coming chapters offers a framework of possibilities that can be used as a measure to evaluate a school; it can also be used to *triage* existing programs, to help school staff identify and talk about what they are doing well, and to help them identify areas of needed improvement. The resilient school framework is a blueprint for building a better classroom, a better school, and a better community. The resilient school framework offers our students, their families and their teachers a hope for a better tomorrow. We hope that the resilient school framework will prove useful in helping schools everywhere to keep focused on their pathway forward and to keep their eyes on their students' futures.

In the coming chapters, each of the essential cornerstones of resilience is presented in more detail: addressing the academic needs of students, addressing the social-emotional needs of students, addressing the human needs of students and their families, and addressing the professional and relational needs of the school staff.

Next Steps

Please complete the following Next Steps, to integrate your experiences within your own schools and communities with the information presented in this chapter.

1. On page 80, figure 4.2 lists several key environmental protective factors of resilience. As you read this list, consider the following questions.

   a. Which of these protective factors are you currently implementing in your classroom, school, or district? How have you seen these efforts impact your students?

   b. Choose one of the factors you are not currently implementing in your classroom, school, or district. In what ways can you change your practice to strengthen your students' resilience?

2. Are there any schools in your district or nearby in your state that have implemented a community outreach approach? You and some of your colleagues might consider a visit to see one of these schools in operation. The Vancouver Public Schools in Washington regularly host seminars and visits to their family-community resource centers.

3. What do you think are the essential elements of an effective school? A schoolwide discussion regarding the essential elements of an effective school might help to identify agreements and disagreements in the school staff's vision of your school purpose and goals.

4. Looking ahead, which of the four cornerstones are you most interested in learning more about, and why?

5. Why did you become an educator? Knowing what you now know about internal and environmental protective factors, which factors played a role in your life and your decision to become an educator?

Chapter 5

The First Cornerstone of the Resilient School: Addressing Students' Academic Needs

If you provide children with quality education options, support families and children holistically in a community setting, and enlist the support of universities as partners with community, you produce better academic results and improved community outcomes. Then what happens? Eventually, the cycle of poverty breaks. One family at a time.

—Gloria Bonilla-Santiago

Any realistic effort to help students break out of the cycle of poverty must address their academic needs. This relates directly to the challenges that students living in poverty bring to school (discussed in chapter 2, page 31) and was the focus of the initial research on high-poverty, high-performing schools (for example, Carter, 2000; Chenoweth, 2007, 2009; Education Trust, 2005; Stringfield & Teddlie, 1988). Addressing students' academic needs is a foundational aspect of any whole-school effort at building student resilience, as academic success is tied to resilience in a self-reinforcing loop. Thus, all aspects of the web of resilience work toward the ultimate goal of ensuring each and every student learns effectively, masters the basics, stays in school, completes a rigorous academic curriculum, graduates, and finds success in postsecondary education or training. Unless this difficult, long-term goal is accomplished, all else is futile. All the efforts to meet students' social-emotional needs, assist their parents and guardians, and provide staff with necessary support and training are only as valuable as their ultimate contribution to students' academic success. Learning effectively and succeeding in school is the ultimate bottom line.

The good news is this: since the initial research in the 1990s on high-poverty, high-performing schools, the consensus among educators has drastically shifted toward an expectation that *all* students, even those impacted by poverty, *can* and *will* learn effectively (Barr & Parrett, 2008; Chenoweth, 2007, 2009; DuFour et al., 2016). This sea change has moved public education from the old *normal curve* perspective, in which teachers always expected some students to fail, to the new *mastery learning,* perspective, in which the focus is on continuous progress, with the belief that any student, regardless of demographics, can learn effectively and achieve high levels of academic excellence. For U.S. public schools, it represents a revolution in teaching and learning. Some have referred to it as the *new American revolution* (Barr & Parrett, 2007).

The consistency of this new perspective should not lead anyone to believe that this shift comes easily. Improving educational outcomes in high-poverty, high-trauma schools is one of the most difficult and demanding journeys of any professional world. However, we as educators and leaders know so much about what we need to do to meet this daunting task, and even largely how to do it, thanks to the considerable body of research and practice available. All it takes, it seems, is the desire to start down the long and demanding road and the will to stay the course until all students find success. The resilient school framework provides a roadmap for navigating and staying on course to reach and teach all learners. The framework identifies all of the complex parts of an effective school and helps school staff as they attempt to triage their school, identifying what they are doing well and areas for needed improvement. The resilient school framework can act as a blueprint or a road map to guide school improvement.

While isolating any single aspect of the resilient school framework is artificial, this chapter presents just the first cornerstone of the framework—addressing students' academic needs—and identifies and briefly summarizes the ten interrelated essentials that characterize effective resilient schools where all students learn effectively and academic achievement gaps are closed. These ten essentials are:

1. Visionary leadership
2. Effective teachers and the Power of We
3. Data, assessment, and accountability
4. Rigorous, aligned curriculum for all
5. Progress monitoring and remediation
6. Extra time for instruction and support

7. Targeted reading and mathematics

8. Positive interpersonal relationships

9. Parent and guardian involvement

10. Trauma-informed practices

While each of these essentials for academic success has power to positively influence student academic success, the truly great power comes when they are all utilized and integrated into a concerted school- and, ideally, districtwide effort. Additionally, it is crucial that these academic essentials take place within the larger environment of a Culture of Hope. In the past, there has been a rather clear separation between students' academic needs and social-emotional needs. This separation has experienced a slow transformation. It is now understood that overcoming students' feelings of helplessness and futility has a huge and lasting effect on their academic successes. In this chapter we detail the *big ideas*, or essentials, that have been documented in the high-poverty, high-performing schools research. Yet, all of the research conclusions regarding the effective instruction of students impacted by poverty are dependent on student attitudes and self-concepts. To seriously address the needs of students impacted by poverty, including the academic needs of students, a culture of hope and optimism must permeate the entire school and its classrooms; it must surround students and the entire school staff, and must also be extended beyond the school into student's families.

To be clear, while this chapter will present each of the ten big ideas in detail and within the context of the Culture of Hope, it will *not* discuss the complex array of factors related to academic learning which are associated with the other three cornerstones: health, hunger, trauma, fear, social-emotional learning, staff effectiveness, and so on. We will address those issues in subsequent chapters. Furthermore, this chapter will not provide a comprehensive presentation of the vast library of research-supported instructional strategies and approaches related to academic learning. According to Richard DuFour and Robert Marzano (2011):

> No single instructional strategy is guaranteed to result in high levels of student learning. Even strategies that have a solid research base supporting their effectiveness are likely to be found ineffective by a substantial number of other studies assessing the impact of those same strategies. (pp. 141–142)

Teachers have a veritable feast of instructional strategies available to choose from, but space simply does not allow for this book to explore approaches such as mastery learning, differentiated instruction, project and experimental learning, self-regulated strategy development, the Workshop Model, and the rich, research-supported strategies developed within each content area. Instead, we encourage readers to continue on their own their exploration of highly effective approaches to ensure the learning of all students.

Academic Essential 1: Visionary Leadership

A survey of studies on school improvement at the school level revealed that effective leadership is one of the most, if not *the* most, important factors in school improvement (Barr & Parrett, 2007). Visionary leadership includes a strong school leadership team and shared decision making involving the entire staff (Hechinger Report, 2011; Murphy & Torre, 2014). The most effective schools, over time, include parents, guardians, and community leaders in school-based advisory groups. Such an expansive view of leadership enables a school to maintain long-term consistency, even through periods of transformation and transition.

Leadership emerged as a critical factor in both the effective school research and the high-poverty, high-performing school research (Hechinger Report, 2011; Murphy & Torre, 2014). Becoming a high-performing school demands visionary leaders with a single burning focus: effective learning for all students, whatever it takes. The effective leader must work with all school staff to develop a commitment to a set of shared beliefs and goals for the school. The effective principal uses data and meets regularly with teachers to review student assessments. Teachers and support staff receive dedicated time to review student achievement data and plan needed interventions and adjustments to instruction. The effective principal may visit classrooms daily and often includes home visits as a normal part of his or her job. Such a leader constantly reviews class and school achievement records and provides regular reports on progress toward school goals to stakeholders. Leadership must also encourage and provide time for teacher collaboration and often establishes local advisory boards composed of parents, guardians, and community members. (For an overview of shared leadership, see Lambert, 2002.)

In order to ensure that all students learn effectively, leaders may have to work with established teachers to help them adjust skills and strategies that once served them well but are no longer effective with shifting student populations. Many teachers may have implicit biases regarding class and race, and effective leaders must help school staff come to recognize biases and prejudices (in addition to recognizing their own) and, through team building, help all teachers and specialists accept and support common schoolwide goals (see Gibson & Barr, 2017; Gorski, 2013).

> **❝❞** Administrators have a moral obligation to stand tall with teachers to do what's right for kids.
>
> **—Former superintendent**

The visionary leader is called on to lead drastic changes in his or her school and in the community. This calls for clear and concise goals; vigorous, visionary encouragement; and comprehensive staff development. It also demands a firm reliance on data, assessment, and accountability. Teachers now expect professional evaluations to include data on student achievement. Most of all, visionary leadership calls for a laser-like focus on academic achievement for all students. That is the major purpose of modern school administrators.

Insights into management, administration, and leadership have shown the power of shared decision making. Effective schools demand a strong and functioning leadership team working together to continually improve performance. Leaders must share visioning, planning, and decision making with a cross section of the school and community stakeholders. As a result, decisions are more able to weather changes in school personnel. Throughout this book, we use the term *leadership* in this larger sense—to convey shared decision making (see Chenoweth, 2010; DuFour & Marzano, 2011).

Academic Essential 2: Effective Teachers and the Power of We

The foundation of any school-improvement plan lies in the effective classroom teacher, who is caring, supportive, and consistently present for students. Yet finding, recruiting, and maintaining effective teachers in high-poverty areas is often a daunting task (see chapter 3, page 49). The demands of working daily in classrooms and schools filled with students impacted by poverty and trauma can be, at a minimum, a challenging experience. Recruitment and retention of effective teachers requires continual staff development and staff support programs, as well as staff collaboration, because people find great strength in being in something together, or what we call the *Power of We* (Barr & Gibson, 2013).

The effectiveness of school staff multiplies when the school leader and the school leadership team help them develop a unified set of common beliefs and goals. It is essential that teachers, professional staff, parents and guardians, community partners, and even students all hold a clear vision of what they are about and what they are working toward. Everyone must know and believe in the importance of goals such as "All students will read at grade level by the end of the third grade," "The achievement gap will be closed at least 5 percent this year," or "Our front office is welcoming to parents and guardians."

Regardless of specific goals, the leadership team is responsible for ensuring that everyone develops, understands, shares, and supports the goals. The team should teach new school or district hires the goals and the underlying reasons for the goals to ensure their buy-in and support. An absence of strong, shared schoolwide goals leaves the door open for mixed signals and reduces the chances that *all* students will experience successful academic learning. And while district goals and objectives must have top-to-bottom consistency, schoolwide goals cannot simply be mandated by the school board or central administration. Instead, schools must develop them through the long and often complex process of group discussion and processing. Research is crystal clear on this issue: nothing builds effectiveness like a schoolwide group of teachers and administrators all sharing common goals (Barr & Parrett, 2008). The school staff must always keep shared goals as the focus of all their work and all their decisions. They must unrelentingly concentrate on where the school is moving and what they will achieve together (DuFour et al., 2010). Research even seems to suggest that if school staff develop shared goals, gather data regularly, and meet often to review progress, goal fulfillment becomes almost a self-fulfilling prophecy (Barr & Parrett, 2008). Few things are as powerful for student achievement as a unified school staff.

Ensuring all students are learning demands a new type of teacher. No longer can teachers simply close their door and go about their business. Instead, they must work together, rely on each other, and share and learn from one another. This looks like teams observing one another and teaching model lessons for one another. It looks like teams of teachers developing cooperative lessons and assessments. In essence, it looks like the PLC process. The power of PLCs has been well documented (DuFour et al., 2016). At its core, a PLC is a whole-school or whole-district effort in which teachers in subject- or grade-level teams meet regularly to compare student assessments, seek help and enrichment from teachers who have been more successful with certain learning goals, and learn from each other. Teachers in well-running PLCs are constantly asking one another, "How can we teach this better? How can we improve?" by organizing their work around the three big ideas and four critical questions of a PLC (DuFour et al., 2016). This development of teachers sharing and working together has proven incredibly productive for academic learning gains (DuFour & Marzano, 2011). Chapter 8 (page 191) describes the PLC process in further detail.

While a local school can often make its way to improved performance working largely alone, having a unified, systematic set of expectations and supports across an entire district vastly improves the chances of significant student achievement. If the school board, superintendent, advisory boards, principal, and school leadership team all hold the same expectations and enjoy the necessary support, truly great things can happen, and happen quickly (DuFour et al., 2010).

Academic Essential 3: Data, Assessment, and Accountability

The No Child Left Behind years greatly challenged school leadership. The NCLB legislation required leaders to not only develop and implement a school or district data and assessment plan but also participate in a statewide data and assessment plan.

This necessitated that many schools first build school- and communitywide acceptance of the importance of data, then create a system for collecting data, and finally understand how they could use data to guide decisions, evaluate school staff, and assess student progress. While NCLB was replaced by the Every Student Succeeds Act (ESSA) in 2015, the reliance on quality data processes remains.

All in the school community must understand the use of data and assessment, know the difference between quality data and poor data, and become assessment literate. They must use assessment data in all activities and decisions, and leaders and educators must use data to equitably and powerfully guide instruction (see Barr & Parrett, 2007). In order to be effective, decisions about what services or interventions a student requires must be data driven or data based. When students only receive support if an adult notices their need and recommends them for services, many students will slip through the cracks, especially the quiet rule-followers and those who exhibit internalizing behaviors. This is why an advisory group or leadership team must meet regularly to review data and identify specific students who need support (Buffum, Mattos, & Malone, 2017; DuFour et al., 2016).

For all students to learn effectively and for achievement gaps to close, the entire school and community must be able to follow the school's progress toward schoolwide goals, such as "All students will be literate by the end of the third grade" or "We will see 95 percent daily attendance for the school." Many effective schools have large posters in the front hallway that are updated each week to document progress toward school goals for all to see.

While assessment will always be used and misused in the emotionally charged environment of politics, school- and district-level assessment should focus on using data to improve instruction and curriculum so that all students are successful and demographic learning gaps are eliminated. The availability of classroom assessment data can also help administrators identify inept or failing teachers or teachers with possible implicit biases. This information helps protect students from ineffective and even destructive teachers, and also assists leaders with the long and often slow process of building a strong, effective faculty that works well with low-income and minority students.

Closing the achievement gap for poor and minority students demands not just a determined focus on the school's shared goals but also widespread agreement in the school community that everyone is accountable for student success—*all* students' success. We cannot accept failure. This means recognizing our individual and collective accountability—developing the mindset that every student is our student and that we are responsible for ensuring all students, not just the ones who will likely succeed with little intervention, become the best version of themselves. Everyone—absolutely every adult on campus—must understand this responsibility, adequately prepare to meet this responsibility, and deliver on agreed-on actions. Over time, the school must provide more and more attention to those students who are still behind until all students achieve the desired learning goals.

While effective schools ensure their curriculum closely follows state standards and assessments, not one of the high-poverty, high-performing schools that Karin Chenoweth (2010), writer-in-residence at the Education Trust, has studied spends "a huge amount of time teaching their students what will be on the state tests or teaching them how to 'bubble in' a scoring sheet" (p. 216). During the No Child Left Behind years, schools often spent hours teaching students how to do bubble tests, how to game the system, and how to figure out what the answer was if you didn't know it. And they often gave out huge rewards for increasing test scores, even medals and gift certificates (Chenoweth, 2010). Fortunately, these practices have largely subsided with the reauthorization of the ESSA (2015).

There is a huge difference between teaching to the test and teaching an aligned curriculum. The first is passive, rote, and designed simply to boost test scores. The second teaches the concepts, ideas, skills, and strategies being assessed and is designed to have students truly learn how to think. High scores on state assessments should be a byproduct of quality teaching, not the focus.

Field Note

 Educators must monitor student progress with an eye toward celebrating success, not just planning for improvement. Focusing on what isn't working without celebrating what is working sucks the life and passion out of an already-taxed staff. With NCLB's emphasis on test scores instead of students, many educators have a bit of PTSD about monitoring assessments and focusing on what still needs to be done. Reaching and teaching every student over the course of a school year is always an endless mountain, a marathon, so we need to acknowledge and celebrate what folks have accomplished before telling them they have twenty more miles to go! —Emily Gibson

Academic Essential 4: Rigorous, Aligned Curriculum for All

In terms of addressing the needs of students impacted by poverty, what we teach is just as important as how we teach it. The Education Trust (Barth et al., 1999) documents that affluent students and poor or minority students may have vastly different experiences of the same course. And too often, students impacted by poverty may be placed (or tracked) into applied classes and career classes, rather than assigned to regular core classes. While some of these courses are essential in helping students prepare for life after high school, they cannot be used as substitutes for core classes.

Schools can no longer offer some students an enriched, rigorous curriculum and others a watered-down, slow-tracked curriculum. For example, teachers often assign students whom they think are unable to pass algebra to courses in *opportunity mathematics* or *general mathematics*, thus dooming these students to academic failure. Each and every student, regardless of family income or social standing, must receive a rigorous, standards-based curriculum that reflects the best knowledge available from the various professional subject-matter associations. Some scholars emphasize the importance of a rigorous curriculum by referring to it as a *guaranteed curriculum for all* (DuFour & Marzano, 2011).

Effective schools do not dumb down the curriculum when students struggle. Instead, they provide the attention and scaffolding to help each student achieve success in a rigorous curriculum. School districts that have shifted to a single common curriculum and also encourage poor and minority students to take advanced placement or International Baccalaureate courses have documented how successful all students can be in these demanding courses (see, for example, Adelman, 1999).

Schools must carefully align a rigorous school curriculum with state standards, national subject-matter standards, and all required student assessments. If they don't, they will effectively doom students' success, for the students will likely be assessed on information that they have not been taught (Drake, 2012; Drake & Burns, 2004; Perma & Davis, 2006; Tyler, 1949). Students must pursue the same rigorous curriculum as all other students in all other schools in the district and the state. Without a common, carefully aligned curriculum for all, students will be handicapped and unable to compete with others on the SAT and state assessments (Parrett & Budge, 2012; Tyler, 1949).

Field Note

The Advancement via Individual Determination (AVID) program seeks to rectify inequities of instructional practices by providing poor and minority students with rigorous, inquiry-based instruction that prepares them for college. Students in AVID graduate and attend college at higher rates than similar non-AVID peers. Their success is tied to the skills they gain in AVID classrooms: critical thinking, collaborative skills, self-efficacy, and a can-do spirit. AVID's strength lies partially in the program's approach to professional development, which directly confronts implicit and explicit biases, helping teachers relate to all students and have high expectations for all students (see www.avid.org for more information). —Emily Gibson

Academic Essential 5: Progress Monitoring and Remediation

If all students are to learn effectively and the achievement gap is to close, schools must carefully and accurately monitor student learning and have an effective program of remediation and intervention in place. This way, they can track each student's progress toward his or her learning goals. This multitiered system of supports (MTSS) is key to student success. As part of the MTSS or response to intervention

(RTI) processes expected in all public schools, teachers and intervention specialists must monitor student progress at regular intervals (typically six to eight weeks) and adjust instruction and interventions in mathematics and language arts as needed (for more information, see https://rti4success.org/essential-components-rti). Quick feedback to students is a hallmark of effective teaching: "Credible and timely feedback from a trusted individual is one of the most powerful influences on human learning" (Lezotte & Snyder, 2011, p. 92). The sooner students recognize their successes and mistakes, the more quickly they can improve their performance. Even more important, ongoing monitoring of student progress leads to immediate identification of students who falter and fail. The sooner this happens, the faster interventions can occur and the more quickly students catch up.

In addition to monitoring learning, schools must have a systematic process for addressing the identified needs. In his numerous presentations and throughout the work he did with schools and districts, Rick DuFour is often quoted as having said, "Don't tell me you believe that all students can learn—tell me what you're doing about the kids who aren't learning." It is the action that matters most for student learning.

Effective schools have a system to immediately address the needs of particular students whenever they falter or fall behind. Many schools have systems in place to address identified deficits at least before the week ends. These may be intense one-on-one instructional sessions, they may be groups helping one another, or they may be guided homework support sessions. Often the focus is on providing guided reteaching sessions or help in mastering skills.

> " If you don't continually assess student progress and wait until the end of the year, all you will be doing is conducting an "autopsy" rather than a weekly "checkup."
>
> —Craig Jerald, the Education Trust

The aim of all assessments should be to determine progress toward learning goals and provide interventions and remediation as quickly as possible to keep students on track for learning. Every time instruction occurs for anyone at any age, some achieve the learning, others only partially achieve the learning, and some fail to achieve the instructional goal. Yet in our time-driven public schools, the curriculum or instructional train never stops moving down the tracks, thus leaving behind many students who either did not get on the train or only just got on it and failing to provide new, enriching destinations for those students who mastered the learning goals. If teachers do not quickly identify the students who need some remediation or even reteaching, they will fall further and further behind. This is why regular and accurate assessment and rapid responses are so essential. Some call this *just-in-time intervention* (Lezotte & Snyder, 2011).

When educators first confront this concept of remediation and reteaching, they often ask, "When will we do this?" Veterans on the closing-the-gap battleground answer, "You must do it as soon as possible," "You must do it today," or "You must do it this week." In truth, scheduling time for remediation and intervention is just as important as providing the original instructional time. This presents an enormous challenge for educators early on in the school reform process, seeking to find time in the already-packed school day for this crucial practice.

To answer this challenge, some schools establish *learning labs* and schedule time each day that students may use for remediation, interventions, or enrichment. Learning labs address the specific needs of students through reteaching, one-on-one tutoring or helping, or through guided practice. As soon as a student has resolved his or her learning need, the student moves directly into enrichment activities. Some high schools, modeling college course schedules, plan academic instruction for only four days each week and leave one day for remediation, interventions, and enrichment. In this schedule, Fridays become extremely important: college courses may be offered, special field trips arranged, career explorations made available, time for student project learning provided, and, of course, remediation and interventions offered. The richness of the Friday experiences serves to motivate students to complete all assignments and quickly pass all tests so they might participate in these interesting and attractive learning activities. (For more on interventions and remediation and when and how to employ each, see https://bit.ly/3adlu5b; Michell, 2018.)

Another idea that is growing in popularity and effectiveness is having students participate in setting learning goals and then conduct their own assessment of learning growth. This often includes maintaining and displaying portfolios of work samples that the students feel document their progress toward their goals. The students meet periodically with their teacher to review their work and discuss their personal progress. The portfolios of work samples become essential at student-led parent conferences, where the students display their work and explain to their parents their progress across the semester. Research has found great value in both student-monitored assessments and student-led parent conferences (Barr & Parrett, 2008).

Academic Essential 6: Extra Time for Instruction and Support

Students who are impacted by poverty typically arrive at school behind their more-advantaged peers. As described in chapter 2 (page 31), these students may have a limited academic vocabulary and may not be ready to learn to read because they have less experience with print materials. Unless early, dramatic steps are taken, low-income students will not only arrive at school behind academically but also, without intense intervention, fall further behind each year. Therefore, if we are serious about all students learning, it is essential that these students get additional high-quality instructional time and enriched learning situations as early as possible (Barr & Parrett, 2007). In this section, we provide four types of enrichment that effective schools utilize to ensure students receive the time and resources to catch up: (1) preschool and all-day kindergarten, (2) before- and after-school programs, (3) enriched summer programs, and (4) early family intervention and support.

Preschool and All-Day Kindergarten

Schools urgently need to involve young students in organized, planned educational experiences. Nothing is as important to the successful academic education of students impacted by poverty as preschool, Head Start, and all-day kindergarten. These programs aim to help students catch up in these early school years, effectively prepare for the first grade, and start ready to learn.

Before- and After-School Programs

Students who are behind academically always need extra educational support and experiences, remediation, and opportunities to catch up after being absent. Strong evidence shows that planned before- and after-school programs with professional staff can have a huge positive effect on students who need enrichment and remediation (two sources with extensive resources and information about effective programs are American Institutes for Research, 2008; National Conference of State Legislatures, 2019).

Field Note

In 2016 and 2017, a Vancouver, Washington, school district funded enrichment after-school clubs with Title I monies to enrich students, increase belonging, and build school community. Staff members were paid for offering clubs, the district paid for a limited bus run after clubs, and the family community resource center sponsored snacks and activity supervision before and after clubs. The initial run of clubs, offered twice a week for six weeks, had palpable effects on students' sense of belonging, attendance, and academic effort, and helped staff connect with students at different grade levels, increasing the sense of community felt by staff and students alike. Schools repeated the clubs the following year, due to popular demand. —Emily Gibson

Enriched Summer Programs

When the school year ends, low-income students, unlike their middle-class peers, often return home to academically unstimulating environments. Essentially, the resource faucet of school turns off (Entwisle, Alexander, & Olson, 2000). As a result, students impacted by poverty experience a huge drop-off in learning during the summer months and then return to school in the fall further behind than when they left.

To counter this drop-off, effective school districts, in partnership with agencies like the Boys and Girls Club, provide opportunities for mental and social stimulation during school breaks. Library programs and nutrition, instructional enrichment, and recreation options help students stay engaged in learning during the summer. Such programs dramatically help students return to school ready to learn (Bracey, 2002; National Academies of Sciences, Engineering, and Medicine, 2019).

Early Family Intervention and Support

More and more local schools have recognized the disruptive effects of poverty on learning, and as a result, schools have developed early intervention programs. These may include home visits, parenting classes, and mentoring programs to help parents and guardians as they raise infants and toddlers. Some schools have implemented birth-to-three programs that help mothers support one another with child-rearing in their children's first three years. Other schools have a parent-child home program that sends caseworkers to meet with parents and guardians. These caseworkers bring along high-quality children's books or educational toys and engage children and adults in reading, activities, and conversation designed to promote the development of verbal, cognitive, and social skills. Research following these types of programs up through the early school grades is very promising. Once again, children who are academically behind need extra instructional opportunities that begin as early as possible, and often, this means programs directed at parents and guardians regarding education and parenting (Rowe, 2018).

Field Note

In Mobile, Alabama, the local school district held Kids Days in the downtown park during the summer. During one such day, the park was filled with laughing children, teachers, volunteer nurses, a bookmobile, refreshments, and music and dancing. One child was wearing a T-shirt that said, "I am smart!"

I stopped the little boy and asked, "How do you know that you are smart?"

He thought for a minute and then, with a smile glowing on his face, he said, "I don't know. My teacher kept telling me, 'You are smart, you are smart . . . you can do this!' and you know, I just became smart!" —Bob Barr

" " I don't care who they are or where they come from or what their sad problems are; when they leave my classroom, they will be reading.

—First-grade teacher, Albany, Oregon

Academic Essential 7: Targeted Reading and Mathematics

Reading and mathematics are the foundation of all learning. It is absolutely essential that all students learn to read early and learn to read well and that they gain mastery in mathematics as a way of understanding the world. To meet these important goals, high-poverty, high-performing schools make learning to read and learning to think mathematically a priority. The following are some documented changes successful schools make to ensure all students learn to read and think mathematically as early and as well as possible.

All Students Literate by the End of Third Grade

Ensuring all students gain literacy by the end of third grade requires that each student's reading progress be monitored constantly and that remediation and interventions be immediately available should they falter. Research chillingly predicts that students who do not *learn to read* by the end of the third grade "face daunting hurdles to success in school and beyond" (Zakariya, 2015, p. 1). If students do not read well by the end of the third grade, they are at great risk of failing to graduate (Vasconcelos, 2017).

The transition from *learning to read* to *reading to learn* in middle elementary compounds these students' learning difficulties, as now the focus is on using reading as a tool to access information, where comprehension is critical. Students who struggle to read in middle school fall further behind when they fail to learn content, and many eventually drop out of school altogether. Sadly, it appears that these students are no more successful outside of school than in school. They will likely live out their lives unemployed, underemployed, or unemployable. It is worth repeating that the majority of incarcerated adults are illiterate, school dropouts, or both (Lynch, 2014; Sainato, 2017).

A Focus on Mathematics

A focus on mathematics ensures that students who arrive at school without the basics receive additional time to learn those fundamental skills. Classroom instruction focuses on solving real problems, naturally using mathematics to describe situations, and fostering a curiosity instead of a dread of mathematics. Instead of swinging the curriculum to either computational and procedural skills or problem solving and creativity, effective mathematics instruction ensures both are addressed fully and that each supports the other (Larson & Kanold, 2016; National Council of Teachers of Mathematics, 2014). Mathematics opens the door to higher learning. Fundamentally, "math literacy education must be offered to everyone, child or adult, cognitively gifted, average, or slow. We must champion math literacy (numeracy) as vociferously as we advocate for language literacy" because without it, doors to economic possibilities slam shut (Donovan, 2008, p. 35). Students who learn algebra and geometry are more likely to continue on to higher education than students unable to master algebra and geometry. Students who retain a rote, computational focus on mathematics through middle and high school are far less likely to succeed in the working world (Adelman, 1999; Donovan, 2008). Mathematics is truly a necessary skill for finding postsecondary success.

Restructured Learning Time

Recognizing how critical it is for all students to read early and well and master basic mathematics, many schools have restructured the early grades to provide extra instruction for those who arrive at school unprepared to learn to read and lacking a foundation in learning mathematics. Some schools have recognized the importance of learning to read by guaranteeing parents and guardians that their children will learn to read, often contracting with parents and guardians to agree to do their part in enriching reading at home. Some schools, in an effort to carefully place responsibility and accountability for teaching, *loop* teachers, assigning one teacher a single group of students for two to three years with the express goal of ensuring that all students learn to read. The sustained relationships allow students and teachers to start the new year close to where they left off the prior year (Rasmussen, 1998).

Academic Essential 8: Positive Interpersonal Relationships

The heart of all classroom teaching and learning revolves around interpersonal relationships. The effective school works hard to encourage positive relationships between teachers and students, between students and other school staff, and between students. Many high-poverty, high-performing schools have used classroom strategies that focus directly on interpersonal relationships and that seem to develop a positive atmosphere conducive to learning and make a significant difference in the success of students impacted by poverty (Barr & Parrett, 2008; Budge & Parrett, 2018). Three powerful and effective classroom approaches for students impacted by poverty are (1) caring relationships and mutual respect, (2) high expectations and positive reinforcement, and (3) trauma-sensitive relationships.

Caring Relationships and Mutual Respect

Students impacted by poverty absolutely need a classroom built on caring relationships and mutual respect in order to learn effectively and close the achievement gap with more affluent peers. Serious learning can only occur when all students feel safe and respected and that they belong. This is an essential prerequisite of effective, resilient classrooms and schools. Relationships are the antidote to despair, learned helplessness, and disconnection from learning. Gorski (2013) emphasizes the importance of choosing a resilience view, rather than a deficit view, of poor and working-class families. This means focusing on student and family assets. Many positive traits and perspectives are gained from growing up in poverty (for examples, see figure 5.1), and focusing on these positive factors imparts respect. The next chapter (page 121) more fully shares the importance of relationships, especially for students living in poverty.

1. Knowing how to stretch your food budget

2. Knowing the value of charity (low-income people give more of their income to charity than any other economic group)

3. Pondering big purchases more carefully

4. Fearing debt

5. Requiring less money to have fun

6. Being happy with what you have (not using material things as a way to feel happy)

7. Cherishing things other than money

8. Measuring happiness in meaningful ways (for example, quality of relationships, health, life events, friends, and so on)

9. Valuing hard work

10. Being grateful for your achievements (paying for college through work, saving money for a car, and so on).

Figure 5.1: Ten benefits of growing up poor.

❝ ❞ When you look at your high-poverty classroom, who do you see? If you do not see doctors, lawyers, small business owners, and professional leaders, then it is not the students who are at risk; it is you who is placing them at risk.

—Middle school teacher, Kentucky

High Expectations and Positive Reinforcement

Educators know that students live either up to or down to expectations. Research on effective instruction strongly concludes that high expectations, coupled with positive reinforcement and careful instruction, have dramatic positive effects on student achievement (Budge & Parrett, 2018). High expectations may look like using challenging vocabulary and explaining the meaning within the context, instead of dumbing down the language from the outset. High expectations may look like challenging students to revise one of their pieces of writing—in kindergarten. High expectations may also look like expecting all learners to achieve the standards. Positive reinforcement occurs when adults look at students' attempts from a *glass is half full* perspective instead of a *glass is half empty* perspective. This means recognizing that students do better when they can do better, and our job is to help them do better (this is the core of the collaborative problem-solving work introduced in chapter 6 under seed 3, page 139).

Many middle-class teachers may hold racist or biased attitudes—often unconscious and implicit—toward poor and minority students, which may cause them to unwittingly expect less from these students. When staff find themselves making excuses for students' poor achievement, implicit biases may be at play. High-poverty schools must exercise great care in hiring teachers and in providing professional development to ensure that only teachers who believe minority students and students living in poverty can achieve high levels of academic success work in these schools' classrooms.

These schools must also make great efforts to ensure that they help teachers identify their implicit biases through staff development which includes responding to scenarios, taking surveys, and practicing bias realignment to re-see student and family actions through a more neutral lens (Gibson & Barr, 2017). Principals must counsel teachers with negative or biased attitudes toward people living in poverty to consider other careers or employment opportunities. Educators in turnaround schools often explain it takes a minimum of three to five years for a leadership team to build a faculty that has a shared, unified vision. It takes time to build trust between leadership and staff, to determine what is and is not working, to learn new ways to do things, and to become a team where everyone is pulling oars in the same direction. Such a shared vision is necessary to ensure a high-poverty school becomes and remains a high-performing school. The process of developing a shared vision demands open, honest discussions with the entire school staff, professional development, and often anonymous surveys to help identify individuals who have implicit biases or who fall outside the majority viewpoint of the shared beliefs of the school staff.

Trauma-Sensitive Relationships

All students, but especially students impacted by the traumas of poverty, need to have positive relationships with adults in their school. As a primary instructional goal, school personnel must establish secure, consistent, and caring trauma-sensitive relationships with traumatized students. In trauma-sensitive relationships, educators are aware of the impacts of trauma and are able to support the academic needs of learners impacted by stress and ACEs. Little academic learning will occur until students develop strong relationships with adults and peers and develop their ability to regulate their emotions and needs; these conditions ultimately determine students' learning success.

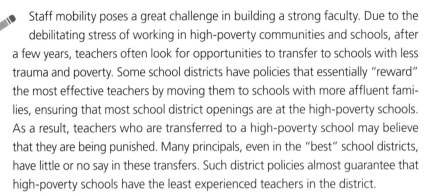

Field Note

Staff mobility poses a great challenge in building a strong faculty. Due to the debilitating stress of working in high-poverty communities and schools, after a few years, teachers often look for opportunities to transfer to schools with less trauma and poverty. Some school districts have policies that essentially "reward" the most effective teachers by moving them to schools with more affluent families, ensuring that most school district openings are at the high-poverty schools. As a result, teachers who are transferred to a high-poverty school may believe that they are being punished. Many principals, even in the "best" school districts, have little or no say in these transfers. Such district policies almost guarantee that high-poverty schools have the least experienced teachers in the district.

High teacher mobility causes principals to have to start over year after year in building a strong, committed faculty that has shared beliefs and supports shared goals. Each year thus ends up being year one in the three to five years needed to make real change. Those staff who stay may begin to feel like they are stuck in a time warp, reliving the establishment of expectations and never moving on to the rewarding, positive outcomes of sustained effort over time. —Bob Barr

Academic Essential 9: Parent and Guardian Involvement

While schools increasingly play a vital role in addressing the human needs of students' families, it is equally important that they recognize the vital role families play in teaching and learning. Research concludes that parental involvement and engagement leads to increases in academic achievement, high school graduation rates, positive social skills and classroom behavior, and increased self-confidence and motivation in the classroom (Cotton & Wikelund, 1989; Waterford, 2018). When schools take the time to work closely with families, including listening to them and soliciting their input, there is a direct payoff in student learning. Unfortunately, teachers may misunderstand the actions of parents and guardians living in poverty and assume that they just do not care about their children or the school, when, in fact, they care deeply (Gibson & Barr, 2017). As an example, if a parent doesn't show up for a parent-teacher conference, and the parent is unemployed or works at a fast food restaurant, the assumption may be that they could have come but don't care enough about their child's education to do so. But if the parent is a doctor or a college professor, the assumption may be that they care but something important came up. That underlying assumption can then color follow-up communication, or even affect if follow-up communication occurs at all. While chapter 7 (page 155) explores interrelationships with families in greater depth, the following sections mention a few essential staff practices that boost academic achievement by promoting parent and guardian involvement.

A Welcoming Atmosphere

In order to overcome the uneasiness that many low-income families feel when they enter school, effective schools go to great lengths to develop a welcoming atmosphere for parents, guardians, and students. This often includes murals, bilingual notices and posters, and student greeters at the front door.

Encouragement of Involvement

Some teachers in high-poverty schools lament the lack of parental involvement in school. School staff can do two things to encourage parents and guardians from poor communities to step through the school doors. First, they can persistently reach out to families; over time, when staff continue to extend invitations, the families are more likely to get involved. Second, parental and guardian involvement increases when staff ensure that poor and working-class families have access to a variety of opportunities for family involvement, not just the traditional volunteering in the classroom or helping with class parties or field trips (Gorski, 2013). For example, schools that are serious about including all families might provide kits of things to do, such as assembling booklets, preparing materials for an art project, or cutting out manipulatives for math, which families can sign up to do at home.

Two-Way Communication

Two-way communication, where staff and families can both send and receive information, helps develop better relationships with parents and guardians. Staff must enrich more traditional one-way communication strategies like notes, robocalls, and emails home with strategies that engage parents and guardians in two-way communications, with apps like ClassDojo and Remind or a classroom Twitter feed.

Field Note

Teachers, administrators, and specialists absolutely must listen to parents and guardians and actively solicit their ideas and issues. Too often, when family members come into school, they are immediately told what to do, what is wrong or right about their child, and what the school is going to do. Educators rarely pause and ask what the parents or guardians are concerned about or what they want to celebrate.

Coordinators of family community resource centers often explain that centers are started with few expectations other than to identify families' needs and to solicit their ideas regarding how the center can be of help. The coordinators listen to the families and, as they say, "do everything possible to meet their needs." The information they glean from listening and the connection and belonging that they create are invaluable. At any meeting between school and family, it is essential to ask what the family wants to focus on. It is also essential to listen closely to the parents' or guardians' concerns. —Bob Barr

Parent and Guardian Education

Family members want to help their students be successful in school, but may lack an understanding of how they can help, especially if they themselves struggled in school. Effective schools strengthen student learning through parent and guardian education and information on a variety of topics, from how to help your child with reading to using shopping trips to boost math, from helping your child speak in complete sentences to strategies for helping children solve problems (see chapter 7, page 155, for more on family education).

Home Visits

More and more staff in effective schools conduct home visits to get to know parents and guardians, help engage them in their children's education, and increase staff knowledge about students' home situations and home lives. Some schools plan home visits during the summer and the week before school starts in the fall, or during in-service days or early release days. In community service schools, the community resource coordinator often plans home visits, and in other schools the EL teacher conducts home visits as part of their work day. In one school we visited, teachers sent notes home inviting families to invite them to their homes, when they were ready, because the EL teacher learned that families wanted to host their child's teacher but were uncomfortable reaching out and worried about being rejected.

Field Note

A teacher came to me and complained that she had a parent who never showed up for her child's individualized education program (IEP) conference. Since part of my job as our school's family and community resource coordinator is to be the liaison between the school and families, I made a home visit in order to meet the mother and asked her about the IEP meetings. She hung her head and cried, saying, "I am so sorry, but I have nothing to wear to the school and do not want to embarrass my little girl." We solved the problem in a heartbeat. "Come in to the center," I told the mother, "and we can help you." (For more information on the resources available at family and community resource centers, see chapter 7, page 155.)

When she arrived at our school's community resource center, we arranged for her to take a shower and then pick out some new clothes to wear. She was overwhelmed with the choices we could provide her and had difficulty selecting something to wear. She was so thankful. She left for her IEP meeting with this huge grin on her face and thanked me for our help.

> It was not that the mother did not care; it was, in fact, just the opposite. She cared so much she did not want to do anything that would hurt or embarrass her child. Many of our parents and guardians do not speak English or speak it poorly. Only after they have improved their language skills in our English language classes do they feel comfortable in meeting with teachers. Often, after their language skills improve, parents and guardians begin volunteering in their children's classes. Some started working as playground supervisors.
> —Family and community resource coordinator, Garfield Elementary School, Boise, Idaho

Academic Essential 10: Trauma-Informed Practices

Much of the literature on the effects of trauma and adverse childhood experiences has, rightly so, focused on students' behavior and social-emotional needs, and chapter 6 (page 121) covers these needs. But more recent research on high-poverty, high-performing schools highlights the relationships among trauma, adversity, and academic performance. This research provides a better understanding of how the symptoms of trauma impact student learning, and how schools can become trauma informed to better meet learners' academic needs (see Cole et al., 2013, and Sporleder & Forbes, 2016). Once again, this research documents the importance of a whole-school approach.

This research indicates that students who have experienced trauma may have changes in the brain that can interfere with organization, comprehension, memory, and engagement which disrupt their ability to learn effectively and consistently (Cole et al., 2005). Thus, in our classrooms and schools, we must create brain-friendly and socially welcoming environments to avoid triggering these brain changes and help build new neural networks more conducive for learning (Hammond, 2015). In addition to the previous "what works" ideas and strategies, trauma-informed or trauma-sensitive schools and classrooms have awareness of the impacts of trauma and use strategies that support the academic needs of learners impacted by stress and ACEs (Cole et al., 2013). The following sections briefly summarize some specific instructional qualities that effectively mitigate the overriding effects of social and behavioral issues related to the traumas of poverty: relevance of instruction, predictability, academic expectations, independent learning, behavior supports, and adjusting language-based instruction (adapted from Cole et al., 2005, pp. 61–68).

Relevance of Instruction to Students

Experienced teachers know the importance of relevance to students, but may not know that perceived irrelevance can be a trigger for students. The often-heard questions "When am I ever going to use this?" or "Why should I care about this?" are a key to what matters most to students: their own lives. We can increase student motivation and effort and decrease traumatic responses to academic demands by identifying student interests, abilities and competencies, and focusing instruction on these attributes, connecting them to academic content. For example, recognizing that students were very concerned about climate change, a local high school provided a science course on climate change in which students developed a local guide to what people could do in their homes and lives to help. In another example, a teacher focused a series of physics lessons on skateboards and snowboards because half of the students were aficionados of one or both.

Predictability

Provide predictability in routines, schedules, transitions, expectations, and consequences to provide order in students' school lives. As described in an earlier section, students impacted by trauma and poverty especially benefit from predictability in their environment. For example, ensuring that the day's schedule is clear and visible, preferably with visual cues; starting out the day with an overview of any changes to typical routines; having clear signals for nonverbal communications of basics (drinking water, visiting the bathroom, sharpening pencils, and so on); and being consistent with expectations such as the expected response to a quiet signal (and the reinforcement and practice of that signal if response lags).

Academic Expectations

Present consistent academic expectations for all students, and scaffold support to get there. For example, if students require adapted work, ensure they know what they are having difficulty with, why they are struggling, and what they can do to meet the expectation (more practice, tutoring, and so on). Eliminate gray areas, eliminate comparisons between students, and eliminate public displays that make individual students' academic struggles visible, such as homework charts that show which students are or are not meeting expectations. Instead, post classwide data.

Independent Learning

An external locus of control often manifests in learners as a dependence on the teacher to carry the cognitive load of tasks (Hammond, 2015). Dependent learners are typically unsure of how to tackle new tasks and will often sit and wait passively when stuck. Their quiet passivity may mean they get overlooked in the bustle of the classroom. Being an independent learner requires executive function skills. Teachers foster independence through the specific teaching of strategies, processes, and systems and giving students scaffolding when they need temporary support (Hammond, 2015). For example, after learning different organizing frameworks for different types of writing, such as cause-and-effect, chronological, opinion, or problem-solution, students can then use those frameworks to write, and select a framework that suits their purpose for writing. Or, a teacher might introduce the process of a Socratic seminar to teach students how to debate an issue, learn how to take on an opposing side, and use evidence to back up statements. Then, the Socratic seminar process can be used to deepen understanding and review content in any subject (see www .facinghistory.org/resource-library/teaching-strategies/socratic-seminar for an example of the Socratic seminar process).

Behavior Supports

Too often, behavior interrupts learning. Effective schools employ a schoolwide positive behavioral interventions and supports (PBIS) system, and supplement it with clear, specific, positive feedback and reinforcement to students, provided by caring adults. (For more information on PBIS, see www.pbis.org.) Having clear, visible expectations for behavior, which are understood and reinforced by every adult in the school building, creates a predictable environment for both students and adults. Being able to identify student triggers to disruptive behaviors can lead to the anticipation of, preparation for, and avoidance of student disruptions over time. For example, when behavior data collection at one elementary school showed that students struggled the most with expected behavior after any disruption to routine, such as a holiday or a snow day, staff brainstormed ways to support students before and after such disruptions.

Language-Based Teaching

Students exposed to trauma may pay more attention to nonverbal signals than verbal ones (see chapter 2, page 31). As a result, they can easily become lost and frustrated in language-based classrooms that emphasize verbal over nonverbal information. Here are some specific strategies for helping students process language-based information and instructions.

- Present information or instructions in multiple formats—written, auditory, physical (kinesthetic), or visual.

- Preteach vocabulary and concepts, and use common English language learner strategies that focus on story, sequence of events, cause-and-effect relationships, prior knowledge activation with questions, visual or tactile activities, and so on.

- Teach students how to identify and process their feelings, and give them self-regulation strategies that work to calm themselves when their feelings are elevated. (For more information, see www.zonesofregulation.com/index.html).

For more in-depth information on these and other academic strategies that are effective with students under the influence of trauma, see volumes I and II of *Helping Traumatized Children Learn* (Cole et al., 2005, 2013).

> **" "** You know the purpose of the school is not just to raise test scores, or to give children academic learning. The purpose of the school is to give children an experience that will help them grow and develop in ways that they can be successful, in school and as successful adults. They have to grow in a way that they can take care of themselves, get an education, take care of a family, be responsible citizens of the society and of their community. Now you don't get that simply by raising test scores.
>
> —James Comer

Conclusion

Since the 1990s an amazing transformation has occurred in U.S. public education. In only a few decades, the misguided belief that schools could not overcome the debilitating effects of poverty has quite simply shattered, and an entirely new spectrum of knowledge has shown the way to better, more effective U.S. public schools. The evidence can be found in high-poverty, high-performing schools across the United States: students who live in poverty can and do learn when provided the proper supports and interventions. Thousands of high-poverty, high-performing schools at all levels have closed the achievement gap so all students are learning effectively.

In this chapter, we presented ten academic essentials—part of a schoolwide systematic approach that readers can use to address the academic and cognitive needs of students in poverty to raise academic achievement. These big ideas include visionary leadership; a reliance on data, assessment, and accountability; a rigorous, aligned curriculum for all; and extra time for instruction and support, among others.

In the next chapter, our focus shifts from the academic needs of students—what we call the *first wave* of research on high-performing, high-poverty schools—to meeting students' social-emotional needs, what we call the *second wave* of research. We now understand that public education must look beyond just ensuring that students have a successful academic experience in school. Public education must aim to help students break out of the disastrous cycle of poverty and find a pathway to a better life. In the resilient school framework, the academic needs of students are one of the four cornerstones. Once staff and leaders meet the key academic elements of curriculum and instruction, assessment, and appropriate interventions, they can address the other necessary ingredients of school resilience amid high poverty: the social-emotional needs of learners, the human needs of families, and the relational and professional needs of school staff.

Next Steps

Please complete the following Next Steps, to integrate your experiences within your own schools and communities with the information presented in this chapter.

1. In this chapter, we presented ten academic essentials for addressing students' academic and cognitive needs.

   a. Which of these essentials is your school currently implementing? What has been the effect on teaching and learning?

   b. Which of these essentials is your school currently lacking (or would you like to improve on)? What steps can you take to begin implementing this big idea?

2. What are your school's unified beliefs, which you think 90 percent or more of staff would agree upon?

3. How does your district or school monitor student learning and provide interventions? Are there any insights from this chapter which you would like to incorporate?

4. Does your school utilize a distributed leadership model? If so, what has your experience been?

The Second Cornerstone of the Resilient School: Addressing Students' Social-Emotional Needs

Teaching reading and the basics is demanding, and closing the achievement gap is our ever-present schoolwide goal, but our main challenge is the social-emotional and mental health issues of our students. . . . If we can help students to see a glimmer of hope in their life, to become more positive about the future, teaching them the academics is a slam dunk.

—Principal, Ohio

In chapter 5 (page 95), we presented ten essential academic strategies from the high-poverty, high-performing school's *first wave* of research that have proven effective in helping schools raise their students' academic performance and results. During the 1990s and early 2000s, as schools began to apply the strategies from the first wave of research and hundreds successfully began to close achievement gaps, thousands more failed to see any results. Educators also noticed that even when they were able to help elementary students achieve established standards of excellence, these same students began to falter and fail as they later moved on to middle and high school. Slowly across the United States, educators searched for additional answers to these troubling situations. Almost everywhere, educators and researchers wondered, "What are we missing?"

Schools working hard to implement the academic ingredients of successful high-poverty schools without seeing effective results found many answers to the question

"What are we missing?" in a second wave of research on high-poverty, high-performing schools that began in the early 2000s, which illuminated social-emotional factors like relationships, learned helplessness, cultural clash, and belonging. As educators recognized that students living in poverty often developed despondent, helpless attitudes, it became evident that they had to address these overpowering attitudes before they could seriously expect that students would learn effectively and achieve high academic standards. It became increasingly evident that social-emotional needs were essential to success in both school and life (ASCD, 2007; Jensen, 2009).

The challenge of addressing learned helplessness led educators and researchers to take a closer look at students' social-emotional needs. Notably, they found that school settings could, in fact, address social-emotional learning and integrate it with academic instruction. Schools could teach social-emotional skills and attitudes. Through school observations, interviews, and careful review of existing research, it became evident that many high-poverty, high-performing schools were already focused on the social-emotional needs of students who were most vulnerable to failing due to socioeconomic status, ethnicity or race, language, sexual orientation, gender identity, and other variables (Chenoweth, 2009; Lezotte & Snyder, 2011). These schools not only engaged in high-quality academic programs and instruction but also utilized the value-added component of meeting students' social-emotional needs. They did this by developing an optimistic, supportive, caring, and trusting atmosphere; encouraging students to participate in new experiences and activities; and teaching students new, essential skills to build their personal resilience. These schools were surrounding students with what we, the authors, call a Culture of Hope (Barr & Gibson, 2013).

When a school successfully integrates academic and social-emotional learning into an effective educational experience, what emerges is a school culture that surrounds students with an optimistic atmosphere of hope of self-fulfillment (Aspen Institute, 2018). The resulting Culture of Hope helps confront and transform the feelings of hopelessness and apathy that so often characterize students impacted by poverty (Barr & Gibson, 2013).

In this chapter, we begin with a discussion on hope and some general considerations for teaching and measuring hope in schools. Next, we present our framework of social-emotional assets called the *Culture of Hope* and the five seeds of hope that effective schools can use to support students' development of social-emotional assets.

Field Note

 As Bill Parrett and I were finishing our 2007 book, *The Kids Left Behind: Catching Up the Underachieving Children of Poverty*, we sent the manuscript to a number of educational researchers whom we respected and asked them to review our work and offer their reactions. Almost immediately, we got a note back from Rick Stiggins (see *Student-Involved Classroom Assessment*, Stiggins, 2001), one of the United States' most respected assessment experts. He said, and I paraphrase, "While you have prepared a powerful and useful book, you've missed the main point: so many children and youth living in poverty do not believe that they can learn, and they arrive at school with a learned helplessness and often simply do not try to learn." His conclusion was that while the book's high-poverty, high-performing schools research was essential, it would not be of much value until schools addressed this foundational issue of learned helplessness. Stiggins's short critique of our work ultimately motivated me to return to the research for another review of effective high-poverty schools, this time with a focus not on schools' instructional programs but on students' social-emotional needs. —Bob Barr

An Emphasis on Hope

Educators may intuitively understand the interrelationship between the academic and the social-emotional needs of students, but instruction tends to emphasize what is measurable. Report cards focus on academic progress, school districts and states primarily measure academic learning, and teacher evaluations and even salary increases are based on academic measures. So the gravitational pull of testing pressure and administrative emphasis may lead educators to overlook or de-emphasize students' social-emotional learning—not from a perceived lack of importance for student growth, but from a lack of time. What gets measured matters most. Also, it is far less straightforward to measure social-emotional learning growth than it is to measure academic progress.

More comprehensive standards like the Common Core State Standards (National Governors Association Center for Best Practices & Council of Chief State School Officers, 2010a, 2010b), the College and Career Readiness Standards (anchor standards embedded within the Common Core standards), and the Next Generation Science Standards (NGSS Lead States, 2013) reinforce the value of social-emotional learning (Adams, 2013) by requiring safe classroom environments where students can comfortably engage in collaboration, personal analysis, and intellectual discussions. An emphasis on college and career readiness encourages students to not just stay in school but also learn how to thrive in a school and job environment. This strong emphasis on college and career success teaches students that simply staying in school and getting by is not enough and puts their focus on the future and setting realistic dreams for their lives. Students are encouraged to develop detailed plans to a better life, taking into account where they are, where they want to go, and how they can navigate the journey from here to there. In essence, a focus on social-emotional learning, engagement, hope, and resilience requires a paradigm shift within schools—a shift from test scores as the ultimate measure of success to communication, problem solving, and self-awareness as a measure of potential success after high school. This shift must be done at a school-culture level if it is to take root at all.

Field Note

At the beginning of the 2018–2019 school year, I started serving a small group of three students who had some anxiety about coming to school. We met at a table inside, and played various games or did brain teasers and puzzles. When the whistle blew, they walked to their classroom, avoiding the bustle of outside lines. When staff looked at behavior data in October and noticed that a number of students were struggling with expected behavior at the very beginning of the day, before school even started, the search for a solution began. Administrators and other staff began inviting students who were not successful at outside recess in to what we now called Brainiacs Club. Soon we needed two tables, and eventually we moved into a corner of the gym as the numbers swelled to fifteen, then twenty. As word spread, other students who had anxiety about school, or who preferred a more cognitive start to their day, asked if they could join.

Several parents and guardians remarked that before Brainiacs Club, their child would do anything to delay leaving for school, but now their child often dragged them out the door so they could get to school in time for their favorite part of the day. As a result, the parent-teacher association provided a grant to purchase more games, tools, and puzzles to ensure the program continued. During the 2019–2020 school year, the program expanded into the library, with thirty or more students attending each morning. This has reinforced our understanding of how students will do better if they can do better: if they struggle with expected behavior, there's a reason, and if there's a reason, we can find a solution. —Emily Gibson

An Institutional Culture Versus a Culture of Hope

Helping students overcome some of their most basic, internalized understandings of the world, when they work against students' achievement, represents a challenge for schools. There is no textbook to study or instructional strategy to utilize that will help students overcome deep feelings of helplessness, despair, an external locus of control, and hopelessness. Rerouting these negative feelings requires schools to surround students with an atmosphere or culture of optimism and hope that permeates every corner of the school.

Over the years, researchers have taken a growing interest in institutional cultures and the effects these cultures have on the people who inhabit them. As education and psychology researcher Seymour Sarason (1971) explains, all institutions, public entities, and corporations, including schools, have what he calls an *institutional culture* that considerably affects the people working in that environment. He defines institutional cultures as "patterns of behavioral regularities" that have a powerful "conforming force," which leads to uniform behavior and attitudes (Sarason, 1971, pp. 27–29). The institutional culture of schools tends to shift teachers toward the schools' behavioral norms—new teachers do not change their schools as much as their schools change them. This research has long helped explain the difficulty in significantly changing schools as well as other institutions. As former president Woodrow Wilson once said, "It is easier to change the location of a cemetery than to change the school curriculum" (PowerQuotations, n.d.).

While much literature has focused on the negative aspects of culture, especially institutional culture's resistance to change or improvement efforts, educators have more recently recognized how powerful a school's culture can be in influencing student attitudes and behavior (see Darling-Hammond & Cook-Harvey, 2018; Jensen, 2009). Effective high-poverty schools create optimistic atmospheres as an antidote to the negative, defeatist attitudes students too often have when they arrive at school. These schools aim to surround students with such hopefulness that, over time, students replace old, fatalistic beliefs with the belief that they can learn effectively and succeed in school. This schoolwide atmosphere of optimism is what we describe as a Culture of Hope (Barr & Gibson, 2013).

As we have repeatedly emphasized in this book, whole-school efforts and shared beliefs are essential. Developing a Culture of Hope requires that school staff share strong, schoolwide beliefs and values about what really matters (Barr & Gibson, 2013). If a school's staff agrees on the belief that all students can learn and achieve high levels of academic success, students will benefit significantly (DuFour et al., 2010) because, wherever students go or turn, staff will meet them with optimism, positive reinforcement, and high expectations. As Sarason's (1971) work on institutional cultures illustrates, when a can-do, failure-is-no-option attitude saturates the school, student attitudes have no alternative but to make that shift as well.

Research clearly emphasizes the importance of a schoolwide, unifying approach focused on social-emotional and academic skills (Aspen Institute, 2018; Trauma and Learning Policy Initiative, 2019). Such a schoolwide effort or culture surrounds students with a community of trust, respect, and care that is especially powerful in buffering the effects of trauma (Trauma and Learning Policy Initiative, 2019). In such a school, all students feel safe and feel like they belong. The goal in such a school is for each student to feel connected to the school or classroom community and at least one caring and supportive adult. Each student is part of a school family of support and hope.

In schools where leaders take a schoolwide approach, such as the trauma-informed schools model, staff are more likely to integrate social-emotional learning into the fabric of the school, instead of treating it as an optional add-on to squeeze in when they have time. Schools cannot treat social-emotional learning as anything less than an urgent priority—instead, social-emotional learning is a *prerequisite* for academic learning. Additionally, staff who work in schools with supportive, caring cultures are more likely to create similar cultures for students in their classrooms, and are likely to have their own relational needs met as members of their school community.

The Teaching of Hope

In addition to building an institutional Culture of Hope, schools must engage in the process of *teaching hope* in order to positively influence student attitudes and behavior. Scholars see hope as not just another human emotion but rather a way of thinking about one's life—a "process of thinking about one's goals, along with the motivation to move toward those goals, and the ways to achieve those goals" (Snyder, 1995, p. 355). Hope can be taught, but in order to truly change students' life trajectories, this teaching must include helping students consider where they want to go in life, where they are now, and what they have to do to get from here to there. So many highly effective high schools build this process into their everyday curriculum. Students learn to hope by developing a personal plan for their life after high school.

Field Note

 When holding a collaborative problem-solving conversation with a fifth grader, the following exchange took place.

"So, it seems like you haven't been enjoying school as much lately. What's up with that?"

"Nothing. I just don't really enjoy anything."

"What *do* you like?"

"I like science. But I don't want to just learn about things, I want to actually do things, do experiments. I really want to do chemistry."

"Did you know that next year, when you go to middle school, you will get to take lab sciences? High school, too."

His eyes got huge, and he sat up tall. *"WHAT? Are you serious?"*

"Yes, it's one of the great things about middle and high school."

We then looked up experiments he could do at home with things in his kitchen, with adult approval. He bounced off, filled with hopes and dreams about next year. —Emily Gibson

And if the goal of public education is not to just teach students academic knowledge and skills but to help them find a pathway to a better life, the combination of teaching hope and helping students develop a strong purpose for their life will help them find this pathway. Both these approaches involve setting personal goals, figuring out how to get from where they are to where they need to go, and monitoring progress toward their goals. This is, in fact, the pathway out of poverty or the pathway to a better life.

Learning hope can have a powerful, positive effect on student's lives both in school and outside school. In fact, more hopeful students tend to stay in school, graduate, perform better in college, and have better physical health and mental health (Jensen, n.d.; Newell & Van Ryzin, 2007).

The Culture of Hope and the Seeds of Hope

We developed the Culture of Hope framework through observations and interviews in high-poverty schools across the United States. Our school studies helped us identify common characteristics of successful school and classroom cultures that, upon review, seem foundational to human nature: in successful schools, students were surrounded with optimism, belonging, pride, and purpose (Barr & Gibson, 2013). Additionally, these characteristics fit almost seamlessly into Abraham Maslow's (Huitt, 2007) hierarchy of needs, a well-known construct that provides a visual depiction of human needs and dramatizes the ascending importance of these needs, with each level being a prerequisite for the next (see figure 6.1, page 128). Maslow's hierarchy provides a basic framework for understanding the critical importance of the basic physiological needs of food, water, and shelter, but also integrates the social-emotional needs of safety, belonging, self-esteem, and self-actualization (Huitt, 2007).

In our previous work *Building a Culture of Hope* (Barr & Gibson, 2013), we identify and conceptualize four *seeds of hope*, the essential components of a Culture of Hope. Since publication of that book, with continued review of effective school research and our work in schools, we have determined the need for a fifth seed of hope—a *sense of self-regulation*—to capture the essential social-emotional assets reinforced by a Culture of Hope. As a result, the five essential seeds of hope are:

1. A sense of optimism and hope

2. A sense of place and belonging

3. A sense of self-regulation

4. A sense of pride, self-esteem, and self-confidence

5. A sense of purpose

Figure 6.2 (page 129) depicts these seeds within our model of a Culture of Hope.

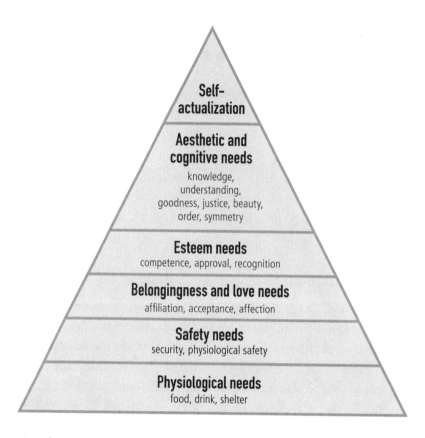

Source: Barr & Gibson, 2013, p. 40; adapted from Huitt, 2007.

Figure 6.1: Maslow's hierarchy of needs.

The seeds of hope, first identified as the common characteristics of high-poverty, high-performing schools' cultures, can help low-income students transition from learned helplessness and hopelessness and an external locus of control to improved self-concepts and more optimistic, capable visions for their own lives. The seeds of hope help students learn executive function skills within the context of academic learning. They are surely essential elements in helping students break out of the debilitating cycle of generational poverty and find pathways to better lives.

One important step in school improvement is building a unified vision among the staff in the school. In our experience with professional development on the Culture of Hope, the seeds of hope provide a simple blueprint for developing or improving effective schools as educators review the seeds of hope, evaluate current practices to see what is already being done, and plan in small groups for seeds and elements of the seeds that they need to add. Since most schools are already doing a few, if not many, excellent practices related to the seeds of hope, such a review provides a boost to staff resilience, which then carries over into enthusiasm and motivation for next steps. This contrasts greatly with the response to an outside professional coming in

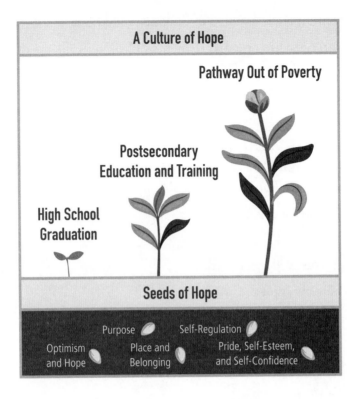

Figure 6.2: The seeds of hope within a Culture of Hope.

to tell a staff what they need to do! The seeds of hope can be a powerful tool for evaluating a school's culture and social-emotional assets.

> " " Based on research and observation, no approach seems as powerful or to have as much potential to help the children of poverty remain and thrive in school as developing and enriching a Culture of Hope in every district, school, and classroom.
>
> **—Bob Barr and Emily Gibson**

Since we developed and presented the Culture of Hope concept in 2013, it has been continuously reinforced by research reports on the importance of social-emotional learning and positive school culture (see, for example, Aspen Institute, 2018; Darling-Hammond & Cook-Harvey, 2018), and by school leaders', education practitioners', and community organizations' Culture of Hope implementation efforts in schools, districts, and communities around the United States.

In the following sections, we briefly explore each of the five seeds of hope. Those wishing to learn more about the complexities of the Culture of Hope, including the numerous ways schools across the United States have supported students' social-emotional needs by implementing a Culture of Hope, can see Barr and Gibson (2013).

The First Seed of Hope: A Sense of Optimism and Hope

Hope and optimism are essential elements in helping students of poverty find success in and out of school (Jensen, 2009; Seligman, 2007). Researchers have increasingly recognized the attributes of human hope and optimism as part of what Maslow describes as essential physiological needs, and as essential for learning (Huitt, 2007; Newell & Van Ryzin, 2007, 2009). Students impacted by the traumas of poverty can experience a transformation from despair to hope in their school. Increasingly, the learned hope and optimism students gain in schools can supplant the negative influences of poverty-impacted homes and communities.

The fundamental aspects of a sense of optimism and hope as evidenced by a school's culture are:

- A unified, schoolwide set of beliefs

- A welcoming atmosphere

- An atmosphere of trust, respect, and safety

- Positive, high expectations

- An emphasis on success

- Dreams for the future

- Communitywide celebrations

- Coordination of human services

(For deeper exploration of strategies and examples for this seed, see Barr and Gibson [2013], chapter 4, pages 45–64.)

A Unified, Schoolwide Set of Beliefs

As with all aspects of school improvement, unified staff who hold agreed-on, shared beliefs are best equipped to implement the seeds of hope. Successfully addressing the helplessness and despair associated with poverty requires surrounding students with an educational atmosphere of optimism. A schoolwide program of optimism cannot be random or occasional; it must permeate the entire school from the classrooms to the hallways, from the cafeteria to the school bus ride home. Everywhere the students turn, they must meet with positivity; a can-do atmosphere of high expectations and hope must surround them. No teacher can create this atmosphere alone. It is essential that all adults in the school share a common set of powerful beliefs that emphasize how each student is part of the school community and family. Though each school will likely have its own set of common beliefs, some examples might include "All students can and will learn," "Parents send us the best children they have," "Children do better when they can do better," "Everyone belongs," "All students will learn to read by third grade," and "Everyone can do algebra." For students to be successful, these schoolwide commitments and focus must exist (Trauma and Learning Policy Initiative, 2019).

> **❝ ❞** One consequence of believing that every child can learn is that as a teacher you have to become a good improviser, adjusting, changing direction, and feeling your way—while maintaining order and projecting confidence when you may still be unsure of the direction you want to take with a particular group of students. The craft of teaching requires the habit of innovation.
>
> —Herbert Kohl

A Welcoming Atmosphere

A school with a Culture of Hope seems to vibrate with optimism. All the staff are positive and welcoming, greeting all students by name and providing hugs or handshakes at the door. The school building is filled with welcoming signs and posters and often student murals. The signage is often in more than one language. The school aims to help students and their families, who may have a history of bad experiences with schools, feel comfortable and welcome; some schools talk about wanting to ensure that the parents and guardians feel that this is *their school*. Many effective schools include home visitations as part of their relentless effort to welcome families and ensure that their first contact with the school is positive. Effective schools work hard to make sure that custodians, bus drivers, and cafeteria workers understand this contagious, welcoming atmosphere and join in.

An Atmosphere of Trust, Respect, and Safety

A schoolwide atmosphere of trust, respect, and safety is very important, and it must occur within the current context of escalating school violence and schools' preparations for worst-case scenarios. School safety efforts typically include limited building access, schoolwide drills for violent events, and more security guards or increased law enforcement presence. All these essential elements in securing a school make the task of helping families and students feel at home and welcome in their school even more difficult—and all the more important. When family members already feel mistrustful of the institution of education, based on their own experiences as children, the act of making it more difficult to enter the school building in the name of safety can be counterproductive to the mission of parent and guardian involvement and engagement. While children may be better able to focus on learning when they know they are safe, family members may fear they are not welcome.

Field Note

At an Oregon school district's school board meeting in 2019, a Mexican-American mother stood up and spoke, in Spanish with a translator, about how disenfranchised her community was due to the heightened safety protocols

at their neighborhood schools. In order to volunteer and participate in their children's learning inside the school walls, they had to go through many hoops of paperwork and evaluation, which were made more difficult with the need for translation into Spanish. She indicated that in their community, the parents felt they did not belong in schools, and were not valued. Her message was one of hope—they felt they had much to contribute to the school—as well as a warning: children will not do as well without parental involvement in the classrooms.
—Emily Gibson

Students who do not feel trusted and respected by teachers and other school staff may simply refuse to learn from them and may, in fact, respond to real or perceived negative teacher attitudes with disruptive behavior and hostility. A fundamental way to boost respect in the classroom is to make time each day for students to share ideas, make recommendations, and provide input into plans. Some schools even provide a suggestion box in the office for anyone to share ideas about ways to improve the school! Poverty-impacted students learn far better in school and classroom environments that foster respect, and teachers, administrators, and families also do far better work in atmospheres of trust and respect (Chenoweth, 2010).

Positive, High Expectations

We now know that students live up to or down to the expectations of the adults who surround them in their life. One teacher's positive regard and expectations can transform a student, so just imagine the effect of an entire school surrounding students with high expectations, trust, respect, and positive reinforcement. Karin Chenoweth (2010) has concluded that high expectations are a key characteristic of high-poverty, high-performing schools. Throughout these successful schools, staff continuously engage students in discussions about their futures, about postsecondary pathways, and about possible careers. It is through these discussions that students begin to consider new and higher levels of what's possible in their lives.

Students living in poor communities are less likely than their more affluent peers to have such positive visions of the future without the intentional work of teachers, administrators, and school specialists. Also, students impacted by trauma and poverty often hear far fewer positive affirmations during the day than more affluent peers do (Hart & Risley, 1995), making school personnel's daily expressions of high expectations and positive reinforcement crucial. This is exactly what researchers mean when they talk about external or environmental protective factors of resilience (page 78).

An Emphasis on Success

Closely related to positive, high expectations is an emphasis on success, which means bombarding students with encouragement and a "you can do it" attitude. In every classroom, teachers approach instruction by focusing on small increments of learning, and when students achieve learning goals, they shower them with positive reinforcement and encouragement: "See! You did it! I knew you could!" Nothing banishes feelings of helplessness like success. And nothing helps build strong self-confidence like real academic success.

Field Note

I always debrief a learning by sitting with students who are struggling and point out to them how well they have done. I have had a lot of success with these students in this way. We have a list in the front hall of all the students who have achieved the mastery level in each of our curriculum areas. When students tell me that they don't think that they can do the work, I ask them who their best friends are and then tell them to go down to the front hall and look at the list of students who have achieved mastery. They always come back and say, "Hey! If those guys can do it, I know that I can do it!" Then we are ready to do the work. The students have to believe they can do the work and succeed, or all our hard work will just be for naught. —Teacher, California

Dreams for the Future

Encouraging students to dream—to think about the vast array of opportunities available and to believe they can reach their dreams—is a powerful strategy for building hope in students. According to Eric Jensen (2019), "Managing your destiny is a hope builder" (p. 74). As students explore career opportunities and specific jobs, they can envision all the possibilities and gain an optimistic vision of a better life ahead. With an eye toward the future, students can see how what they are doing in class relates to their goals and dreams.

In encouraging students to dream, teachers should model how to plan for the future daily in the classroom, and they should help students set daily, weekly, and yearly goals. Such long-term planning requires that teachers support students in monitoring progress toward goals, provide feedback, and help students refine and revise their goals over time (Jensen, 2019). This in-depth dreaming and hoping needs to occur at all school levels, within the context of trusted relationships with staff. At the high school level, student advisory groups are a perfect vehicle for this; small groups of students can work with one staff member to build future plans during the four years of high school.

Communitywide Celebrations

Effective schools also create an atmosphere of optimism by inviting the community surrounding the school to celebrate important events for local cultures or neighborhoods. These communitywide celebrations include calendar events like Cinco de

Mayo, Chinese New Year, Martin Luther King Jr. Day, or Día de la Raza, as well as local community events like Rodeo Day, Cherokee Community Celebration Day, Future Farmers of America Day, or a winter carnival. Some schools have regular family nights, curriculum nights, and early-morning "pastries with parents" events. Food, music, free books, health information, and school attendance supports are often woven into the events. The goals are to make families that are uneasy about being in the school feel recognized and important and to have them all participate and become part of the school community. (See chapter 7, page 155, for more on school community events.)

Field Note

My neighborhood school in Boise—Garfield Elementary—had a predominantly white population in the 1990s. In 2020, the students come from around twenty different countries and speak many languages. The highlight of the year is the school's cultural celebration. The evening features a meal and all sorts of activities going on all over the school. There are Basque dancers, Japanese puppet shows, tutorials on how to make Russian dolls, African drummers, and so on. The school is always packed, and it looks like a meeting at the United Nations. Parents and guardians tend to show up in their native dress, so it is a visual wonderland. This school also has a family and community resource center and a childcare program. All these efforts combine to make families, many of whom have only recently arrived through refugee programs, feel that they are part of their new community. —Bob Barr

Coordination of Human Services

We have expanded this aspect of the seed of optimism into a cornerstone of the resilient school, because finding ways to meet the human needs of families (food, shelter, transportation, access to medical care, and so on) is necessary for children to learn. When the human needs of families are met, there are less stress and trauma in the home. Schools build optimism through the coordination of human services by helping families more easily access the resources they need in one streamlined, central location. For example, schools can become the location for food banks, immunization clinics, tax preparation information, and parent education classes. For more information on this subject, see chapter 7, page 155.

The Second Seed of Hope: A Sense of Place and Belonging

On Maslow's (2007) hierarchy of needs, a sense of belonging is third only to physiological and safety needs (see figure 6.1, page 128). Belonging to a group, belonging to a place, and being able to say "I'm from here; these are my people" fulfills a fundamental human need (Brendtro et al., 2019).

It should come as no surprise that a sense of belonging is a crucial prerequisite to academic and social well-being. And while belonging is an essential need regardless of demographics, students living in poverty or exposed to chronic trauma and stress can find belonging as important for learning as food and sleep (Cole et al., 2013). A trauma-informed school, which makes students feel connected to a caring and supportive community in the school and classroom, acts as a great antidote to trauma. Helping students know that they belong, through the development of positive interpersonal relationships, develops a foundational building block of resilience.

If school staff do not make a concerted effort to ensure that students feel they belong, many will feel left out, isolated, and alone. Too often, when low-income students and students of color enter the white, middle class–influenced institutions of public schools, they and their families immediately feel like outsiders. The task of welcoming all students and their families into the school and ensuring that all students feel like an essential part of the school is absolutely critical for student success in school and life.

> **" "** No one leaves the ninth grade—I mean no one—until we have helped them find a place where they belong.
>
> ## —School counselor, Corbin High School, Kentucky

Research in psychology, sociology, and education documents the benefits of having a sense of belonging. Students with strong social connections to peers, groups, and organizations tend to have better grades, attendance, and prosocial behaviors, and engage in less bullying, less violence, and fewer risky behaviors (Barr & Parrett, 2001; Brendtro et al., 2019; Newell & Van Ryzin, 2007)According to Russell J. Quaglia (n.d.), educators contribute enormously to a student's sense of belonging and connection when they truly listen to what the student tells them, reflect on it, and take action. When students' *voices* matter, *they* matter. Enhancing student belonging has a tremendous return on investment. The positive results of developing students' sense of belonging go far beyond initial investments: "In school, positive peer relations and teacher/student relationships are vital to maintaining high levels of motivation, engagement, achievement, and positive behavior. . . . Belongingness also has a profound impact on adolescent mental health and well-being" (Newell & Van Ryzin, 2007, p. 467).

A synthesis of our observations in effective schools and examinations of research literature has resulted in a number of specific approaches for increasing students' sense of belonging and place (Barr & Gibson, 2013). These include:

- Developing a school-based "surrogate family" atmosphere
- Fostering a strong schoolwide community
- Helping every student find a connection to a talent or interest outside academics
- Helping students connect with a career interest within academics
- Monitoring and supporting transitions carefully

(For more strategies and examples, see Barr and Gibson [2013], chapter 5, pages 65–84.)

The School as a Surrogate Family

Developing a familial school atmosphere of connection and support through small group sizes can have an enormously positive effect on students, especially students living in poverty and high-trauma environments. For many students, the school, and more specifically the classroom, provides much of what a healthy, functional family provides: belonging, being seen and known, being able to contribute to a group, being needed and depended upon, problem-solving opportunities, and support. They are surrogate families that stand in for families during the time students are at school. Most research on schools as surrogate families has come from studies of small, available-by-choice alternative public schools, magnet schools, and charter schools, but educators working in bigger schools can still utilize this option by forming career clusters or *schools within schools* (Barr & Parrett, 1995, 1997). Low-income students often report that they feel lost in large schools, as if they are invisible to teachers and staff. Feelings such as these make it easy for students to fail to come to school and even drop out, so educators need to address and prevent these feelings by creating a surrogate family atmosphere and ensuring students are seen, known, and heard.

> **❝ ❞** When I left the big middle school and came to this small, little alternative program for students at risk, it just changed my life. I went from a place where no one knew my name and no one cared to this place, where it's like a happy family. I have gone from the "invisible man" to the "family man"!
>
> **—Middle school student, Meridian, Idaho**

Small-group learning environments in high schools, such as career clusters where students work on content areas through the lens of a particular career (health services, engineering, education, restaurants, and so on) with other students interested in the same career, provide students an opportunity to work for much or all of the school day with a smaller number of students and teachers than they would in a more traditional school environment. Often, the teachers in these programs specifically choose to work with students impacted by poverty and trauma, and have unified core beliefs that support students more fully. These small programs evolve into learning communities or "schools within schools" of thirty to two hundred students where everyone knows, trusts, and supports one another. Interviews with students in these small programs inevitably reveal that the students feel they are part of a supportive family. This represents the ultimate feeling of belonging, which can have an immediate and powerful impact; it can transform students' attitudes and improve their learning (Barr & Parrett, 2001).

❝❞ In all places on campus, students must feel safe and connected to adults and peers—not just in one program or with one adult. Though the impact of one caring adult cannot be overemphasized, it is the impact of an entire school community which has the power to truly change lives and help our most traumatized students find success.

—Susan F. Cole, Anne Eisner, Michael Gregory, and Joel Ristuccia

Strong Schoolwide Community

Research on trauma and adverse childhood experiences emphasizes the importance of building a schoolwide community where every adult in the school recognizes the symptoms of trauma and adversity and actively works to make every student feel that he or she is connected and belongs (Cole et al., 2013). This school community, often referred to as a *trauma-sensitive* or *trauma-informed school*, represents a schoolwide system of care and support. A schoolwide system of care and support aims to have every student feel safe and connected to adults everywhere in the building, and to have staff know the most supportive and effective ways to respond to students impacted by trauma (Cole et al., 2013). Typically, a school's Positive Behavior Interventions and Supports (PBIS) work supports this effort, by identifying students in need of social-emotional or behavioral support and making sure that expectations throughout the building are clear and understood. Strong peer tutoring, mentorship, and class buddy programs can help build schoolwide community. In one school, we observed workshops where, twice a year, K–5 students would register for a workshop with a staff member on a variety of topics, including cartooning, robots, animals, dance, and jewelry making. For six days, students would meet in classrooms for one period to study the topic of their choice with other students and staff also interested in the same topic.

> **❝❞** I always felt like a weird outsider in every school that I ever attended. But since I got here, I don't feel weird anymore. I just seemed to have been accepted and "disappeared" into this really happy family!
>
> —High school student, Portland, Oregon

A Connection to a Talent or Interest Outside Academics

Schools should make it a goal to have all students connect with some activity outside classroom academics (Cole et al., 2005). Students' areas of strength may not be academic, so schools need to have extracurriculars in the arts, athletics, music, and potential job pathways or skills as options. These activities help students connect with personal interests and discover and develop unique talents. Schools that commit to offering students a wide array of clubs, activities, and extracurriculars make a commitment to belonging. Extracurricular and cocurricular activities are important for developing self-esteem and confidence in all students but especially in those impacted by trauma (Klitsch, 2010; Kremer et al., 2015; Youth Law Center, 2019).

A strong connection to sports, music, or any of the many clubs and activities that a school might offer can have a great effect on school attendance and academic success. And the development of talent and interest is directly connected with students' finding a motivating purpose in their lives, often leading to college and career dreams and opportunities. In our observations of effective high-poverty middle and high schools, some reported having as many as 90 percent of their students involved in a nonacademic activity (Barr & Gibson, 2013).

Field Note

 The reason these poor kids get up and get dressed and come to school is not history, mathematics, or English. They come to school each day because of this band program. These kids are up early to hang out here in the band room, play, and practice. And they are here every afternoon after school. I can't tell you how many of my students, who learned to play on these used, beat-up, donated music instruments in this shabby band room, have received college scholarships. Our program is not just teaching music—we are transforming lives. —High school band director, Covington, Kentucky

A Connection to a Career Interest Within Academics

For low-income students who may feel that their middle school or high school curriculum is far removed from real life, discovering a career interest can ignite motivation. Connecting talents and interests with potential career pathways fosters a surge of relevance for schooling. Many effective high schools have organized their academic programs around career clusters to provide a direct relationship between academic study and students' career interests. In elementary and middle schools, teachers can help students start to connect with the world of jobs and professions by attaching content to potential careers (for example, "If you like learning about earthquakes and tsunamis, you might like being a seismologist!") or by bringing in family members to talk about their jobs. As students see how to get from where they are in their life to where they want to be, they also begin to develop specific plans for making their dreams become reality.

Support During Critical Transitions

Students' lives include critical points at which school personnel and families should focus their attention on the students' sense of belonging. At these times, students are more likely to feel disconnected from the school or their peers and more likely to struggle with belonging. The first critical transition is students' first days in kindergarten, which may be their first experiences away from the comforts of home. From there, the transitions from elementary school to middle school, middle school to high school, and then high school to college, postsecondary training, or career are critical points during which creating a sense of belonging for incoming students is tremendously important. Equally important, both school staff and families can help by giving students time to process any sense of loss they have in moving on from a place that they found positive and comforting; this may include celebrations, ceremonies, tokens, memory books, and so on. Without careful recognition of the issue of belonging, and programs to help students make these critical transitions, many students may simply drift away from school, becoming increasingly absent and finally dropping out, seeking to fill the need for belonging in other ways with groups that may not support positive life choices.

Promoting belonging and optimism begins to fulfill students' social-emotional needs and build resilience. It also prepares them for the next seed, that of self-regulation.

The Third Seed of Hope: A Sense of Self-Regulation

The need for self-regulation has gained more prominence, thanks to the growing knowledge base on neuroscience, executive function skills, childhood trauma, and adversity (see Cole et al., 2013; Jensen, 2019; Sporleder & Forbes, 2016). Due to the prevalence of trauma, all adults in the school community who come in contact with students need to be well informed about trauma's impact on behavior and alert to how trauma manifests in children and youth. Exposure to trauma is not always evident from the outside, and adults best serve students when they operate from the assumption that *every child* may be impacted by trauma. Sadly, without conscious efforts, schools, classrooms, and school buses can seem like battlegrounds that unwittingly reinforce "traumatized children's assumptions of the world as a dangerous place," which "sabotage their ability to develop constructive relationships with nurturing adults" (Cole et al., 2005, p. 32).

Traumatized students may act out, become confrontational, or exhibit hypervigilant behaviors, or they may be worried and withdraw. Sometimes, they dissociate and seem numb or depressed (Cole et al., 2005). All these symptoms point to struggles with regulating emotions and self-soothing. The adults in a school must stay ever alert to these behaviors, and they must ready themselves to support students in developing their lagging self-regulation skills. Without appropriate interventions, these behaviors will not only greatly challenge students' academic and social learning but also likely disrupt their classrooms and their peers' learning and development.

> 66 99 In my school, we experience severe behavior daily. Room clears happen several times a week at my building. These events disrupt everyone's learning. All students lose out while the room is cleared. After the room has been put back together and the students return, many cannot get back on track. I notice that the students are louder and less on task. Some speak about being fearful and not wanting to be at school.

> ## —English language development specialist, East Portland, Oregon

The need for self-regulation skills is, of course, not limited to students who have experienced trauma. We all experience frustration, distress, and other emotions that challenge our equilibrium. Anytime we really care about something, or anytime we are invested in a particular outcome, we are bound to experience roadblocks, difficulties, and wrong turns, all of which may trigger frustration, what Quaglia (n.d.) calls "enthusiasm in need of an attitude adjustment."

Public education includes the goal to help all students, especially traumatized students, develop self-regulation skills. These skills primarily involve students' recognizing when emotions or triggers have deregulated them and dropped them into their *reacting brain*, and doing things that help calm their bodies and minds, regulate their systems, and reactivate their *thinking brain*.

To achieve this goal, schools must actively work with students to find tools and strategies that help the students self-regulate. Before they do this, schools need to create a foundation of trust and safety by ensuring that each student feels safe, develops trusting relationships with adults, has positive relationships with peers, and feels a strong sense of belonging in the school community and classroom. (See The Second Seed of Hope: A Sense of Place and Belonging, page 134.) And schools need to provide regular social-emotional learning opportunities where students can gain skills and strategies they can use when they feel deregulated.

Educators have a growing range of strategies for helping students gain the ability to recognize deregulation and then do something about it, such as the following (adapted from Cole et al., 2005).

- A focus on evidence of competence
- Predictability and consistency in environment and communication
- Positive behavioral interventions and supports
- Social-emotional learning curriculum taught in all classrooms
- Regular use of classroom circles and class meetings
- Regular use of mindfulness exercises and self-regulation tools
- Efforts to strengthen internal and environmental protective factors

A Focus on Evidence of Competence

Educators in successful schools work to find students' areas of ability, competence, and expertise, rather than emphasizing test scores and failure or success. Trauma-influenced students are more likely to have low self-worth or sense of their positive abilities. By drawing attention to what students have done well, educators can build neural pathways for optimism and resilience, which fosters self-regulation. This doesn't mean sugarcoating student achievement, but it does mean focusing on what students know and can do and building from there. For example, this may involve writing *+5* on a test, instead of *−10*, because this makes it clear that the most important part is what the student *knew*, not what he or she *didn't know*. When students get discouraged, they can be reminded of what they did well and what they can do next.

Predictability and Consistency in Environment and Communication

Traumatized students need clear, taught routines and predictable expectations (Cole et al., 2013). Teachers should post schedules, review them, and refer to them throughout the day or class period. They should clearly define, reinforce, and recognize student expectations. Teachers must also carefully plan and preview transitions, and support students who need to be able to anticipate regularly scheduled breaks each day.

For example, a middle school administrator may walk through the hallways the day before assembly day, holding a clipboard with the schedule and reminding students the next day is altered schedule. Students may walk up to him, saying, "Yeah, I need to know when lunch is. I really have a hard time on assembly days." When possible, school staff should share any changes to the plan in advance and give students an opportunity to ask questions and create a plan for self-regulation if needed.

Positive Behavioral Interventions and Supports

A strong schoolwide PBIS system works for all students, but it especially benefits students who have experienced trauma and adversity in their lives because it enhances predictability in the environment and clarifies expectations (for example, Pennsylvania Community of Practice, 2018). Students know what to do and why. It also helps provide specific student feedback, such as "I noticed you were able to focus for ten minutes on reading by yourself today!" rather than general feedback like "Nice job during reading."

PBIS systems within a school or district can incorporate a number of other models which foster students' self-regulation through teaching them how to solve problems and how to make amends for mistakes. Restorative justice and restorative discipline practices, which emphasize learning from mistakes and making things right with those who have been harmed, ensure students continue learning (instead of getting pulled out of class to receive discipline, such as detention or suspension). A developing, highly successful approach for responding to behavior challenges is the Collaborative Problem Solving—or Collaborative and Proactive Solutions (CPS)—process developed by psychologists Ross Greene and Stuart Ablon. This process helps adults and students deal with problems by sharing perspectives and needs and coming to a solution that works for all (Greene, 2008). (See Ablon's work at www.thinkkids.org and Greene's work at http://cpsconnection.com to learn more about the CPS process.)

Social-Emotional Learning Curriculum Taught in All Classrooms

Social-emotional learning is the epitome of self-regulation, being "the process through which children and adults understand and manage emotions, set and achieve positive goals, feel and show empathy for others, establish and maintain positive relationships, and make responsible decisions" (CASEL, n.d.). Effective schools make social-emotional learning a high priority, as evidenced by their curriculum, staffing, and professional development. Many high-poverty schools now have social-emotional learning specialists who teach classes and provide interventions and supports for social-emotional learning. Teachers teach regular social-emotional learning lessons each week and also integrate social-emotional learning concepts into academic content. Schools and districts provide staff with professional development opportunities designed to strengthen social-emotional learning, such as yoga for students (see, for example, Yoga Calm at www.yogacalm.org), Collaborative Problem Solving (http://cpsconnection.com), class meetings, mindfulness, and more.

" " I find that when I lead my students in a breathing exercise or a yoga pose during transitions, I am doing it for myself as much as my students!

—Elementary teacher, Oregon

Regular Use of Classroom Circles and Class Meetings

Teaching self-regulation includes teaching students how to communicate about problems in ways that serve to calm, not elevate, emotions. Classroom circles (see *Circle Forward: Building a Restorative School Community*; Boyes-Watson & Pranis, 2015) and class meetings (see Developmental Studies Center, 1998; Nelson, Lott, & Glenn, 2013) provide regular structures and times in the schedule for resolving conflicts. These help students let go of problems in the moment, knowing they will be able to come back to them later. Regular circles and meetings also reinforce the notion that having problems is normal, not a problem in and of itself. We all have disagreements, misunderstandings, and hurt feelings as a normal part of working with other people. We all benefit from learning effective communication strategies for resolving these problems.

Regular Use of Mindfulness Exercises and Self-Regulation Tools

Effective schools teach students and staff a variety of mindfulness exercises and self-regulation tools that they can use at any time to promote self-regulation. These exercises and tools include breathing exercises, stress-relief balls, calm-down corners, exercise corners, sensory pathways, yoga rooms, quiet rooms, check-ins with a caring adult, break passes, and headphones for listening to music. Some schools have *sensory rooms* or *sensory labs* where students (and staff) can explore their sensory pathways and discover what is regulating or calming, elevating or energizing, and overstimulating or triggering for them. In an exemplary sensory room we observed in Bend, Oregon, students explored activities along eight different pathways (auditory, visual, oral-motor, proprioception, vestibular, tactile, olfactory, and cognitive) and then practiced using different pathways to self-regulate. School leaders can boost the use of mindfulness exercises and self-regulation tools like stress balls, breathing, or aromatherapy by making them a part of staff meetings and other adult gatherings to further model the importance of these tools for daily living.

Efforts to Strengthen Internal and Environmental Protective Factors

In chapter 4 (page 71), we presented information about the protective factors that foster resilience. Educators can utilize the list of internal protective factors (see page 75) in conversations with students as a source of self-regulation while students learn how to use their strengths in times of adversity. Schools can use the list of environmental protective factors (see page 80) to evaluate practices and ensure maximum student resilience and self-regulation.

Helping students develop self-regulation skills and competencies is closely associated with both a sense of belonging and a sense of pride, self-esteem, and self-confidence, which is the next seed of hope.

The Fourth Seed of Hope: A Sense of Pride, Self-Esteem, and Self-Confidence

To counter the debilitating effects of prolonged exposure to poverty, this seed of hope helps each student develop a strong sense of pride, self-esteem, and self-confidence—the very antithesis of feelings of despair and helplessness. The need for confidence and self-esteem appears in the fourth level of Maslow's (Huitt, 2007) hierarchy of human needs (see figure 6.1, page 128) and represents an essential building block for success in school and life. Note that a sense of pride and self-esteem does not come from pep rallies, interactive team-building activities, or school buttons, posters, or pins (Chenoweth, 2010). While these efforts may boost a sense of belonging or enjoyment, feelings of pride and self-esteem arise through personal satisfaction of a task well done—the result of genuine effort and real accomplishment.

> **" "** If we believe that it is of paramount importance that each student has self-worth, is actively engaged in their learning, and has a sense of purpose, then we will invest the time it takes to ensure all students reach their fullest potential.

—Russell J. Quaglia

A number of schoolwide social-emotional learning strategies, when used consistently over time, can powerfully boost self-esteem and pride. These strategies include the following.

- High expectations and positive reinforcement
- Positive personal connections with adults
- Leadership and the assumption of responsibility
- Service learning projects
- Academic success and personal monitoring of progress

(For more strategies and examples, see Barr and Gibson [2013], chapter 6, pp. 85–106.)

High Expectations and Positive Reinforcement

The most powerful approach to helping students develop strong feelings of pride, self-esteem, and self-confidence is surrounding students with high expectations and positive reinforcement while ensuring they experience successes in the classroom. Research documents the almost-magical power of high expectations and positive reinforcement (Chenoweth, 2007). Surrounding students with these two attitudes can have profound positive effects on both learning and self-confidence over time.

Positive Personal Connections With Adults

Research has often documented how important it is for children and youth to have a positive personal connection with an adult (Newell & Van Ryzin, 2007). This is especially true of children who are impacted by poverty or who may not have regular positive, undivided attention from adults. Too often in our busy world, parents and guardians in low-income families have to work two or three jobs, are under tremendous stress, deal with health issues or substance abuse issues, and lack the time or ability to be present for their children. Connecting with a teacher or another adult in school can lead to increased academic achievement and positively influence these children's behavior and self-concept. For students who have experienced trauma and other adverse experiences in their lives, personal connections with adults in the school are essential.

Almost all successful students can point to an adult outside their immediate family who has had a clear influence on their life. This adult may be a teacher, counselor, principal, coach, band director, janitor, or bus driver, someone the student respects and wants to be around. Some students will explain that they come to school every morning and "put up with all the boring classes" just to arrive at one particular point in the day when they are with that significant teacher or adult in the classroom or school setting. To have a respected adult believe in them, care about them, and take an interest in them provides a tremendous boost to their pride and self-esteem. Strong personal connections with adults have positive, lifelong significance for students.

Leadership and the Assumption of Responsibility

Students crave engagement and active learning. This may be why sports, the arts, and science labs have such a powerful effect on student engagement—in these activities, students get out of their seats and actively participate in a task that relates to or creates an area of interest or talent. Another common factor in these activities is the assumption of agency or responsibility for outcomes—artists, athletes, and scientists engage in acts of doing which are based in desires to do, perform, or entertain. Unlike previous agricultural generations, where students had farm and household chores and responsibilities, students today often have fewer direct, personal responsibilities beyond schoolwork. Having responsibility for completing or performing a significant activity may be totally outside a student's life experiences. But it appears that having a responsibility and performing that activity well leads to great personal pride that may also help ensure the student feels a sense of belonging (Barr & Parrett, 2008).

In terms of equity, schools need to provide a range of opportunities so that each and every student might experience some type of leadership role. Students living in poor neighborhoods may have fewer opportunities than their middle-class peers to experience leadership or responsibility. To have the responsibility and vote of confidence of being chosen class president, club chairperson, lead cellist in the band, or starter on the football team may be outside the realm of possibility for students in comprehensive high schools. Small alternative public school settings have had effective results in increasing student engagement because these schools, often developed specifically for at-risk students, provide a greater range of student leadership opportunities (Barr & Parrett, 2001).

Effective schools develop students' pride and self-esteem by finding ways for students to assume leadership roles in the school and take on responsibilities in the school and community. These schools have students assume real responsibilities through service learning, community volunteer work, and jobs throughout the school. Some schools give students opportunities to serve on committees that interview and hire teachers as well as school disciplinary committees.

Field Note

When I was teaching in a large high school in Fort Worth, Texas, I was asked to take a student who was causing great disruptions almost every day through his behavior. The student had a sorry record of school attendance, failure, and classroom behavior issues. I think some teachers were even afraid of this young man. When he arrived in my class, he saw that some of my students came into my class during study hall and before and after school to serve as teacher assistants. I had made this a really significant honor for which I selected students. When he said that he wanted to be a teacher assistant, I told him that to become an assistant, he would have to attend class every day, and his behavior would have to improve. He was not happy.

As I thought about it, I decided to give him an opportunity to serve as one of my teacher assistants. I asked him to take responsibility for stamping my signature onto school paperwork and student passes. He was also responsible for taking roll in our class and calling, from the office, any student who was absent. Over time, I gave him more and more real responsibilities, and in every case, he performed higher than my expectations. As my attendance clerk, he dramatically improved the class's attendance through his supervision. It seemed students would do almost anything rather than get a call from my clerk. —Bob Barr

Service Learning Projects

Service learning offers students a chance to assume responsibilities, and a chance to serve their community in some necessary or meaningful way. This might include working at the county health department to gather water samples over time and record pollution of community streams and lakes, or it might include working as an aide in a local hospital, mental health center, or homeless shelter. The idea is to get students out of the classroom and into the community, where they can have a rich experience, gain pride from doing needed tasks, and discover added relevance and motivation for their studies at school. Service learning projects can often lead to unexpected career pathways and open doors to students' futures. Service learning projects enhance students' pride, self-esteem, and self-confidence as students do real work for others and are able to see the impact their efforts have on their community.

Field Note

The PeaceJam Foundation, a worldwide effort to involve students in service learning projects, connects youth to Nobel Peace Prize recipients, who represent an incredibly diverse group of people from all corners of the earth. The PeaceJam curriculum introduces students to the incredible stories of Nobel recipients and inspires students to find a way to make the world better. (Visit www. peacejam.org for more information.) —Emily Gibson

Academic Success and Personal Monitoring of Progress

Effective schools use a wide variety of instructional strategies to ensure that each student experiences early academic success and then builds on that success with repeated accomplishments. Schools often break down curriculum content into small, manageable units so that all students can master even the most demanding content, one small step at a time. Schools can also involve students in self-monitoring their own learning. To self-monitor learning, each student participates in establishing the current unit of instruction's learning goals and records where he or she is and what he or she needs to achieve. Students then follow their progress daily and weekly as they work toward achieving their learning goals. At student-led conferences, students report their progress to their parents or guardians and describe what their next steps will be. Such strategies enhance learning and build pride, self-esteem, and self-confidence.

Building student pride and self-confidence in various settings is often a school-wide or communitywide endeavor, complete with mentoring, job shadowing, and more. Even though academic success is directly related to pride and self-esteem, these programs go far beyond classroom learning. Success in these pride-building activities often helps students find great motivation for their academic studies as well as a purpose in their lives, which leads to the final seed of hope—a sense of purpose.

The Fifth Seed of Hope: A Sense of Purpose

Helping students find a strong, personal purpose in their lives relates directly to the highest level of Maslow's (Huitt, 2007) hierarchy of human needs—self-actualization. While the elementary and middle school years focus more on career exploration and the many work and professional roles that might be available to students, the high school years push students to select their initial career interests and finally make detailed plans for their lives after they graduate. Just as financial advisors help adults moving toward retirement develop detailed, long-range plans for achieving their goals, teachers and counselors help students on the cusp of adulthood plan for their future and open the door of opportunity. It is through this final essential level of development that students find hope in their future—hope for breaking the cycle of poverty that may have weighed down their families for generations.

While research on human purpose is limited, psychologist William Damon (2008) conducted an intriguing study on purpose, which he reports in his book *The Path to Purpose: How Young People Find Their Calling in Life*. In his study of American teenagers, Damon (2008) finds that only 20 percent of the students he studied were *purposeful*, being able to express a sense of purpose or direction in their lives. In addition he describes 25 percent of the studied students as *dabblers*, who did a little bit of many things without committing; 31 percent as *disengaged*, who did not find purpose in doing; and 25 percent as *dreamers*, who had ideas and plans but did little to engage in action.

Separately, Quaglia (n.d.) describes *dreamers* as students who have lofty goals but take little action to achieve them, while *doers* do strong work in school but have little vision of where they want to go in life. When dreaming and doing come together, they create aspirations, or purpose. As Quaglia (n.d.) says, "Students with strong aspirations show that they have dreams for the future, and are inspired to do what it takes in the present to work toward their fulfillment." A student with purpose is a student with unlimited promise. Having a purpose is essential for success both in school and in life.

> **" "** The most successful students I know are clear about who they are and what they believe in; they are not afraid to show it and are confident they will make a difference in this world.
>
> —**Russell J. Quaglia**

Schools' challenge is to help the students who do not have purpose in their lives (approximately 80 percent of students, according to Damon [2008]). This is a daunting goal, but effective schools see it as a great opportunity to make a significant contribution to students' lives and the larger world. The literature on how effective schools are helping students find guiding purpose for their lives by exploring career options, narrowing their focus to areas of interest, and making their plans for the future includes a number of powerful strategies, including the following (Damon, 2008; Jensen, 2009; Newell & Van Ryzin, 2009).

- Development of talents and interests
- Career exploration
- Provisions for learning options, career clusters, and high school academic majors
- A personal plan for the future
- Pathways to the future

(For more strategies and examples, see Barr and Gibson [2013], chapter 7, pp. 107–138.)

Development of Talents and Interests

When students realize that something personal and important to them connects to the larger world of possibilities and opportunities, it often boosts their motivation. In effective schools, exploring personal talents and interests also leads to serious thought about possible future professions and jobs. Since students are typically drawn to school sports, music, clubs, and other extracurricular activities because they are interested in them or have talent in the area, extracurriculars can provide a launching point for serious consideration of a student's future and provide purpose.

" " I wanted to expose them [students] to dozens of jobs, each of which employed a modest number of skilled people. My idea was to spark in each student, one by one if necessary, some inner desire for satisfying work, and through that desire and the connection to ways to realize it, help them see a way out of the poverty they lived in.

—Herbert Kohl

Career Exploration

Effective middle and high schools fill up their calendars with career fairs, opportunities to hear professionals talk about their work, visits to large and small businesses in the area, and trips to community colleges, technology schools, and universities. Students are so isolated from the contemporary work world that many good jobs and careers remain largely unknown to students, hidden in the urban and suburban sprawl. Few things are more exciting for students than leaving the classroom and having experiences in the world of commerce. Here, they make connections, discover interests, and see the beginnings of long-term possibilities.

Provisions for Learning Options, Career Clusters, and High School Academic Majors

A growing number of effective districts are providing students with a menu of learning options by replacing a basic college preparation curriculum with a number of small alternative programs, magnet schools, or charter schools that offer diverse curricular experiences. Examples include schools for the arts or performing arts, often established in cooperation with local professional artist groups; stand-alone high school baccalaureate programs; law or legal high schools; and schools for the culinary arts. Some schools have gone even further, diversifying their entire curriculum with several broad career clusters (law, medicine, technology, and business, for example) that relate to possible professions.

These types of learning options give students the opportunity to begin thinking about their futures and to engage with a school curriculum that actually connects academics with career interests. They also allow teachers to connect with other teachers and students who have similar interests and to relate their academic area to real-world applications. In the same way that college students select an academic major to guide their work in college, high school students can make decisions about their life and future, which typically increases their personal motivation and effort to move toward their goals.

A Personal Plan for the Future

Some high schools have gone far beyond simply offering students curricular options. These schools have implemented a mandatory senior project or graduation project that requires a four-year effort. For this project, each student explores career options, identifies general areas of interest, participates in business and college tours and visits, conducts detailed investigations (including interviews, job shadowing, service projects, and internships), and finally, during senior year, develops and presents a detailed plan for life after high school. These students leave high school knowing exactly where they will go to school or to work next, how they will finance their education, and what they will do to forward their dreams. (For more information about how high schools specifically support purpose, see Barr and Gibson [2013], chapter 9.)

Pathways to the Future

Educators can also spur students at every grade level to develop their sense of purpose by presenting them with possible pathways to the future. These pathways are general directions that students should think about and hopefully consider in their life choices (Barr & Gibson, 2013). Pathways include the following.

- Leaving school without a high school diploma
- Graduating from high school and entering the world of work

- Entering the military after high school

- Completing job training after high school

- Obtaining a one- or two-year certificate or community college degree

- Gaining a four-year college or university degree

- Receiving a professional certificate or degree that requires graduate school

Schools may outline these various pathways on charts around the school and in classrooms so students and their families can explore each pathway, look at anticipated salaries and long-term opportunities, debate the pros and cons of each pathway, and make decisions about students' general desired directions for their lives.

Finding purpose is the ultimate goal of the seeds of hope, and of our public schools. Graduation from high school represents a huge transition into a world of postsecondary training and education, a world that people impacted by poverty, especially generational poverty, may have little or no experience navigating. As a result, graduation can represent a frightening step into the unknown. For this reason, implementing a high school project or personal plan for the future can act as a significant capstone, supporting this last, greatest transition. If a student has developed the plan truthfully and with care, it will provide the student with a huge foundation for personal resilience and a road map for the future.

Conclusion

Addressing the social-emotional needs of students, especially students impacted by poverty, gives each and every student a strong foundation of personal resilience. The five seeds of hope provide students with the tools to overcome poverty's traumatic effects and the associated sense of helplessness that cripples so many public school students. These seeds encourage students to develop the foundational strength necessary to break out of the sticky cycle of poverty and find success in school as well as life. They represent a massive twine in the rope of relationships, resources, and reasons that students in high-poverty, high-trauma communities need in order to bypass the quicksand of poverty.

In the next chapter, attention shifts to the third cornerstone of the resilient school: meeting the human needs of students and their families. This cornerstone underlies the other cornerstones of a resilient school. Without this cornerstone, all other efforts to boost students' academic and social-emotional needs may fall flat.

Next Steps

Please complete the following Next Steps, to integrate your experiences within your own schools and communities with the information presented in this chapter.

1. After reading about the seeds of hope, share with other teachers how well you think your school is addressing these essential social-emotional needs. What do you think you and your school are doing well? Which seeds do you feel it would be important to work on?

2. Use the seeds of hope as a guide to talking to your students about the effectiveness of your school. You might develop a short anonymous survey in which the students are asked to reflect and comment on how well they think the school is meeting their social-emotional needs. You might also use the same survey with adults in the school and then see the degree of agreement there is among the teachers and how much they agree or disagree with the students. This always leads to powerful conversations. You can find sample student surveys online (see www.solutiontree.com/free-resources/schoolimprovement/bacoh).

3. Purpose is so important for high school students. In your school, or the area high school, do you feel that staff are helping students develop, clarify, and pursue purpose in their lives? Do you feel some of the tasks described in this chapter relating to *purpose* would be worthwhile to discuss with the school staff in your school as well as with students and their parents?

4. For each seed of hope, create a three-coumn diagram with columns titled "Doing," "Change," and "Add." Fill out this chart, preferably with colleagues or as part of a PLC meeting, for each seed of hope. Consider what you are doing in your school that already addresses each seed of hope, things you are doing that you want to change (either eliminate because they are counterproductive, or further develop), and things that you would like to add. These completed charts can guide your practice.

5. Which SEL or sensory practices are in place in your school? Which would you like to implement?

Building the Resilient School © 2020 Solution Tree Press • SolutionTree.com
Visit **go.SolutionTree.com/schoolimprovement** to download this free reproducible.

Chapter 7

The Third Cornerstone of the Resilient School: Addressing Students' and Their Families' Human Needs

How can I worry about teaching my students multiplication tables and reading and the concepts of science when they are sick and hungry? When they are frightened and stressed from conditions in their home and neighborhood? How can I teach children who do not believe that they can learn? If we are serious about teaching, there are issues here that we simply cannot ignore. We must find ways to deal with them. If we don't, who will?

—School Social Worker, Salem, Oregon

Throughout our public schools, a revolution is in progress, redefining the roles and responsibilities of the neighborhood school. Schools across the United States are transforming themselves through a focus on addressing the human needs of students and their families. More and more schools have come to recognize that no matter how effective they make their instructional program, no matter how much they strengthen their curriculum, and no matter how well they address students' social-emotional needs, factors outside the school have a profound effect on learning in the school. In particular, the factors of absenteeism, family mobility, food scarcity, and home or community trauma, which arise when students and families cannot meet their human needs, affect learning. These and other factors can all be major contributors to school failure and dropout rates. As a result, schools have begun to turn their attention outside the classroom and school walls and take dramatic steps to address students' and their families' human needs. This is what we, the authors, call the *third wave of research* into high-poverty, high-performing schools, and which is the third cornerstone of the resilient school.

Meeting human physiological needs is an essential prerequisite to achieving personal resilience. Before a student has any real hope of achieving social competence, autonomy, or a sense of purpose, he or she must have food, clothing, and a place to live. Addressing families' and students' human needs appears as the foundation of all other needs in Maslow's (1970) hierarchy (see figure 6.1, page 128). Communities and schools must start here. To have any hope of learning effectively and becoming socially competent, students cannot be hungry, cold, sleepy, or frightened. This is the bottom line; this essential issue undergirds all others. Since 2000, as schools in districts like Vancouver Public Schools began to struggle with how to address and eliminate the root causes of sickness, hunger, absenteeism, and family mobility, they turned their attention toward coordinating a wide variety of social and health services to make them more easily available to families in need, no matter the underlying reason.

> " " One in every four students sitting in your classrooms right now comes from a family in which one or both parents or guardians have significant problems controlling their addictions. These students are five times more likely to be victims of sexual or physical abuse. They have a much higher likelihood of becoming addicts themselves or of entering into destructive relationships than do their peers from addiction-free homes. In addition, children from addicted homes are three to five times more likely to be referred for treatment as learning disabled or behaviorally disordered children.

—Richard R. Powell, Stanley J. Zehm, and Jeffrey A. Kottler

From New York to Oakland, Nashville to Portland—in urban, suburban, and rural schools grappling with the complex and insidious impacts of poverty—a grassroots movement is well underway, led by educators and administrators and community members set on bringing hope to families in need. And community outreach is an essential cornerstone of a resilient school. The hub of the resilient school is a complex network of community partners coming together with the school to address the human needs of families living in poverty and provide students with a real chance to break free of generational poverty, achieve success in school, and find a pathway to a better life.

In this chapter, we share the third cornerstone of the resilient school: addressing the human needs of students and their families through what we call *community outreach*. This chapter first outlines the origins of community outreach and its recent growth surge before delving into the five steps necessary for setting up and maintaining a community outreach center.

1. Identifying the needs of families

2. Establishing the school as a hub of coordination

3. Setting up the community outreach center, including hiring a coordinator

4. Monitoring the community outreach center's outcomes

5. Funding community outreach

The chapter will conclude with a discussion of what the literature has found regarding the impact of community outreach on student learning.

The Emergence of Community Outreach

Since the late 1990s, research in high-poverty, high-performing schools has sought to find just the right mix of curriculum, instructional approaches, school policies, and professional development for teachers and administrators to best reach and teach poor and minority students. While great progress has been made in reaching and teaching all students, we now know with great certainty that actions limited to the classroom will surely not disrupt poverty, regardless of the quality of the curriculum or the effectiveness of the teacher.

In spite of the often-herculean efforts of dedicated staff, many schools have been unable to close the achievement gap between poor and affluent students or to sustain their successes over time. The search for better results in the wake of poor results after implementing the first wave of research, starting in the late 1990s and early 2000s, led innovative leaders and educators in places like Kentucky; Cincinnati, Ohio, Indianapolis, Indiana; and Vancouver, Washington, to look outside the school's walls—to focus on the human needs of students and their families. According to Joy Dryfoos (1998), these educators' early "full-service schools" focused on resolving families' struggles with homelessness, hunger, unemployment, addiction, health and dental needs, family trauma, abuse, family mobility, crime, and so many other issues arising from lives in poverty. Through resourceful, creative, and perhaps initially clumsy efforts in partnering with service providers within the community, these schools found that investing energies in helping families meet their basic needs of food, shelter, and health care had tremendous, reverberating positive effects on student attendance, behavior, and, ultimately, academic achievement.

In the beginning, as schools learned more about the needs of families in their communities, they sought out and stumbled across government agencies, organizations, and groups that provided the types of supports and services that families so desperately needed. These agencies, organizations, and groups were, coincidently, seeking ways to provide services, but often could not connect easily with families in need. The coordination between schools and service providers represents a bold leap forward for public education. In conversations with school personnel in school districts in a number of states during the years between 2010 and 2018, a few themes emerged—common conclusions that each of these districts seemed to have arrived at independently.

- If schools truly want to address the needs of students and their families and ensure that all students are learning to their capacity, they must look outside the school walls.

- Family mobility, chronic absenteeism, lack of reading readiness, low student achievement, and failure to graduate are directly related to issues in the home and community.

- Schools often lack the skills, funding, or knowledge to seriously address the needs of families and communities.

- Agencies and organizations in the public and private sectors can provide services poverty-level families desperately need, but families can have difficulties finding and accessing these providers.

- Little or no coordination exists between classroom teaching and learning, families' needs, and community providers of supports and services.

While neither the schools themselves nor their already-stretched-thin educators were equipped to provide every service students and their families needed, they discovered that schools could act as a hub for organizing services already provided within the community. As school districts attempted to connect the dots by linking classrooms, homes, and community service providers, a complex network of inter-related services emerged that helped low-income families become more resilient and their children become better able to stay in school, thrive in school, graduate, and find postsecondary success. These schools essentially redefined their role and function and created a new vision for public education in the United States—one with the school as the emotional center of life in the neighborhood.

Field Note

In 2016, a Peoria, Illinois, school district leadership team concluded the schools only had students for 7–10 hours a day, depending on a student's activities, and the rest of students' time was spent in their homes and communities, where

> traumatic events and experiences threaten to overwhelm all the hard work and effort of teachers and school personnel. Under the guidance of leadership professionals from the Centergy Project (see thecentergyproject.com), Peoria schools began to survey and interview students in order to identify their needs firsthand. These bold efforts to collect student voices (concerns, needs, problems, and so on) and to develop vigorous efforts to address the students' concerns led the Peoria schools to connect with community partners that could provide support and assistance in the areas of identified student needs. The district then created a "wraparound center" that connected students to available services in the community. —Bob Barr

Since the late 1990s, schools' abilities to successfully respond to the human needs of families spread slowly across the United States, often emanating out from the original beacon schools or districts. A true pioneer in this wave of first responders was the state of Kentucky. In the early 1990s, Kentucky had the United States' highest illiteracy rate, ranked near the bottom in per-pupil spending, and placed forty-ninth in students continuing to college. As part of its "education revolution" at the time, the state helped equalize school district funding and mandated the creation of family assistance centers in all of Kentucky's eight hundred schools. These centers provide preschool programs, extended school services, vocational programs, family literacy services, health services, substance abuse and mental health counseling, and other services. Kentucky's family assistance centers were still serving students and families in 2019, with well-documented positive results. The state's high school graduation rate is more than 86 percent—the United States' fourth highest—and nearly two-thirds of Kentucky's high school graduates are considered ready for credit-bearing college courses (National Education Association, n.d.a).

Field Note

When working in a Kentucky school district during the winter of 2019, I was hit with a rather dramatic insight. While talking with a number of high school principals about their family assistance centers, I kept hearing them explain that over the years funding in Kentucky for these centers had been cut at the state level again and again, and as a result, their programs had diminished significantly. What struck me was that some of the most successful family assistance centers that I had visited and studied around the country had started and been operating on budgets that were dramatically less than the Kentucky centers. It seems to me, in my very limited visits to community outreach programs, that the most effective programs, even the most ambitious, seemed to be those who had to depend on coordinated funding form a variety of local sources, such as the United Way, Title I, housing authorities, food banks, churches, Boys and Girls Clubs, and others, in partnerships with the school districts. Such combined, coordinated funding may well provide a far stronger resource base than relying solely on external grants or government funding. —Bob Barr

Likewise, in Camden, New Jersey, the LEAP Academy University Charter School applied a communitywide, full-court press to ensure K–12 students have a chance. Beginning with its first high school graduating class in 2005, the LEAP Academy has had a 100 percent graduation rate and 100 percent college acceptance rate (compared with the 50 percent graduation rate in neighboring public high schools in Camden; Bonilla-Santiago, 2014). The LEAP Academy, although a charter school that falls outside our focus on regular neighborhood schools serving high-poverty populations, began as an attempt to stop the hemorrhaging of youth from schools in Camden, where two of the city's five high schools have less than 50 percent graduation rates and where gang activity and drug use is rampant. In Camden, LEAP Academy educators are building an "educational pipeline" to a better life by providing *cradle to college* supports for black and Latino children in one K–12 school, including a health center, a community outreach center, and a college and career assistance center. See *The Miracle on Cooper Street* by Gloria Bonilla-Santiago (2017) or visit leapacademycharter.org to learn more about the LEAP Academy.

Remarkably, this outreach between schools and communities has spread across the United States without a federal mandate or law requiring its development, and in most cases without designated state funding. It has truly been a quiet, national grassroots movement spread through word of mouth and positive results. Although their specific details and names vary from school district to school district, and state to state—including *family community resource centers, family access networks, integrated student supports, full-service schools,* and *community schools*—we refer to all these schools and programs with the universal term *community outreach* or *community outreach schools* in this chapter, as all centers and programs entail outreach into the community to connect families with services.

Development of community outreach is an essential piece of the school-improvement process, without which a school cannot seriously confront the long-term effects of poverty and help students find pathways to better lives. Districts all across the United States have community outreach programs. And although there is some disagreement regarding the number of community outreach schools in the United States because these schools often operate with a wide variety of names, the Coalition for Community Schools reports more than five thousand community outreach schools in the United States in a wide variety of settings (Coalition for Community Schools, 2019; Zalaznick, 2017). See figure 7.1 for examples of such schools.

Examples of the vast range and variety of community outreach schools, districts, and programs we have visited or discovered within the Coalition of Community Schools (2019) work include the following.

- Small and medium-sized school districts like Escambia County, Florida; West Chicago, Illinois; and Boise, Idaho

- The many small and rural schools in Kentucky, and rural schools in central Oregon, where seven school districts scattered across three counties joined together to form the Better Together (2018) community outreach partnership

- Larger districts like Evansville Vanderburgh School Corporation in Evansville, Indiana, which began with one Title I school in the 1990s and has since expanded into community outreach in every school in the district; and Albuquerque Public Schools in New Mexico, which has twenty-three community outreach schools partnering with city and county governments and the University of New Mexico

- The Marietta Student Life Center in Georgia, which was created to address the needs of high school students. The center was built on a set of priorities taken directly from student voices in the school, and the center used the priorities to connect to very specific partners in the community who had the expertise and the ability to address students' needs. See thecentergyproject.com for more information.

- The Cincinnati, Ohio, schools designated in 2001 as an *academic emergency* district. Using community outreach models, in nine years this Cincinnati district transformed itself into the only urban district in Ohio to earn the *effective* designation. Graduation rates climbed from 51 percent to 82 percent, and achievement gaps between white and African American students were eliminated.

- United Way of Central Indiana (n.d.) in Indianapolis, Indiana, which increases student success by channeling volunteers in the community to make quality childcare accessible, to foster early reading skills, and to support students through graduation. United Way serves as a tracking center, monitoring childcare centers and enrolled children, kindergarten readiness and third-grade reading levels, and attendance rates, graduation rates, and annual goals.

- Schools Uniting Neighborhoods (SUN) in Multnomah County, Oregon. Eighty-five SUN community schools at all levels work with the SUN program, in cooperation with Multnomah County, the City of Portland, the Parks and Recreation Department, six school districts, the Oregon Department of Human Services, nonprofits, and community members. See https://multco.us/sun to learn more.

- Vancouver Public Schools in Washington. Starting in 2008, Vancouver Public Schools established family and community resource centers in two high-poverty schools; by 2015, the district had expanded centers into eleven elementary schools, two middle schools, and two high schools, as well as in a community learning center. These schools serve more than half the district's students. The district has added two mobile family and community resource center vans in order to serve the needs of students and families at the remaining district schools. The district's long-range plan focused on establishing the centers in all thirty-five schools by 2020.

Figure 7.1: Examples of the diverse variety of community outreach schools and districts.

When turning a school into a community outreach center, the first and most crucial step is to establish the needs of the families. This, of course, will guide the sorts of services the outreach center should aim to provide, as well as the service providers operating in the community. In the next section, we will discuss several ways to determine the needs of the students, their families, and the wider community.

> 66 99 Our major challenges all fall in the arena of the mental health issues of our students. Curriculum and instruction have their daily challenges, but the social and emotional needs of our students, the crises and trauma that so many experience growing up in a home of poverty can simply overwhelm a classroom at any time.
>
> **—April Whipple, principal, Peter S. Ogden Elementary School, Vancouver, Washington**

Step 1: Identifying the Needs of Families

Scholars agree on the needs of low-income families (see Barkan, 2016; Lindsey, 2009; Moore, Redd, Burkhauser, Mbwana, & Collins, 2009; Ratcliffe & McKernan, 2010). Most debilitating issues associated with poverty can be organized into a few broad categories.

- Food, clothing, and shelter issues
- Physical health issues
- Mental health issues
- Parental or caregiver issues
- Family and community trauma
- Cultural issues

These very issues directly affect students' ability to attend school and be alert and industrious while in school.

> 66 99 With my students impacted by the traumas of poverty, I'm not sure what has happened that morning or the night before, or if they even slept in a bed. I'm not sure what they witnessed. That sometimes is transparent with kids; you can see there's something going on. And other times, they're really good at disguising that, especially when they get to the middle school level.
>
> **—Teresa Martin, sixth-grade teacher, Oregon**

In addition to noting the high-visibility issues of absenteeism, family mobility, and trauma that so often mobilize staff efforts to address specific family and student needs, community outreach schools become extremely creative in identifying the underlying issues that often lead to absenteeism, movement in and out of a school district, and even classroom disruptions. They turn to the *real authorities* and ask the parents and guardians, teachers, and students how they can help them; what they need.

Families Identify Their Needs

When starting a community outreach center, schools solicit input from families. They do this through the creation of *community advisory boards*, which meet regularly to talk about needs and evaluate services. When these community advisory boards commence at the district level, the membership is typically designated by the various school and community groups that co-fund and provide direction and vision to these ambitious efforts. These almost always include professionals from throughout the community who know the world of poverty and who have extensive experience in working with families living in poverty. Over time, participation on these district boards are enlarged to include parents and community leaders. To be effective, each local school must also have an advisory board, and these always start with concerned parents and community leaders who join in efforts to identify family needs.

These local boards gradually come to evaluate the success of programs, plan program expansion, provide volunteer support of community members, outreach, and so on. This work has a great empowering effect on parents as they come to consider the local schools as "our school" and become active participants in the school programs both in the school and in the community. At the school level, it is the parents who provide the foundation of support and success for these community outreach efforts. In some schools, like Marietta High School in Georgia, students themselves become advisory board members and provide the guiding force for school and community outreach.

In addition, schools may use parent surveys, community meetings, and focus group discussions to gather family input. Schools have found that parents and guardians may ask for everything from English language courses to childcare to help with income taxes, public transportation, children's vaccinations, or even adult addictions. Over time, as the outreach center is up and running, parents and guardians may come to feel that the center *belongs to them*, that it is their center. They may help decorate and paint the center; in cooperation with the center coordinator, they may help plan and schedule activities and events and become true partners in the operation of the center.

Teachers and Staff Identify Their Students' Needs

Few people know students like their classroom teachers and school staff. The teachers and support staff are who recognize when a student is suffering from trauma and becoming a disruption to the class and school. The adults in the school recognize when a student needs a warm winter coat or shoes or is hungry or sleepy. School personnel are the front line in identifying when students may need to see an optometrist, a dentist, or a mental health provider in order to learn more effectively. Typically, staff share concerns or potential needs with the community outreach coordinator as the needs arise. The coordinator then reaches out to the family to build rapport and see what services may benefit the family.

Students Voice Their Needs

A very interesting approach for determining human needs was first developed in a high school in Marietta, Georgia, beginning in 2013, and has since evolved into the Centergy Project, which helps schools and districts access student voices and design community outreach centers which meet those needs. In an effort to raise Marietta High School's rather dismal 67 percent graduation rate, the school's principal proposed asking the students what was good about their high school, what they thought could be done to improve the school, and what specific assistance and support they felt would help. This process of seeking student voices led, in 2015, to the creation of a wraparound community outreach center almost completely focused on the students' stated needs—the Marietta Student Life Center (see figure 7.1, page 161). By listening to the students, and making sure the students recognized how the school was addressing identified needs, the community outreach center became a huge part of the high school experience and quite different from other outreach centers in that the services focused on mental health, substance abuse, and restorative discipline in addition to basic needs. During student interviews and focus groups, students shared about their parents' addiction problems; domestic abuse and sexual abuse in the home; drugs, violence, and gang pressures in their neighborhoods; sexual identity issues; and so on. To best handle these sensitive issues, the center utilizes counselors, mentors, service providers, and therapists, who work with students in confidential, supportive, and sometimes therapeutic relationships. Many of these issues rarely emerged when talking to parents or staff. From 2013 to 2017, the high school's four-year graduation rate rose by 12 percentage points and their five-year graduation rate rose by 17 percentage points. (Visit the Centergy Project's website, www.thecentergyproject.com, for more information.)

As school community outreach centers identify families' and students' specific needs, the community outreach coordinator then turns to the community for help in filling these needs. The needs of families and students lead directly to very specific partners in the community—partners who have the expertise and the budgets to deliver the needed services at the center.

Field Note

We sometimes forget that even in some of our most affluent communities, there are pockets of extreme poverty scattered all around that are largely "out of sight, out of mind." Working in Ames, Iowa, Dr. Clemmye Jackson and her husband George spent their careers helping school boards, university leadership, superintendents, professors, principals, and even teachers recognize that there were under-represented students who need support and assistance. In Ames Community School District, Dr. Jackson's work led to strong special programs focused on the needs of students and their families, and ultimately led to the creation of a new position that was funded and initiated in high poverty schools in Ames: the family resource counselor. These counselors were traveling responders visiting homes, identifying needs, seeking out services to address those needs, and serving as advocates for families and students. The family resource counselor was the forerunner of today's community outreach school, a huge milestone in the effort of schools to serve the needs of students and their families.

Clemmye's husband, Dr. George Jackson, spent his life across town at Iowa State University addressing the needs of students. At a memorial service following his death, a university vice-president talked about seeing George coming down the hallway flashing his beacon of a smile, invariably asking for a small donation to help some student in need: a winter jacket for a southern student, money for a Greyhound bus ticket so that another student could go home and see a sick mother, or donations for a student who could not afford his textbooks. There seemed to always be some student in need. The vice president said he learned to always carry a twenty-dollar bill in his shirt pocket just in case he saw Dr. Jackson in the hallway. That day, the memorial service was packed with Clemmye and George's former students—lawyers, doctors, educators, and religious and business leaders— all there to share what their education meant to them and how Clemmye and George had changed their lives. —Bob Barr

Step 2: Establishing the School as a Hub of Coordination

For every family issue described in step 1, most communities have agencies, organizations, and community groups already at work providing direct services to families in the neighborhood. Though many existing community outreach schools initially lacked the capacity to work with numerous agencies, they quickly developed a leadership role in coordinating these services. The schools began to transform the way communities responded to the needs of their families and their children. Instead of placing the burden to find and access resources on parents and guardians, agencies came to rely on the schools to provide access to needy families. Schools became an intermediary, providing a hub of connection. Suddenly, this made the complex problem of distributing services far easier for providers.

To be effective, a local neighborhood school serving a high-poverty community must become the coordinating hub of a broad range of new activities and responsibilities—the emotional center of the neighborhood. The principal, teachers, and specialists all must adjust the way they do things and make room for new roles and responsibilities. The school must create new jobs and advertise and fill new positions. It must revise and expand budgets.

Schools that have started community outreach centers have shown remarkable creativity in finding funding. Some school districts reallocate Title I funding, others are funded by community organizations like United Way, but most are ultimately co-funded by numerous community organizations, government programs, and even local churches. Since these various groups see that using the school as an organizing hub for the delivery of services is an unusually effective and efficient way to achieve their own goals, they have been willing to use their budgets to help fund the school's outreach efforts. Most community outreach centers start rather piecemeal, perhaps beginning with working with a local church or food bank to provide *weekend backpacks* filled with nutritious food for the student and their families, and using community volunteers to do the work. Over time, the center expands to work toward other identified needs and with other community partners, such as a Lions Club or Rotary Club, for help with purchasing a washer-dryer for the school or for the local food bank to use the school as a distribution center once a month. Over time, as the school identifies new needs, these efforts inevitably expand, leading to the creation of a school-community advisory board and a coordinator jointly funded by a variety of school and community groups.

The school connects family needs with available social services and integrates these efforts into the teaching and learning process. Staff now must observe students with an eye toward unmet needs that they or their families may have. The school must become involved in marketing and communication and come face to face with families, agencies, organizations, and foundations. It means developing trust with a wide variety of individuals and groups. And it means developing partnerships with agencies and organizations, and it may even involve inviting some partners into the school building and sharing space between an instructional program for both students and their parents or guardians and outside community groups. Community outreach demands that public educators go where they have rarely gone before—out into the world of poverty and social services.

Initially, the effort to provide coordination between the school and community or government programs can seem overwhelming. Yet, most of the community outreach programs begin small, and over time the early efforts led to a broader and broader set of community connections. For example, as mentioned previously, efforts to provide food-filled backpacks for students over the weekend might lead to discussions with community food banks. Programs often start with local Boys and Girls Clubs or with local churches. They might expand as the school realizes that their students' families are homeless or having to move again and again to find affordable housing. This realization leads to contacts with housing authorities. Teachers' concerns for students suffering from stress and trauma may lead to a search for organizations who can provide added mental health providers for the school. Sometimes, community outreach begins with a government program or community organization that approaches the school with a simple request: "How can we help?" What is so remarkable is how community outreach grows out of all the things that any high-poverty school tends to already be doing as they work to ensure that all children and youth are learning effectively. It is a very natural development that is occurring more and more in communities all over the country.

Field Note

In December 2018, in Vancouver, Washington, an elementary school's core leadership team and family community resource center coordinator began talking about a neighboring low-income housing complex's upcoming closure for restoration. Its yearlong restoration was slated to begin that summer. Though the neighborhood would close only two or three units at a time, each family would face a tremendous burden in securing housing and was not guaranteed to find a place in the complex again after restoration. Knowing this would disrupt about thirty families attending the school, the coordinator and school principal spoke with the district family community resource center coordinator and local housing entities to plan ahead for where these families might go. The coordinator and principal wanted to know how the district could ensure these students would remain at their school, instead of being uprooted from both home and school. By March, the school principal and coordinator held a meeting at the neighborhood recreation center to share information with families and help them begin to apply for housing and make plans well in advance of the closing. This is a beautiful example of how school leadership can support already-overwhelmed families and anticipate things that may impact students' ability to be successful in school. —Emily Gibson

While professionals can quickly be overwhelmed with the complexities of various service providers, low-income families are unlikely to even know about, let alone be able to find and access, the many programs that provide direct assistance. For poor families, the multitude of organizations and agencies in any community represent a bewildering array of inaccessible services and supports, complicated by the added burdens of transportation, hours of operation, and childcare demands. Some families also have additional complexities related to being undocumented immigrants, including concern about services access, legal difficulties, and even deportation.

Field Note

For a middle-class parent or guardian with a car and a full-time job with benefits, getting a child to the doctor can be a scheduling challenge. For a low-income parent or guardian working two jobs who relies on public transportation, getting a child to the doctor can quickly become a nightmare, requiring juggling bus schedules, securing time off from jobs, arranging for pickup and drop-off at school, communicating with the school about the reason for the absence, and budgeting for the costs. Add in inclement weather, the sickly child, and the need to deal with social service offices about insurance or Medicaid, and it is understandable why a doctor appointment requires a child to miss an entire day of school. Imagine the relief when a child can see a doctor or get their eyes checked at the mobile health clinic that comes to school once a week as a community partner. Suddenly, the arduous daylong journey becomes much more manageable for a stressed-out parent or guardian. —Bob Barr

As a school begins working with its neighborhood community partners and services and supports improve, trust develops, and something remarkable occurs. Over time, the school becomes the one-stop center to which families can turn for help. It provides coherence to the bewildering array of government, social service, nonprofit, and faith-based organizations that provide supports to families. It simplifies and coordinates family needs with partner providers. The school serves as the go-between for families, service providers, and classroom teachers.

The level of coordination that emerges over time has rarely existed in schools before. The coordination enables the school to efficiently cut through much of the confusion and bureaucracy of the many isolated, independent service providers. This streamlined approach maximizes the way the most appropriate partners address family needs, it cuts through the paperwork, and it improves the speed of response. This is possible because, over time, school coordinators develop specific human contacts throughout the community. One community outreach coordinator working at Garfield Elementary School in Boise explained it this way:

"Remember the old Rolodex with all of your phone numbers and contacts on little cards? That is what my head looks like. Any time we have a problem or need, my brain just starts spinning through all of the organizations and government offices and churches and individuals we have worked with in the past, and a name pops up. I don't call organizations. I don't contact government offices. I don't stand in

line and fill out applications. I call people in those organizations or offices who I know can cut through all of the bureaucratic red tape and requirements and simply get the job done. I know my contacts will get the job done effectively. We may not get all of the paperwork completed or work our way up through a network of requirements, but dealing person to person, we can address the need. I shudder to think about a poor mother, perhaps even a refugee with poor English skills, trying to find a government office that could help them, let alone provide all of the detailed requirements that are prerequisites to services. I could not do my job serving kids and their families without my network of contacts—contacts who know how to quickly get the job done!" (Community outreach coordinator, personal communication, October 1, 2019)

Community outreach services tend to fall into four broad areas: (1) family services and supports, (2) family education, (3) community development, and (4) wraparound educational programs.

Family Services and Supports

The most visible and essential services and supports coordinated by schools relate directly to families' complex human needs. These services almost always include food pantries, clothing closets, washers and dryers, scheduled eye and dental checkups, and childcare.

Field Note

On the days when a school becomes the hub for a community food bank, an army of volunteers descends upon the school cafeteria or gymnasium as soon as the lunch rush is over and the floor is cleaned. The food bank coordinator arranges for the delivery of a variety of healthy foods, including fresh produce, dairy, canned goods, cereals, rice, and dried goods, and the army of volunteers unpacks and arranges the food on tables, spread out for easy access. At the end of the school day, the community is invited to come and fill their bags with needed, essential food for their family. Families with children who attend the school are given first priority and invited to use the food bank before picking up their children at the end of the day.

These food banks become major community events and inevitably improve school-community relations. Over time, food bank officials and school officials may realize the relative ineffectiveness of such occasional food distribution and instead create a local *food pantry* somewhere in or near the school, making food available to families in need on an ongoing basis. At Garfield Elementary School, a portable frame building houses the Community Outreach Center. The Center has an entire wall that looks just like any grocery store, with all sorts of essential food. The center has a rule regarding the pantry: "Come as often as you need, take as much as you need." After families realize that the pantry is available every day, they tend to reduce the size of their collections on a day-to-day basis. The local county food bank refreshes the stock each week. The school district also provides free child care for all school programs and events and for parent education classes, utilizing high school students seeking volunteer credits for service learning. The Garfield Center is an amazing place that is a hub of activity and filled everyday with the parents of this community, taking classes, washing their clothes, or meeting with mental health providers. —Bob Barr

A school's efforts bring the services and supports that are distributed throughout a community to the community outreach center so that families do not have to find and access each service separately. Rather than having parents and guardians try to go to the organizations and agencies, the services and supports come to the centralized location of the school, where students and their families go every day.

In order to address the mental health needs of children, youth, and adults suffering from the effects of trauma and poverty, community outreach centers often make mental health supports a priority in their program of services. Students experiencing stress and anxiety in their daily life, or even trauma, violence, or other forms of adversity, are in great need of mental health professionals, but are often unable to access them in the greater community. When schools are able to provide confidential meeting areas, such as a small conference room with a private entrance, service providers in the community are able to come to the clients.

Field Note

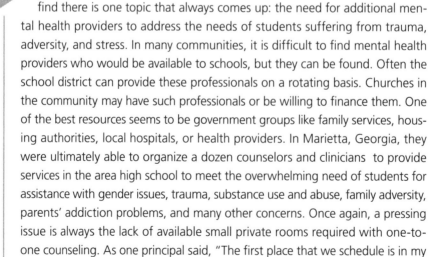

In discussions with local teachers and principals in high-poverty schools, I find there is one topic that always comes up: the need for additional mental health providers to address the needs of students suffering from trauma, adversity, and stress. In many communities, it is difficult to find mental health providers who would be available to schools, but they can be found. Often the school district can provide these professionals on a rotating basis. Churches in the community may have such professionals or be willing to finance them. One of the best resources seems to be government groups like family services, housing authorities, local hospitals, or health providers. In Marietta, Georgia, they were ultimately able to organize a dozen counselors and clinicians to provide services in the area high school to meet the overwhelming need of students for assistance with gender issues, trauma, substance use and abuse, family adversity, parents' addiction problems, and many other concerns. Once again, a pressing issue is always the lack of available small private rooms required with one-to-one counseling. As one principal said, "The first place that we schedule is in my office. The kids' counseling needs far outstrips my administrative needs." Another principal said, "There is always 'no space available' for private counseling; but in any school, if you are creative enough, and tough enough, you can always find the space." —Bob Barr

Family Education

Directly related to the family services and supports coordinated by the school are a whole series of "programs to attract parents, establish a welcoming climate for them, and help them learn how to be involved in and supportive of their children's education" (Children's Aid Society, 2011, p. 3). Family education will often include English as a second language classes, a host of parenting classes, employment opportunities information, job counseling, recreation, health and wellness classes, and birth-to-three support groups.

Community Development

Some community outreach schools go even further and help communities develop neighborhood associations and learn effective means of supporting needed community developments. For example, center coordinators may advocate at city council and school board meetings and support the election of individuals invested in addressing poverty in their communities. In discussions with center coordinators in a number of states, it seems that community development grows out of local advisory boards and the empowering of parents. As parents and guardians in high-poverty communities become more involved in providing advice and volunteer efforts, these local boards often turn their attention to larger issues in their neighborhoods: crime, housing for low-income families, and adequate funding for the local school are often included in their concerns. A center coordinator, seeing this interest and support, may help parents and community leaders find ways to focus their energies and to help them arrange contacts and meetings with appropriate school, government, and community organizations.

Wraparound Educational Programs

The community work of schools is always supplemented and supported by effective programs that research on effective schools and high-poverty, high-performing schools identified long ago. These wraparound programs include preschool and all-day kindergarten, before- and after-school programs, programs that assist both students and families, and supports for transitions between schools and to post-secondary opportunities. Research suggests that connecting families early with resources that address family and student needs will help more students find success in school and beyond (Ratcliffe & Kalish, 2017). Invariably, before- and after-school programs, summer support programs, and counseling programs are consolidated at high-poverty schools. Local churches may also provide funding or essential volunteers to staff the programs. If near a college or university, schools coordinate with teacher-education courses to staff essential programs.

Field Note

At the high school in Marietta, Georgia, the primary mechanism developed to better address student-identified needs is the Marietta Student Life Center, started in 2015, which eventually took up an entire wing of the school. This center was unlike most other centers in the United States; all the services made available in the center directly related to students' identified areas of need in mental health and substance abuse. But since most or all of the needs fell outside school staff expertise, the leadership team sought out community agencies and organizations that had the necessary skills and resources and already provided outreach services and supports in identified areas of need—they were the experts. Natural connections were found, and the bonus was the providing agencies, not the school, supplied the funds and resources for these services. This meant that, at a high school with only a few counselors for the entire student body of 2,500 students, the center was able to provide access to eight to twelve licensed mental health providers on campus. These counselors gave students opportunities to schedule individual appointments to receive therapy or counseling. Small support groups were formed, and almost overnight, students began receiving the help that they had cried out for in their interviews and surveys. While the center in Marietta delivered the usual services of other outreach centers—food pantry, clothing closet, washers and dryers, parenting classes, and health services and referrals—its primary effort was to serve the students as a counseling center. —Bob Barr

Step 3: Setting Up the Community Outreach Center

Based on the experiences of successful family and community outreach centers in the United States, as well as research, evaluations, and support from national organizations like the Coalition of Community Schools and the National Education Association, we have identified a number of critical components involved in setting up outreach centers. These components include the resource coordinator, center facilities, the local advisory council and board of directors, and community partners.

The Community Resource Center Coordinator

As schools have developed community outreach centers, a new position has emerged not previously seen in public education: the center coordinator. Whom should community outreach schools select for the post? Initially, schools must address the critical issue of whether the coordinator will be a school employee or someone from a community agency. While the center coordinator might not need to be a certified teacher, administrator, or specialist, the union contract might demand it and staff might expect it, even though groups outside the school district may, in fact, pay part of the salary. Regardless, family and community resource center coordinators need to have experience working with both schools and families. They also need a track record of working in communities and some knowledge of the various agencies and organizations that are available in the community. They need communication and presentation skills as well as skills in managing projects, gathering data, and reporting data. A center coordinator needs to be a person who can work well with educators, low-income families, and service agencies.

A typical family and community resource center coordinator's job description includes these roles and responsibilities (adapted from Cincinnati Public Schools, 2012).

- Lessen burdens of the principal and teaching staff to meet students' basic needs.

- Help the principal utilize community resources to improve student learning.

- Market or "sell" the idea of the community resource center by preparing newsletters, making presentations to groups, and "motivating community influencers to act on behalf of the school" (Cincinnati Public Schools, 2012, p. 7).

- Develop and manage partnerships.

- Promote trust and collaboration among the school, the district, and external partners.

- Help families trust the school to help with their problems and needs.

The coordinator is the nerve center of any successful community outreach program. He or she must gain the trust of teachers, district leaders, families, and agencies, and, above all, the school principal. The coordinator must work closely with all stakeholders, under the grace of the principal. The coordinator brings all these individuals and groups together, and this can lead to improved resilience for neighborhood families as they only have one person to interface with and build a connection with. In essence, the success or failure of this endeavor ultimately rests on the shoulders of the coordinator.

Family and community resource center coordinators we have worked with explain that their job boils down to developing an extensive network of personal relationships, phone numbers, and email addresses they use to cut through the bureaucratic red tape; it comes down to knowing exactly who in an agency or organization can get things done quickly and efficiently, and knowing who to avoid. It is one-to-one diplomacy. They create a contact network of professionals all trying to respond to family needs, and they develop personal trust with families. It is this network of contacts that makes community outreach work quickly and well. In schools we have worked with, staff report having far more time to focus on teaching and students' learning when the community resource coordinator is at work.

Field Note

The Family Assistance Center at Garfield Elementary in Boise provides low-income families with all sorts of help. One thing that they do is provide parent education regarding taxes, and even a tax specialist who volunteers their time to help the parents fill out their forms. This year, one family found out that they will receive a nine thousand-dollar refund, and three other families received more than seven thousand dollars each. Similarly, in Vancouver, Washington, family and community resource center coordinators have provided information to families about Lighthouse Community Credit Union's free tax service for families. What a wonderful gift of support from the local outreach center, and how these refunds will help these families through the winter! —Bob Barr

Center Facilities

Community outreach centers come in all shapes and sizes. Many centers are little more than a *concept* of services that are administered out of a small office buried somewhere in a school building. From this office, the coordinator plans and provides all sorts of events and services such as food banks, Muffins With Moms, clothes drives, and immunization clinics. Other centers have an actual classroom within the school, or even a separate portable building located on the school's property. Community outreach centers that have such facilities are able to provide a daily food pantry, a clothing closet, washers and dryers, and room for classes. Over time, these centers can become like a club for parents and guardians in the neighborhood. In addition to providing services daily rather than periodically, some centers are able to provide a private entrance so parents and guardians do not have to go into the school to access services.

Field Note

Leigh Colburn and Linda Beggs, both now consultants with the Centergy Project, have helped schools throughout Georgia and several other states start community outreach centers. They make no bones about it: a center must have its own space. So much of a center involves very personal mental health issues; thus, an essential center requirement is many small areas where privacy is available for one-on-one mental health services as well as larger areas for small support groups and meetings.

The first thing that Colburn and Beggs encounter when helping start a new center is the response "We have no room!" Inevitably, they find room. They laugh and say schools and teachers are "hoarders." They always find rooms filled with old overhead projectors, hopelessly out-of-date encyclopedias, and

even mimeograph machines. They find rooms filled with books long unused. They find some schools can simply reorganize their media centers and transform these large areas into computer centers and all sorts of small meeting spaces. One school obtained a grant to transform a media center into a health and wellness center, which provided a food pantry and a nutritionist, a registered nurse, and a staff of counselors to address the students' emotional needs. Need space for an outreach center? Look around and be creative.
—Bob Barr

Local Advisory Council or Board of Directors

Once a district has identified family needs associated with concerns related to attendance, behavior, and student achievement, discussions should begin involving a broad range of leaders from the community. These discussions typically lead to the creation of some type of local, school-level advisory council or board of directors. This council or board usually includes representatives from businesses, agencies, and organizations; school personnel; parents and guardians; high school students when applicable; and other community groups (local churches, community associations, and so on). Initially, the advisory council or board of directors develops interrelationships and professional friendships; this often involves visiting effective community outreach schools in other districts. The advisory council or board of directors also serves as a visioning group to develop goals and plans for the future. The representatives on the advisory council become the primary contact between their particular agency or organization and the families and school, and they lead efforts to evaluate and monitor the success of the council's work.

> **" "** We have just been shameless about stealing ideas from other districts. I even called and asked if they had a job description for the local center coordinator. They were so kind, I received it in a few minutes with a note that said, "Use anything or everything that might prove useful." We used it almost verbatim. It is so great when professionals are willing to help others.
>
> **—District coordinator, Boise, Idaho**

Field Note

The Garfield Elementary School Family and Community Resource Center in Boise is housed in a large, portable wooden building behind the school. Parents and guardians do not have to go through the school to access the center, and next door is a childcare center. Open the door of the center, and you step into this huge room. There is a set of couches and easy chairs in an inviting conversation area, much like someone's living room. There is a huge oak table that looks exactly like an old-time farming family's dining table, but this table must seat about twenty people. Some classes are held in another area, where chairs are arranged in a semicircle. African art hangs on the walls, and bright, colorful pillows that parents have made are scattered on the chairs. At the back of the room are restrooms and a laundry area with industrial-sized washers and dryers that are in use every day. The center is a warm, inviting place that says, "Welcome! Come on in."

The center provides an on-site food pantry, clothing closets, and a pantry for hygiene and household sanitation products (even diapers, which cannot be purchased with food stamps). Any family can walk into the center and receive any of these products. The center's motto is "Come as often as you want; take as much as you need."

The center helps parents and guardians with their income taxes, school forms, English language classes, parenting, and housing. It has also organized soccer teams for the students. And rather than have dozens and dozens of parents and guardians trying to find their way across town to some government office or agency, the center tries to bring the services to the families; services like inoculations, health checkups, mental health services, and legal advice are brought right to the center. When services require transportation or childcare, the center also provides those. —Bob Barr

Community Partners

When educators begin to look outside their schools, they often find a bewildering array of city, county, state, and federal offices and agencies providing services: nonprofits, faith-based organizations, and funded projects. Even in 1989, researchers critiqued the United States' array of providers, concluding that the broad swath of service and support programs was so fragmented as to limit the programs' effectiveness for children and their families (Hodgkinson, 1989). In even a medium-sized city, there are likely dozens of these potential partners, all offering targeted services to low-income families. These various groups may often be working directly with the same families but from different perspectives, each giving direct assistance and services that reflect its own mission and its own funding with little or no knowledge of what others are doing. These various services are found scattered all over a community in buildings, offices, and storefronts that are often even difficult to locate or recognize.

The great benefit of community outreach schools is in how they coordinate access to services that busy, stressed families overwhelmed by poverty desperately need. As the school attempts to support neighborhood families and better serve its constituents, it may partner with a growing number of social service agencies and organizations, or it may form a lead partnership with one agency or organization. The Children's Aid Society (2011) recommends a *lead-partner model*. In a lead-partner model, "a single community partner is recognized by school administrators and other partners as the one agency that deals directly and daily with the school leadership; the lead partner maintains a full-time presence in the school" (Children's Aid Society, 2011, p. 3). In numerous communities, this one agency has been United Way. Regardless of which partnership model is used, it may require joint funding of efforts and sharing of school building space.

For public educators, social services and supports are often a confusing world of bureaucracy and red tape. Most public school educators know little to nothing about this complicated world, and even less about the services that it provides. Talking with government agencies using their alphabet-soup acronyms is truly talking in a foreign language. Often, school counselors or school social workers have a better understanding of this complex arena, but until a school's staff launches out into high-poverty communities to address their human needs, staff are frequently flying blindfolded.

Identifying and developing community partners can be a challenging process. Figure 7.2 (page 178) features a list of potential public and private community partners. Initial discussions with the advisory council or board members may begin with a few of these groups or even a single organization, but the discussions should soon lead to very specific agencies and organizations that provide the identified direct services that families in the community need, often urgently. The needs of families require specific partners, and as such, when new needs emerge, partners may change. Over time, as the community outreach process continues, an ever-growing number of other organizations and agencies may make contact and want to help. Thus, the web of resilience supports grows steadily over time.

Yet, while many partners will make overtures to the school, experienced community outreach schools caution against having too many agencies and organizations become *formal* partners. The advice from many center coordinators always seems to be start small and grow over time; start with a very specific purpose (for example, a food pantry) and expand as other needs are identified. For example, many schools partner only with the United Way, and the organization then coordinates the school or family needs with service providers. Many schools create formal partnerships involving written contracts and joint funding; others seem to be a handshake and a personal commitment. A center must select partners based on their relationship to the school community's identified priorities and for the resources to support these services. The center should find ways to respectfully and politely decline partnerships with service agencies which do not serve those needs—their partnership may be needed at a later date as needs evolve.

Public-Sector Partners

Education service providers: Early Head Start, Head Start, early childhood assistance programs, educational service districts, community colleges, and faith-based organizations

Health and recreation support: YMCA, Boys and Girls Clubs, local free health and dental clinics, and mental health care agencies

Family housing and workforce support: Local housing authorities, homeless councils and agencies, workforce and economic development, various types of career centers, and local community colleges

Family assistance organizations: United Way, food banks, and churches and other faith groups

Public agencies and higher education institutions: State colleges and universities, and various city, county, state, and federal agencies

Private-Sector Partners

Local and national foundations: The many local foundations that operate in most communities as well as many national foundations, such as the Bill and Melinda Gates Foundation, the Robert Wood Johnson Foundation, and the RGK Foundation

Local and national businesses: Everything from national franchise businesses to local independent banks, local retailers and groceries, national chains, a wide variety of banks and credit unions, food companies and distributors, and retail department stores like Target, Walmart, and Costco

Professional clubs and organizations: Lions Club, Rotary Club, and even alumni associations

Figure 7.2: Public and private community partners.

Field Note

In 2018, I was invited to sit in on a discussion at an elementary school in Vancouver, Washington. A local health provider was meeting with the principal to provide information on free health services for the poor. The director of the health program offered to provide bakery goods and coffee at an upcoming Muffins With Moms before-school gathering, and to use the meeting to provide the mothers with information that could prove helpful. The principal took all of the information and had a central administrator check out the organization and determine if the group was legitimate and if a public school could partner for these kinds of services. The principal also told me that over the last few months, she had similar meetings with a local Boys and Girls Club and the largest church in the neighborhood, who wanted to provide a meal for school parents once a month at the school.

Once a community outreach center is open for business, community providers tend to arrive asking, "How can we help?" This is where having clear goals and a vision is critical, so the school and community outreach coordinator are not overwhelmed with help. —Bob Barr

For every family need—whether it is food, clothing, mental health support, eyeglasses, temporary housing or financial support for low-income housing, English as a second language, or job training—one or more agencies or organizations will have that need as their target responsibility. The challenge is for schools and the family and community outreach coordinator to search among the many providers and find the appropriate provider to obtain the needed services.

Field Note

I arrived at Ogden Elementary School in Vancouver, Washington, at 7:30 a.m. on a blustery, rainy March day in 2018 to observe a Muffins With Moms event scheduled to start at 7:45 a.m. The weather was cold and dreary, and it was still dark out, with no one waiting in the school parking lot or outside the school entrance. I was there to visit the school's family community resource center, do some interviews, and observe the daily routine. So I was disappointed that no one was there.

Then, just as I stepped out of my car and into the wind and rain, I noticed all these people walking into the schoolyard and a line of cars turning in. It was the neighborhood moms, aunts, grandmas, and guardians, with all their preschool kids coming for a meeting at the school. The family community resource center had planned for about one hundred moms, but it had learned to always be prepared for whoever walked in the door. That morning, there were easily two hundred women and children. The tables were loaded with all sorts of books and magazines and educational games for the moms and female caregivers to take home for their kids. There was coffee supplied by a sponsoring Starbucks and food tables loaded with muffins and juice, all supplied by a local free health clinic that had staff there to provide information about its available services. The director said with a huge grin, "We don't just sit around hoping that people who need health care will find their way to our clinic; we go out looking for patients."

The school district provided a Spanish translator in case there was a need, and the principal and administrative team were all around the room, meeting and welcoming the moms and the aunts, grandmothers, big sisters, and even dads who had showed up. The principal, April Whipple, finally took the microphone and welcomed the group to the school, described upcoming events, and encouraged the parents and guardians to take as many books as they would like. Many little ones were already snuggled up on adults' laps, being read to while they enjoyed a morning treat. The school newsletter lay on tables, reminding parents and guardians that the food pantry was coming up and the dental van would be there next week. Laughter, smiles, and good cheer filled the room. The connection and trust between the family members and the school leaders was evident. A number of the moms I spoke to all said the same thing (in both English and Spanish): "This is our school! We love our school." In every instance, they said it with a huge smile.

After about forty minutes, the food was eaten, and mothers and kids struggled back into their coats and rainwear to slip out again into the dark morning carrying armloads of books. The principal, the assistant principal, the family community resource center director, the custodian, the volunteers, the health clinic director, and, of course, the visiting educational researcher all pitched in as the cleanup got underway, folding and stacking tables and chairs. It was a massive job to prepare for this event, and an even bigger job to clean up. Someone laughingly said, "Wow, muffins are certainly messy," referring to the muffin crumbs and debris everywhere. After all the preparation work the night before and in the early morning, it took the staff and volunteers another half hour to get things folded, stacked, and cleaned up. Only then were the staff ready to start their school day, content with the feeling that they had reinforced trust and friendship with the neighborhood families and that the parents, the guardians, and their kids would be surrounded by books when they got home. It was just another day in the life of one of the United States' high-poverty public schools. —Bob Barr

Two U.S. organizations support community outreach schools in both their beginning stages and their ongoing work: (1) the Coalition for Community Schools (www.communityschools.org), organized as part of the Institute for Educational Leadership and (2) the National Center for Community Schools (www.nccs.org), part of the antipoverty organization the Children's Aid Society (2005). Both of these groups offer schools a wide variety of checklists, descriptions of specific steps in creating community outreach schools, research summaries, and case studies of effective programs. For example, the Coalition for Community Schools offers an Indicators of Capacity checklist useful for evaluating a community outreach school's capacity for serving student and family needs (see Coalition for Community Schools, n.d.; visit https://bit.ly/3bs4cln for the checklist).

The Coalition for Community Schools also has a Partnership Compliance Checklist, used by the community resource coordinator and the school administrator to evaluate the community partnership and assess next steps (available at multco .us/file/9095/download). The coalition has also established several national networks to help support the continued development and improvement of community outreach schools, including the Community Schools Leaders Network (available at www.communityschools.org//CSLN/) and Community Schools Coordinators Network (available at www.communityschools.org/about/community_school_coordinators _network.aspx).

The next section offers information and resources about monitoring and measuring the outcomes of community outreach.

Field Note

In the early stages of a family and community resource center, the center may have very few or no formal partners. Often, it finds the partners when the center coordinator responds to a specific need in the community. As the family community resource center coordinator at Garfield Elementary School in Boise explained to me, "Our parents and guardians wanted English language classes and classes to help them with income taxes. Parents and guardians arrived needing childcare and transportation in order to take their kids on a long bus ride to get vaccinations. We brought the vaccinations to the school and found specialists in the community who were more than willing to teach some classes. We don't do any of this. We have always been able to find someone really skilled in the community to help in every instance. And over time, we develop all of these contacts who know us and are willing to respond to our requests."

At Ogden Elementary School in Vancouver, Washington, the principal said, "We work really hard to get the word out about all of our services. We send home a print newsletter in English and Spanish each week, and oh boy, do we work the social networks. We constantly use Facebook, Twitter, and Instagram, and all sorts of churches and social service organizations see our posts and show up wanting to help. Over time, we've built this incredible network of community friends who step in and go to work." —Bob Barr

Step 4: Monitoring the Community Outreach Center's Outcomes

As we stated in chapter 6 (page 121), we cannot grow what we do not measure. Every effective transition to community outreach includes a careful plan for gathering data and assessing the outcomes toward targeted goals to support reflective, continuous improvement. Because community outreach is a relatively new concept, and one that involves reallocation of school district funds and responsibilities, central administrators have invested great effort in relating community outreach to improved student achievement and high school graduation rates and monitoring family and community resource centers' impact on student success over time. Some community outreach has included follow-up data on students' success in college and careers. The following are two examples of monitoring community outreach.

Vancouver Public Schools, Washington

Because student success is related to issues that are beyond a district's control, Vancouver Public Schools found it imperative to develop a process for monitoring supports to families with school-level outcomes: school attendance and learning outcomes in reading and mathematics at the third-, sixth-, and ninth-grade levels. The district identified nine causes of chronic absenteeism and tracked these identified causes' relationships to learning, which enabled the district to "measure and understand the value of their investment and, in turn, assess the degree to which that investment" was "paying off in terms of helping schools to achieve the particular goal [of improved attendance]" (Broader, Bolder Approach to Education, n.d.). Over time, the school district developed a district performance score card involving twenty-five performance indicators. Similar to a student report card, it reported such items as access to resources, level and change of family involvement, and extent of partnerships (direct services provided to families by community partners).

Central Oregon

Better Together (2018), a community outreach program involving a dozen partners from school districts, higher education, and support agencies, developed a comprehensive evaluation and assessment plan that regularly reported student data from preschool through college and careers, including data on attendance, achievement, graduation rates, college attendance rates, and so on. The goal of any community outreach center is to improve student attendance, improve achievement, raise graduation rates, and increase the number of students going on to college or vocational training. The difficult and demanding work of a center must have documented payoff in improved learning and education. This is the bottom line; the buck stops here. Especially when a number of school, government, and community organizations are working together amid often co-founded efforts, it is absolutely essential to monitor and assess progress toward agreed upon goals. Better Together in Bend, Oregon, publishes an annual report on improved graduation rates and the rates of students who go on to college. Community outreach centers use assessments to document their progress, but also to help with public relations and communications with area communities (see figure 7.3).

The next section offers information about funding sources for community outreach.

Step 5: Funding Community Outreach

Community outreach involves hiring additional personnel, especially at the school level, and providing a host of services that schools have never offered before. Thus, it requires the reallocation of existing school district funds as well as the search for additional funding through grants and community agencies. Usually, private foundations and government funding sources consider a community outreach effort to

Schools and communities can use the following tools to help them assess the impacts of poverty on students.

The Developmental Assets and Developmental Relationships frameworks developed by the Search Institute (n.d.; 2016; available at https://bit.ly/2wpJ3JN and https://bit.ly/2y7m3j9) can be used by councils or boards to determine needs and evaluate progress over time.

Resilience measures developed by TRACEs Central Oregon (n.d.) in partnership with Oregon State University–Cascades (available at https://bit.ly/2QJVRBo) can be used to measure resilience in target populations and identify areas of need.

The Trauma Responsive Schools Implementation Assessment (TRS-IA; available at https://traumaawareschools.org/traumaResponsiveSchools; Treatment and Services Adaptation Center, n.d.) can be used to measure how strong your school's trauma-informed practices are and to continuously improve (Lander, 2018). This assessment can measure many components of a resilient school, including safety, social-emotional learning, effective classroom strategies, trauma prevention and intervention, professional development for staff, staff self-care and social-emotional learning, and family and community engagement.

Figure 7.3: Tools for assessing a community outreach center's outcomes.

be an attractive target for their investments. Some school districts have been able to fund family coordinators using Title I funding. Most communities have found that service and support providers are willing to invest funds in the local coordination of efforts or co-fund a family coordinator and various services with other organizations and agencies. Since the community outreach center simply helps with coordination so the various agencies and organizations can actually do the work they are committed to doing, it is usually reasonable for the community agencies to supply the resources that will support the services provided at the school. In larger school districts, central administrators and grants writers often have a comprehensive knowledge of local not-for-profits and foundations that would entertain grant proposals. Most grants provide only short-term funding or start-up costs—few would be useful for long-term funding. The best forms of local funding come through school district allocation or from large service providers who see the community outreach center as a logical opportunity to address the group's goals.

Funding examples include the following.

- Central Oregon's Better Together (2018) community outreach program is a coalition of hundreds of partners throughout the region, all working together to improve outcomes for youth. By pooling their resources, they are better able to effect change.

- Vancouver, Washington, funds its family community resource centers through Title I monies, school foundation funds, partners' contributions, and reallocation of district funds.

- United Way has sites in every state in the United States, and provides major funding for the District of Columbia, Maryland, and Virginia, among other states.

The Long-Term Impact of Community Outreach

The Coalition for Community Schools and the National Center for Community Schools offer a set of research conclusions documenting the effectiveness of community outreach schools. Unfortunately, we have not found any large national or statewide study reporting the long-term outcomes of community outreach centers. The Coalition for Community Schools (2020) reports a variety of very positive results.

- Students enter school fully prepared to learn

- Students develop improved work habits, effort, and attitudes toward learning

- Students improve grades and test scores

- Students earn more credits and stay in school

- Students graduate high school and continue learning

- Schools are cost effective and provide a strong return on investment

Unfortunately, each of these very positive conclusions is based on developments found in specific school districts and communities or certain types of schools. Each conclusion is supported by a ragtag assortment of school assessment and evaluation, or data collected in a particular city. The Coalition for Community Schools identify assessments, evaluation, or research in Boston, Cincinnati, Portland, and Tulsa. They occasionally report research on a particular type of program, like Communities in Schools. As a result, while each of the Coalition's conclusions regarding the effectiveness of these schools may be helpful to local communities working to develop or improve community outreach schools, they must be considered suspect for general conclusions regarding effectiveness due to the diversity of programs, the lack of rigor, the fact that so many of the conclusions are based on assessments in a single city, and the fact that few represent longitudinal data. Certainly, the Coalition has assembled a remarkable set of data for each conclusion, and these conclusions may provide a local community or school with rock-hard evidence regarding the success of specific schools and programs. However, it is not possible to draw general conclusions for the many school districts reporting community outreach results (see Coalition for Community Schools, 2020).

This is not to say that at the local level, schools and communities like Vancouver, Washington, and central Oregon are not gathering data and tracking results, and continuing their efforts based on real results. A couple of these local success stories include the following.

- The Coalition for Community Schools describes the Multnomah County Schools Uniting Neighborhoods (SUN) program in Portland, Oregon, as achieving an average daily attendance of 94.5 percent, when the state benchmark was 92 percent. (See Coalition for Community Schools, 2020, and Multnomah County, 2020, for more information.) A more positive development can be seen when comparing rates of chronic absenteeism (defined as missing 10 percent or more school days): SUN schools had a 17 percent rate of chronic absenteeism while the district average was 32 percent. Graduation rates also show a marked improvement (see Coalition for Community Schools, 2020).

- In Bend, Oregon, several school districts, a community college, and Oregon State University partnered with over fifty government agencies and community organizations including chambers of commerce, credit unions, health councils, juvenile justice, and youth clubs to create the Family Access Network (FAN). Started in 2012, this ambitious group reported a mixed set of outcomes five years later: while FAN was able to report the four-year graduation rates improved from 68 percent to 76 percent, they were unable to report improved attendance. (For more information, see Better Together, 2017, pp. 11–12.) The most positive support for the FAN program came from families. In 2016–2017, FAN provided nearly 2,000 families with utilities assistance, over 1,300 with health services, and over 1,700 with housing. In a survey of the 9,017 children and family members served by FAN, 100 percent reported that FAN had improved their lives, and 86 percent reported that FAN helped their children attend and stay in school (Family Access Network, n.d.).

- The Vancouver School District in Washington holds itself strictly accountable for community outreach. It tracks the needs of families, resources it has allocated, and change in parental involvement, along with school indicators (attendance, family mobility and learning). The district has developed a 25-point performance indicator to assess the complicated world of community outreach. Results include (Weiss, 2016):
  - ✦ Between 2006 and 2016, core course failure rates fell by 31 percent in middle and high schools.
  - ✦ Enrolment in advanced placement increased from 792 to 1,325 since 2007, a 67 percent increase. For low-income students, participation in

advanced placement courses increased from 126 to 367, a 200 percent increase.

+ Graduation rates improved from 64 percent in 2010 to a projected rate of 80 percent in 2013.

+ The mobility rate (percentage of students moving in and out of the district) declined in community outreach schools, from 24 percent in 2012 to 16 percent in 2017.

+ Reading readiness in community outreach schools was 16.5 percent higher than in unserved schools.

Further, in a 2001 survey of forty-nine community outreach schools, thirty-six reported academic gains since converting to a community outreach school model. In addition, nineteen schools reported increased attendance, eleven reported decreased suspensions, and twelve reported higher rates of parental involvement (Dryfoos, 2008).

The major research focus has shifted since 2010, from studies of community outreach schools to what has come to be called *Integrated Student Supports* (ISS). Once again, the great diversity of programs and the lack of rigor at the local levels has led to few viable positive conclusions. A major paper in 2017 was coauthored by two leading scholars at the Learning Policy Institute and the National Education Policy Center, and once again, their conclusions were mixed. While reporting considerable evidence to justify federal investment in community outreach schools, many of the schools they studied did not call themselves community outreach schools. And while the study covered all of the key components of community outreach schools, there was only one component that had across the board positive data: after-school programs (Oakes, Maier, & Daniels, 2017).

As the number of community outreach schools has increased, researchers have explored the best ways to implement these schools and "whether and how these efforts have improved outcomes for students, schools and even communities" (Weiss & Reville, 2019, p. 179). Unfortunately, Elaine Weiss and Paul Reville's (2019) nine-year study on the research on the effectiveness of community outreach schools, as well as in-depth case studies of twelve diverse communities, reports this disappointing conclusion: after more than two decades of efforts and an increasing number of studies, "the evidence remains thin. We still lack the definitive data establishing the effectiveness of community outreach schools—data that advocates and practitioners alike rightly consider necessary. The insufficient evidence is a daunting concern for advocates, analysts, and policy makers" (Weiss & Reville, 2019, p. 179). Weiss and Reville (2019) go on to say, "The lack of solid, large scale, and longitudinal data prevents researchers from studying initiatives that identify as community [outreach] schools" (p. 179).

Part of the problem relates to the definition of a community outreach school. Schools using that designation may in fact have a wide assortment of very different programs that vary from school to school, making it difficult to track positive developments across many schools. Also, hundreds of these community outreach schools are very new and still in the development mode. Since these schools go by different names (Community Schools, Full Service Schools, Community Outreach Schools, Integrated Student Support programs, School Development Program, Cities in Schools, and so on), there is a good deal of disagreement regarding even the number of community outreach schools.

Rarely has such a growing and important development in public education had so little concrete evidence to support the investment and hard work it takes to establish and operate a community outreach program. It seems at this time to require a huge leap of faith as local schools react to the tragedies of poverty, to the immediate and long-term issues that children and youth impacted by poverty bring into the school and classroom each day. And while community outreach may have started with very specific goals in mind, over time, it may be the humanitarian instinct of communities to reach out and help struggling students and their families.

One final point: what is being discussed here is truly a grassroots movement. So many of these community outreach efforts are being developed independently and simultaneously in diverse cities and school districts all over the country. Developmentally, it is a mess of different names, programs, and services. But this is a major development occurring with little direction other than attempts to address the urgent needs of students and the families in their neighborhoods.

For those contemplating the development of or who are involved in the process of operating a community outreach school, the best advice is to go to the websites of the two national organizations and seek evaluations and research of public schools nearby. School visits are essential, where exchanges of all sorts of information can occur quickly and organically: how did they get started, what problems have they encountered, how effective have they been, and so on. School districts like Vancouver, Washington, run workshops and schedule visitation to their outreach centers. This district alone has helped dozens of other school districts to create their own programs (Blad, 2016; Webb & Hagley, 2019).

As noted previously, community outreach schools are inevitably started to address one or more specific issues (for example, school attendance, graduation rates, family mobility, and reading readiness). These initial goals vary greatly from school to school and from school district to school district. But once a community outreach school is started, *data must be collected and monitored over time* to provide direction and to help identify areas of needed improvements. When this process of local evaluation is followed and the data collected is distributed widely in the school and community for discussion, it is like a self-fulfilling prophecy: results almost always improve over time.

One telling fact is that we have yet to find a school or district that has established community outreach schools and wants to end the program. Once started, the notion of walking back the coordination of services, regardless of measured student outcomes, is unheard of. This speaks to the "heart work" of meeting the real needs of students and families (see Field Note).

Field Note

Our strategic effort to engage families and mobilize partners in support of community schools is really a matter of heart work. It means even more to me now as a parent. As I think about my own children and realize that they are so very fortunate compared to thousands of the other students we serve in Vancouver Public Schools, I am inspired to do this work. I want all of the kids in our district to feel hopeful and have the same advantages my wife and I are able to provide for our kids.

I have always heard that the best way to help poverty-affected students overcome barriers and develop resiliency is to treat them like they were your own kids. Over recent years, my colleagues and I have come to understand better the size and significance of the challenge. Our commitment to equity is the force that drives our family-community resource centers, and it is why we are working so hard to address the human needs of families struggling with poverty. We also understand that making it happen requires the ownership and participation of an entire community: school board, superintendent, central administrators, principals, teachers, counselors, specialists, custodians, bus drivers, and nutrition services staff, along with parents, partners, and volunteers. We are all in this together, and yes, this work involves matters of the heart. —Tom Hagley Jr., Chief of Staff, Vancouver Public Schools

Although a growing number of school districts throughout the United States have made a significant investment in community outreach, we must remain cautious of any claim that community outreach has disrupted poverty or broken the cycle of poverty. Helping poor students attend school regularly, stay in school, experience academic success, graduate, and transition to jobs or postsecondary education is an enormous uphill battle. When even one student, let alone a small percentage of students in any school or classroom, finds a pathway out of poverty or a pathway to a better life, we must view it as a great human victory.

Conclusion

In embarking on the journey to become a community outreach school, a school comes to reinvent itself and its role in the community. The principal, teachers, specialists, and family and community resource center coordinators develop new roles and learn to work together in new ways. The families see their school in a new light, eventually dissolving prior perceptions and barriers. Community service providers spend more time helping families and far less time finding those who have needs.

In the journey toward developing community outreach schools, a school district will also experience fundamental changes. School boards and superintendents will need to share their authority, responsibilities, and funding with outside groups and agencies. New professional positions that fall outside the traditional staff roles will challenge the status quo of certificated staff, administrators, and classified staff, and may involve renegotiating union contracts and developing formal relationships with other school districts and many agencies, organizations, and individuals to fund positions.

Within the larger community, neighborhood associations and faith groups may take on larger leadership roles and find new energy and invigoration in the increased activity afforded by the school's invitation for partnership. Community groups may learn new political strategies for gaining support and services as well as develop new forms of communication and organization, all to serve students, families, and schools.

Fortunately, innovative schools and districts provide a blueprint for transforming into a community outreach school, with a clear five-step process for getting started on this complex, necessary work. If schools need help along the way, a wealth of resources exist (see appendix, page 217, for examples), and likely, another school or district within a day's drive has navigated this journey and is eager to help other schools learn how to leverage the essential components of community outreach: the district, the school, the social service agencies and organizations, and the neighborhood community. These components combine to confront the debilitating effects of poverty and assist families living on the fringes of society. Working together, they will reach out and engage families, all to help students find a pathway to a better life.

In this process, the local school transforms into a new, more effective social, educational, and service institution; it becomes the emotional center of the community, and staff become the first responders for the human needs of families living in poverty. However, being on the front lines of poverty, as explained in chapter 3 (page 49), comes with a price to staff resilience. It can decrease staff's job satisfaction, which is based on their ability to successfully carry out their roles and responsibilities as they envision them, and their ability to develop the professional and personal relationships that they desire. Decreased job satisfaction is tied to staff turnover and attrition. In chapter 8 (page 191), we explore how resilient schools address these relational and professional needs of staff (the fourth cornerstone of the resilient school framework) and how they ensure staff are strengthened, not diminished, by their work.

Next Steps

Please complete the following Next Steps, to integrate your experiences within your own schools and communities with the information presented in this chapter.

1. The first step in improving a school is to review data about the school and find areas of needed improvement. This might be poor attendance or low graduation rates, or students arriving far from reading ready. What would your school or district's goal areas for improvement be? How could community outreach support meeting these goal areas?

2. Few schools decide to start a major community outreach. After reading this chapter, we encourage you to use this information to triage your school. Ask: "What are we already doing and doing well? What are some interesting program ideas that we read about in this chapter that we might want to consider? Where do we start?"

3. Have you visited a community outreach school? It is an incredible experience to witness a new type of public school and hear the praise from parents, students, and teachers. See if you can find a community outreach school nearby and make contact.

Chapter 8

The Fourth Cornerstone of the Resilient School: Addressing Staff's Relational and Professional Needs

Teaching is an emotional matter as well as a moral and academic one; being with children day after day over a school year means that the emotional tone of your presence affects the nature and quality of what is achieved in the classroom.

—Herbert Kohl

In chapter 6 (page 121), we introduced the concept of the Culture of Hope and its five seeds of hope (optimism, belonging, self-regulation, pride, and purpose). These seeds are the social-emotional assets that enrich schools and build resilience among students. These same five seeds of hope are also necessary for staff resilience, especially among staff working at high-poverty, high-trauma schools. The best way to inoculate staff against the negative effects of secondary trauma or compassion fatigue, the grinding toll of a heavy workload, and the real and pressing needs of students is to support staff using the five seeds of hope. This chapter begins with a discussion of how leaders—administrators and teacher-leaders—can support staff, and how staff can support each other, using the seeds of hope. It then discusses fostering staff resilience in difficult times and meeting staff's professional needs.

Field Note

 We just can't keep doing this anymore. I have a family. I have church responsibilities. I do a lot of work in my community. But this job . . . with these kids . . .
they demand so much out of me. Some days, I come home too exhausted to
even talk to my own kids. Yet, to me . . . this work is so important. I sometimes
feel that I am the only hope some of my students have. Nobody knows the tragic
stories that I hear from my students that I carry around in my heart. But I need
something. I need support and appreciation and encouragement. Yet all I hear
on the news is how bad our schools are, how bad our teachers are. I need to
somehow be rejuvenated. —Teacher, Mobile, Alabama

Supporting Staff With the Seeds of Hope

The seeds of hope are closely connected to schools' concerns about staff turnover, job satisfaction, and morale. As presented in chapter 3 (page 49; Evans, 1997;
Senechal et al., 2016), teachers' sense of satisfaction comes from how well a particular school context fits with their perceived professional roles and responsibilities
(the intellectual or cognitive aspects of teaching) and their expected professional
and personal relationships (the relational or emotional aspects of teaching). As discussed in chapter 3 (page 49), job satisfaction is one of the most frequently cited
reasons for leaving a teaching job, or leaving the profession entirely. Utilizing the
seeds of hope with teaching staff provides a boost to staff engagement and overall
satisfaction—similar to the effect of the seeds of hope on student engagement and
learning—which theoretically can help reduce staff attrition and turnover. In the
following sections, we consider how the five seeds of hope can support staff in meeting their relational and emotional expectations.

" "   The discipline of hope: the refusal to accept limits on what your students can
learn or on what you, as a teacher, can do to facilitate learning.

—Herbert Kohl

Seed 1: A Sense of Optimism and Hope

An early casualty of trauma and stress is optimism, or the belief that tomorrow
will be better. Even if most of the day was great, having one negative encounter can
ruin a whole day. Over time, a negative perception can become the norm because, as
human beings, we are hardwired to negatively assess things (Jennings, 2018a). Thus,
having an optimistic mindset is a conscious decision. When schools and districts
focus on building optimism among staff, they keep despair and hopelessness at bay.
When staff have optimism, they may be more likely to have a high morale, looking
ahead to expect the school context will be a good fit for them in the future. If staff
have optimism in the face of adversity, they are more likely to keep going.

Ideas for encouraging a sense of optimism among staff include the following.

- Build optimism and fun into staff meetings. In a school in Bend, Oregon, the administrator puts trivia questions into the staff meeting agenda and tosses out gifts (stress balls, chocolate, a fancy pen) to the winners. At a school in Vancouver, Washington, the administrator starts the staff meetings with photos of current middle-school students when they were in Kindergarten. At another school in Bend, Oregon, meetings begin with sharing what staff members did over the break, weekend, or summer. At a school in central California, staff meetings began with glows or special moments from the week.

- Insert trivia, knock-knock jokes, or puns into agendas, newsletters, and bulletins.

- Utilize PBIS and restorative discipline processes.

- Have monthly celebrations.

- Surprise staff with a coffee wagon or treats.

- Keep healthy snacks available in the staff room, so people can snack without guilt (and keep plenty of forks in the staff room because it seems like every school seems to have a shortage of forks).

- Keep the staff room bright and welcoming.

- Acknowledge what is hard, and encourage reframing and laughter.

- Celebrate accomplishments, no matter how small.

- Encourage positive mindsets.

- Encourage growth mindsets.

- Welcome people to school, and use names.

- Recognize milestones.

- Keep communication channels open.

- Have open-door policies or office hours (for support and administrative staff).

Field Note

I came to Boise, Idaho, in 1981, and the neighborhood school near where we built our home was a small elementary school: Garfield Elementary. I recently found some of my very old notes documenting conversations I had with teachers back then. The following is a sample from my old notes:

"Over the years, the faculty at our high-poverty elementary school developed into a really tough core of dedicated teachers. Oh, there have always been teachers who could not deal with the challenges here—they would come and go—but our central core of teachers has stayed the course and worked together here for more than a third of their careers. We also have a great, supportive principal. We have all become best friends. This school has become a real part of each of our families. We feel that we have found our place; we belong here."

"We can't say that we have whipped poverty, but we sure have given it a good fight. We have had some blazing victories and some tragic defeats. But we have also won a lot of hard-fought battles. We have helped so many kids during our professional lives; we have help so many break out of poverty; to break free for a better life."

"This is our community; it is our neighborhood. Many of us live here, and we see the kids after they leave our school. So many come back to check in, update us on their lives, and often ask for our help. And over the years, we can see the ones who made it; see the many who have found their way to a better life. That makes us so proud, that's what we are about. We like to think that we are a part of the modern-day American Dream. We believe that we have something really good here; we believe that we are making a difference in the lives of kids."

In 2020, I visited Garfield's family assistance center and attended school functions. In my recent conversations with the school staff and the staff at the family assistance center, I was struck by the similarities between the teachers then and now. In fact, I could almost interchange my notes. In 2020, the school has, of course, a very different school staff, but their commitments sound almost the same. Garfield Elementary reminds me of the long and demanding process of becoming a resilient school. —Bob Barr

Seed 2: A Sense of Place and Belonging

Human beings are social beings, so school personnel need to feel a sense of belonging among their school community, colleagues, and students. They gain this by building meaningful relationships with students and with colleagues, which is one of the two primary needs of education professionals (the other being the ability to fulfill their professional duties). Belonging is, in essence, the relational and emotional aspect of the profession, and it is critical for teacher job satisfaction and morale.

Not just teachers but all school personnel need to feel a sense of belonging and connection to their colleagues and their school context. In the busyness of the school day, it can be easy to lose contact, rushing from task to task, from emergency to emergency. The custodian hurries from cleaning the cafeteria to addressing emergency cleanups and rushing outside to deal with slippery paths. The principal rushes to help with a student's emotional outburst, then dashes into a class for an observation before being called to the office to respond to a parent or guardian right before the scheduled earthquake drill. Front-office staff bounce from treating a sick student to reminding subs to turn in attendance and answering the phone before smiling at the student who walks in looking for her lost backpack. Too soon, the day is done, and staff hurry into the evening to pick up their own children and prepare for dinner with their families.

Field Note

At Long High School in Longview, Washington, the hallways and rooms are filled with posters with slogan and quotes—some for teachers, some for students. I watched students coming into the building at the end of the summer, and so many stopped to read these inspirational messages. The principal told me, "The best investment I ever made was to purchase a large-scale poster printer." It just changes the school atmosphere and reminds everyone, "This is your school. This is where you belong." —Bob Barr

Without intentional attention on belonging or connection, a staff can become disjointed. If the adults in a school do not feel belonging and connection, students are not likely to feel it either. When schools and districts work to ensure that school personnel feel connected, they combat turnover and stress and support the social-emotional needs of staff.

Ideas for fostering a sense of belonging among staff include the following.

- Use names to address one another.
- Learn about each other's lives.
- Have a school motto, or create a new one each year.
- Create a school cheer, song, movie, hand signal, or handshake.
- Design a staff shirt.
- Have staff bingo or trivia games (with the questions being about staff).
- Encourage staff to eat lunch with each other.
- Have time to celebrate milestones (such as births, graduations, weddings, and monumental trips).
- Take and share photos of staff teams, groups, events, and professional development.
- Find out what staff like, and use that knowledge to connect in some way.
- Mix up groups at staff trainings, meetings, and events so everyone gets to know each other.
- Hold after-school events.
- Utilize some form of mentoring or advisory program where every staff member is responsible for a group of students.
- Say hello and goodbye.
- Smile with your eyes.

Field Note

In 2018, at an elementary school in Bend, Oregon, I experienced a most creative team-building method at the start of the school year. Rather than doing the traditional review of information typical at the first staff meeting (including the nurse's report, custodian report, reading specialist report, and cafeteria report), staff members were split into eight teams of five to six people. The administrators created the staff teams with great mindfulness, crossing grade levels and staff assignments and mixing certificated and classified staff. Following clues, these teams traveled to different locations in the community to hear eight school staff give short presentations to the whole school.

At school, teams received their first clue, which led them to one of the stations, where they enjoyed the presentation and connected in a more personal way with the staff member sharing information. They then received their next clue and went off to find the next station. As they rotated through the eight stations, they drove together, talked, laughed, got lost, and shared excitement for the new year and new students. The last clue brought everyone to the location of a staff picnic and celebration. Oh, and everyone was dressed up as pirates, the clues were written in pirate limericks, and everyone was given a pirate name! This took an enormous amount of the administrative team's creativity and time to prepare, but it got the staff off to a hugely positive beginning to the year that everyone would remember for the rest of the year and beyond. —Emily Gibson

Seed 3: A Sense of Self-Regulation

Like students, school staff members thrive when they are able to regulate their own emotions, thoughts, and needs. Teachers' ability to regulate their feelings is critical because the sheer number of important decisions they must make in a workday rivals that of air traffic controllers and emergency room staff. When staff cannot self-regulate, they may sometimes disregard bodily needs to eat or use the bathroom, and they numb or ignore their feelings just to get through the day's schedule and tasks. This can result in professionals who are on a hair trigger, who overreact more than they'd like, and who slowly fall into unhealthy habits over time, just waiting for summer break to "live" again. When schools and school districts emphasize self-regulation for staff, they create a buffer against turnover and low morale, supporting the relational and emotional aspect of job satisfaction.

Ideas for fostering a sense of self-regulation among staff include the following.

- Present wellness information in staff bulletins and meetings.

- Teach staff about the modes of regulation (see figure 8.1, page 198), and experiment with different modes.

- Begin and end the day with optional wellness activities, like a walk in the park or quick yoga.

- Create a break corner for staff somewhere in the school, outfitted with items similar to those found in student break corners, such as stress balls, kaleidoscopes, a balance board, some aromatherapy samplers, some tactile puzzles, a beautiful picture book, breathing exercises, some yoga poses, and a chime.

- Encourage reflection in staff meetings and team meetings.

- Share difficult moments and what you did to get to a better place.

- Laugh often.

- Share ways people prefer to handle stress, and encourage teams to support each other in ways that are most regulating (see figure 8.1, page 198).

- Have an emergency code word across the school that, when used, lets others know a staff member needs a quick five-minute break.

- Explore sensory needs as a staff.

Field Note

At an elementary school in Bend, Oregon, the administrators plan a "December to Remember" for staff during the three weeks of December between Thanksgiving and Winter Break. Each week has a schedule of activities to look forward to, with special snacks in the staff room, elves hidden around the school to find, a coffee cart one morning, and weekly dress-up themes. During one of the most stressful times of year, these administrators treat their staff well, knowing their resilience is priceless. —Emily Gibson

How do you self-regulate? To find out, use the modes of self-regulation chart in figure 8.1 (page 198). Developed from a framework designed by child psychologist Rick Robinson (2018), this chart claims that regulating activities have two poles: (1) sensory/cognitive and (2) social/solitary, creating four quadrants (sensory-social, sensory-solitary, cognitive-social, and cognitive-solitary). It shares example activities in each of the four quadrants. By using this chart, staff can discover their own and their colleagues' regulation styles. Participants simply place a check mark beside all the activities that they do or would like to do to calm themselves when they are upset or deregulated. In this way, they can discover their preferred modes of regulation.

Seed 4: A Sense of Pride, Self-Esteem, and Self-Confidence

As professionals, educators take great pride in how their students are doing, both academically and behaviorally. Sit down to talk with any teacher, and you will hear stories of when they made a difference, and stories of when they felt sorrow because they could not make a difference. When educators do not feel they are making a difference, or do not feel proud of their work with their students, they may struggle

	Self-Regulation via Movement and the Senses	Self-Regulation via Use of the Brain
Self-Regulation via Activities With Others	Performing progressive relaxation in a group Attending movement or yoga class Singing with a group or choir, or playing in a band or orchestra Participating in a drum circle Mirroring movements Playing team sports Attending dance groups Walking and talking with others Performing karaoke Going to the gym or a workout group Bird-watching with a group Cooking for others Participating in group activities like tug-of-war, human knots, or jump rope Smelling candles at a store with others Sampling food or drinks with others	Playing card games with others Playing board games with others Making conversation or talking with friends, family, or colleagues on the phone or in person Playing Simon Says or I Spy Reading out loud to someone Performing theater or acting Writing letters to pen pals Playing *Mad Libs* or *Words With Friends* Watching a film with others and talking Attending a book club or writing group Attending a class of some sort Receiving group counseling Playing or watching *Jeopardy!* or *Wheel of Fortune* with others Playing video games with others Teaching or leading a class or group
Self-Regulation via Solitary Activities	Doing breathing exercises Singing to yourself or playing an instrument by yourself Making pottery Playing with kinetic sand or a zen sand garden Gardening Listening to music, books on tape, or relaxing nature sounds Changing lighting Using fidget spinners or stress balls Smelling candles, incense, or scented lotion Chewing gum or eating hard candy Eating crunchy snacks Using a yoga ball or balance board Playing hidden picture or visual puzzles Using a heated or scented eye or face mask Looking at art, photos, or sculptures Wearing soothing clothes (velvet, silk, or cashmere) Drinking tea Playing individual sports Taking a long soak in a warm tub	Doing pencil-and-paper puzzles Solving hand puzzles (such as a Rubik's cube) Playing solitaire Making origami Hand knitting Performing needle arts (embroidery, crochet, or quilting) Coloring Making visual art (drawing, painting, and so on) Reading Writing a story, journal, or poetry Watching a video Making photo albums or scrapbooks Cracking codes Playing individual sports Solving crosswords Playing sudoku Seeing a counselor Playing a video game or solve-it game

Source: © Emily Gibson, 2020.

Figure 8.1: Modes of self-regulation chart.

Visit ***go.SolutionTree.com/schoolimprovement*** *for a free reproducible version of this figure.*

with resilience and self-worth. As a result, their job satisfaction can take a hit. Sadly, educators are often asked to do work that does not make sense, or to document (again) the work they are doing, instead of doing more pressing tasks related to student learning. When schools and school districts make sure educators have reasons to be proud, when they value educators' professional judgment, and when they consult educators on policy decisions, they are fostering resilience among staff and increasing the likelihood of job satisfaction and high morale.

Ideas for fostering a sense of pride, self-esteem, and self-confidence among staff include the following.

- Implement a true PLC at Work process in your school district (DuFour et al., 2016), with staff setting the goals for their teams.
- Share what is working, and share successes often.
- Ensure that policy makes sense to those enacting it.
- Use collaborative leadership.
- Celebrate accomplishments, such as new degrees, training, or certifications.
- Have staff lead professional development opportunities instead of outsiders.
- Share data, and celebrate growth.
- Hold staff talent shows with students as the audience.
- Provide support to those impacted by stress, trauma, or loss (staff, students, or families), which can be rewarding and inspire a sense of pride and satisfaction.

Seed 5: A Sense of Purpose

Most educators and school staff are drawn to the profession for personal reasons, often based in a calling, a sense of duty, a moral obligation, a passion, or a high need for creativity and agency in their work. This fuels their vision of the professional roles and responsibilities they hold for themselves. Also, this fuels their expectations for the relationships they will develop with students and colleagues. Educators come to teaching because they are drawn to making a difference and investing in the future through connection and relationships. Too often, the very policies and mandates educators are charged to uphold reduce creativity, agency, and the human aspect of teaching and learning. When educators are faced with the choice of doing what they are told or doing what is right, they may lose interest or become less willing to do the hard work because they do not feel like they are able to make a difference. This inability to fulfill their ideal of the profession contributes to teacher turnover and attrition, low job satisfaction, and low morale. When schools and school districts protect teachers' sense of purpose, they are creating a buffer against staff's leaving the profession by enhancing job satisfaction and morale. While it can be difficult to protect staff members' sense of purpose, in the face of policies and mandates that are often even out of the control of school administrators, there are ways to do so.

Ideas for fostering a sense of purpose among staff include the following.

- Have staff set goals based on data (instead of having outsiders set goals).

- Share successes regularly in team meetings, staff meetings, newsletters, grade-level meetings, and so on.

- Take time to understand how a new district, state, or federal policy relates to current work and goals; debate its merits; and decide as a team how to incorporate the policy.

- Share reasons for working in schools.

- Interview or survey previous students or graduates, and share the results.

- Build staff consensus and commitment around shared goals.

- Conduct surveys of students, staff, and families on relevant topics, such as seeds of hope. Share results with students, staff, and families; develop goals based on the results; implement the plans; and follow up to measure the results. (See the section On Coming to Consensus in *Building a Culture of Hope*, pp. 154–159, for more information about using surveys.)

     ❝ ❞   One day, true purpose will be revealed to you, like the sun rising. When you find your purpose, you will find yourself. When you know your purpose in life, you will never have to work in quite this way again. It doesn't mean things won't be challenging once you find your purpose . . . they will. But the hard work you must do now will change because you will be aligned to your purpose and to your gifts.

—Don Coyhis

Fostering Staff Resilience in Difficult Times

Two specific actions, already embedded throughout the five seeds of hope, deserve special recognition for their importance in fostering staff resilience in difficult times: (1) support and (2) self-care as a moral responsibility.

Support

School personnel often talk about the bonding that occurs as they work through difficulties and see results. When everyone is in it together, buoying each other and sharing the load, staff can find it easier to keep going. In a study of secondary traumatic stress among staff in high-stress schools, over 90 percent of staff report they look to colleagues for support, but only 42 percent report their job requirements encourage talking with colleagues (Caringi, 2012). Leaving this crucial component of support to chance risks decreasing staff job satisfaction and morale. Thus, school leadership and team leaders should emphasize the role of support and sharing the load. Creating networks of support among school staff reinforces all five seeds of hope.

> **❝ ❞** Fostering resiliency in young people is ultimately an "inside-out" process that depends on educators taking care of themselves.

> **—Bonnie Benard**

Self-Care as a Moral Responsibility

In several resources, the idea of practitioner self-care as a moral responsibility has emerged. Similar to the rule on airplanes about putting on your own oxygen mask before trying to help others, teachers and other school staff need to develop social-emotional resilience, self-awareness, and self-regulation in themselves first (Jennings, 2018b). Only then can they truly teach these tools to students (Jennings, 2018b). Staff who work in high-stress environments have a responsibility to prepare themselves through self-care. As teachers, giving to others gives us a sense of satisfaction, but we must be sure to give to ourselves as well.

Self-care is not a luxury or selfish or self-indulgent—it is a necessity, and it can improve one's teaching capacity far more than another professional development on how to teach more or teach better. However, professional development rarely includes, let alone focuses on, how to develop and commit to self-care practices. (Gunn, 2018a). We should make it a goal to practice self-care before it becomes a critical need because this will save us recovery time. Self-care should not be another item on a to-do list that gets pushed to the end and creates more negative feelings.

Said another way, "self-care is an ethical imperative. We have an obligation to our clients—as well as to ourselves, our colleagues, and our loved ones—not to be damaged by the work we do" (Saakvitne & Pearlman, 1996, p. 49). Setting healthy, realistic limits for ourselves and others ensures a more relaxed and mutually supportive environment (Costa, 2012). Educators can use the self-care assessment found online at https://bit.ly/2rwE9bv (Saakvitne & Pearlman, 1996) to strengthen their self-care.

> **❝ ❞** You are a light in the lives of your students, your family, and your friends. In order to shine for others, you must take care of yourself.

> **—Jennifer Gunn**

Meeting staff's relational and emotional needs through the five seeds of hope, and through an environment of collaborative relationships and self-care, in the face of trauma (see chapter 3, page 49) helps foster job satisfaction and high morale. The other piece of the puzzle for reducing teacher turnover and low engagement requires meeting staff's cognitive and intellectual needs, which the final section of this chapter covers.

Meeting Staff's Professional Needs

Teaching is a profession where those who carry out the profession's duties have little input in what those duties are. To enhance teachers' sense of agency and job satisfaction (which leads to greater engagement and greater student growth), policymakers must take into consideration the realities of public school learning environments and be more responsive to teachers' perspectives and concerns. Place any educational policy in front of a panel of teachers, and they will be able to quickly explain the potential unintended consequences of enacting the policy. To fail to consult teachers on policy communicates that the policymakers undervalue educators' professional knowledge and expertise.

As discussed earlier, individuals are often attracted to the education profession, and choose to stay, because they consider it a calling, a mission, or a moral purpose. Education is emotionally intense work, and emotions are central to professional experiences, identities, and values (Bosso, 2017). Professional self-efficacy, identity, and engagement are closely linked with a teacher's self-image and sense of moral mission. Thus, ensuring teachers can reach their vision or ideal roles and responsibilities and enact their moral mission is closely tied to student outcomes.

> **" "** The top-down, bureaucratic and behaviorist nature of many education reform policies has inhibited the moral and affective aspects of teaching and learning. The inherently controlling nature of external educational reform policies influences teachers' work lives, often causing lower levels of efficacy, motivation, autonomy, morale, commitment, and job satisfaction. . . . Paradoxically, this effort at control causes teachers to become more controlling, more frustrated, less efficacious, and less motivated.
>
> **—David Bosso**

Every day, teachers face external directives, mandates, and controls that can interfere with the moral and affective purposes of their work. The bureaucracy of education and the structures and external trappings of schools threaten to overrun the humanity of teaching and learning. Too often, education reformers fail to consider the people a reform effort is seeking to shape, and fail to tap into the knowledge and perceptions of the professionals working in schools. Too often, educators are forced to enact policies that they know will have detrimental impacts on learning and learners. The effects of high-stakes accountability, in the No Child Left Behind legislation specifically, decreased curricular autonomy, increased pressure on standardized test performance, and increased workloads related to data reporting, all of which diminished role fulfillment and job satisfaction for educators (Senechal et al., 2016).

As with other professions, practitioners should have a role in shaping practice in ways that advance teaching as a science, transforming what doesn't work, and keeping what serves students well. We would not want to be treated by a doctor who is still practicing medicine as it was done in 1950, and we also would not want to be treated by a doctor who is more focused on insurance company mandates than on what our symptoms indicate. So, too, should we want our educators to utilize the best, most up-to-date information about teaching and learning without being too constrained by soulless mandates.

In this section, we explore the structures and strategies that can enhance teachers' ability to live up to the expectations they hold for their roles and responsibilities in classroom and school contexts. These strategies include ensuring that the policy rollout includes teachers' agency and voice and that structures support job satisfaction and morale.

> **❝ ❞** Teachers touch every part of the learning process [from planning lessons, teaching, interacting with students, motivating and tapping into students' passions, to assessing learning and re-teaching or extending lessons and communicating with families].
>
> —Terry Heick

Policy Rollout Includes Teachers' Agency and Voice

The rollout of new policies and procedures that govern teachers' work can either encourage agency, voice, and value or encourage passivity, compliance, and second-class status. According to the *Understanding Teacher Morale* study (Senechal et al., 2016), teachers typically evaluate new policies or procedures by balancing consideration of the following five concepts. Any rollout of new policies or procedures would do well to predict teachers' answers to these questions.

1. **Coherence:** Do the policies make sense? Do they have a purpose or reason? Do they meet the intended goals? Do they help students?

2. **Autonomy:** Do I have freedom to exercise professional judgment? Can I provide what students need, or am I curtailed by the policies? Are there restrictions?

3. **Burden:** Is the amount of work required overwhelming and overloading? Are there already too many students and responsibilities? Do the policies add to my burden without taking anything away?

4. **Fairness:** Are the policies and policy implementation fair to all? Do they create an unfair distribution of work, positions, or resource allocation across the system, between schools, or between departments?

5. **Compensation:** Is the pay commensurate with the work?

School and district leaders and policymakers can take the preceding concepts into account when developing a new policy, rolling out a new policy, or both. This way, they can ensure the rollout will enhance teachers' job satisfaction, professionalism, and morale, instead of pushing more teachers out of the profession due to a lack of voice, agency, and professional judgment. Beyond policy development and rollout, the day-to-day structures of schools and districts (such as curriculum teams, PLCs, and early-release days for collaboration) are critical for supporting the roles and responsibilities of professionals, as discussed in the following section.

Structures Support Staff Job Satisfaction and Morale

Teacher job satisfaction and morale can be greatly enhanced through structures at the school and district level that tap into the cognitive or intellectual aspects of teaching. These structures include professional learning communities; the Power of We; professional identity, agency, and voice; professional development; and teacher engagement and staff surveys. We consider each of these in the following sections.

Become a Professional Learning Community

Easily the most effective and important school-improvement process, a professional learning community requires ongoing staff engagement and collaboration. A PLC is defined as:

> An ongoing process in which educators work collaboratively in recurring cycles of collective inquiry and action research to achieve better results for the students they serve. PLCs operate under the assumption that the key to improved learning for students is continuous job-embedded learning for educators. (DuFour et al., 2016, p. 10)

PLCs meet the intellectual and cognitive aspects of teaching by engaging teachers in inquiry and action research, by giving them time and structures to engage in their roles and responsibilities with their colleagues, and by fostering voice and agency so teachers can plan, implement, and assess their ideas for improving learning. PLCs also meet the relational and emotional aspects of teaching by giving teachers time and structures to develop professional relationships with colleagues, to help and be helped by each other, and to strengthen their connections and commitments to each student's learning. PLCs lead to job satisfaction and high morale, when utilized as intended.

Unfortunately, as with many other effective processes, some schools have implemented the PLC process without truly understanding how and why they work, which has led to them labeling a wide variety of staff groupings as *PLCs*. They might call mandatory grade-level meetings, data meetings, core team meetings, and staff meetings *PLCs*, but to truly *be* PLCs, schools must have some essentials in place.

First, they must understand that a PLC is an ongoing process, not a program or a package that can be bought or implemented for one year. PLCs are never done or finished. The PLC process is a way of doing the business of teaching and learning in schools.

Second, the PLC process requires transforming the traditional notions of teaching and learning. Instead of concentrating on making sure students are *taught*, schools that operate as PLCs concentrate on making sure students *learn*. It seems a rather simple turn of phrase, but the implication changes everything.

According to DuFour and colleagues (2016), three big ideas define PLCs.

1. PLCs ensure that students learn by identifying what students will learn, what evidence teachers will use to measure learning, and what the school will do when a student does not learn.

2. PLCs create a culture of collaboration by giving it a time and place in the schedule.

3. PLCs focus on results instead of effort, care, and reasons why students didn't learn that are external to the classroom.

These big ideas of PLCs explain how this structure clearly fits into the resilient school model. PLCs address student academic needs and staff relational and professional needs.

The big ideas of effective PLCs are a collaborative culture with a focus on learning for all, collective inquiry into best practice and current reality, an action orientation (or learning by doing), a commitment to continuous improvement, and a results orientation (DuFour et al., 2016). Members of PLCs engage in a six-part cycle of inquiry. After identifying a specific standard (or standards) as the focus of a cycle, team members then study the standard as a team, select evidence-based instructional strategies to help students meet the standard, and create a lesson plan as a team. Then they implement the lesson plan and gather evidence of student learning, analyze the evidence as a team, and adjust instructional strategies after reflection (Provini, 2012).

From our observations in high-poverty schools, we have learned that members, not outside forces, must drive the purpose of the meetings. Too often, in the No Child Left Behind era, meetings labeled *PLC meetings* were thinly veiled attempts to make teachers comply with district policy, or to shame teachers whose students were not meeting learning targets, rather than to truly assist educators in understanding why students were or were not meeting learning targets and what to do about it.

Not mentioned in the preceding list of core elements is one essential piece: *trust*. PLCs work only when staff trust each other and trust leadership. As a result, successful PLCs begin with excellent leadership. The bottom line is that resilient schools are professional learning communities. It is outside the scope of this book to explain how to implement PLCs for school improvement. Instead, we refer you to the resources available on AllThingsPLC (www.allthingsplc.info) and DuFour et al. (2016) to learn more and get started, or to fine-tune existing PLC structures.

Field Note

 One district the authors observed during the 2010s in the Pacific Northwest was divided up into *silos* of practice—different departments that operated independently of each other with a lack of collaboration and a tendency to compete for the same resources—and teachers were expected to communicate with each silo separately rather than collectively. It was nearly impossible to get the silos to communicate with each other or share information, and teachers' voices were silenced by the silos' tall walls. One byproduct of the silos was they concentrated power in distinct areas. At district-level meetings or trainings, the silos often came up in discussions of implementation of policies: "Well, the curriculum department will never agree to that" or "The Title I team will need to approve that." Instead of teachers having the power, the departments far from the work of students made the majority of decisions. —Emily Gibson

Understand the Power of We

Staff who work together in PLCs talk about the *Power of We*—as in, "We are in this together, and we are stronger as a group than we would be as the sum of our individual strengths." Beyond the PLC process, the Power of We includes professional activities such as team teaching (teachers leading a lesson together), staff observing one another, and collaborating on school-improvement teams. In one school we observed, equity, PBIS, family engagement, and leadership teams met once a month. Another school encouraged every staff member to serve on one school-improvement team each year. The Power of We fulfills teachers' relational and professional expectations. The Power of We is described in detail in *Building a Culture of Hope* (Barr & Gibson, 2013, chapter 8, p. 141).

Magnify Professional Identity, Agency, and Voice

Teachers are professionals, and their voices and opinions need to matter at a school and district level. PLCs definitely provide an avenue for teacher voice, identity, and agency. Another way staff exercise agency and voice is through unions and collective bargaining. Teacher dissatisfaction is evidenced in the growing number of school walkouts and strikes across the United States as teachers and other personnel call for better wages, better working conditions, and more services and resources for students (Senechal et al., 2016). The collective-bargaining process magnifies the voices of school personnel so they cannot be ignored.

Encourage Professional Development

As written into the Every Student Succeeds Act (U.S. Department of Education, 2015), professional development is collaborative, ongoing, job embedded, and student centered (Autio, 2019). PLCs are a form of job-embedded professional development, as are mentoring programs and instructional coaches. Professional development must take into consideration the needs of teachers at different stages in their careers, with new teachers needing far different professional development than seasoned veterans. Some professional development should be mandatory for all, and other offerings should be optional for those who see a need. Book clubs, webinars, optional after-school professional development presented by staff in response to staff-identified needs, and summer district trainings are other forms of relevant professional development. Any professional development should refer to the ESSA's provisions for professional learning. A good place to start is Learning Forward's (n.d.) website (https://learningforward.org/get-involved/essa).

Field Note

Orientation programs for new educators are becoming commonplace in districts. In Vancouver Public Schools in Washington, all new educators to the district, regardless of prior teaching experience, were treated to a full-week orientation in the summer before the 2017–2018 school year began. It was a large district, and the new staff numbered about 150 people. They started out as strangers, but throughout the week, the new staff teamed up by school, subject, grade level, experience level, and interest. By the end of the week, they were beginning to form professional and personal relationships with other staff throughout the district, they had met their mentors who would support them throughout the year, and they had been inducted into the district and the ways it operated.

This orientation program supported the relational and professional needs of these new or new-to-the-district educators. District leadership explained that the district mentors, through an organic, grassroots effort, created the orientation a few years earlier as a way to meet new staff's needs. In other words, in creating the orientation, the mentors were also meeting their own relational and professional needs! —Emily Gibson

Sustain Teacher Engagement Through Staff Surveys

According to a 2015 Gallup poll, just 31 percent of teachers are engaged in their work, meaning they are involved with, enthusiastic about, and committed to their work and their school. Meanwhile, 56 percent are simply not engaged and are going through the motions. They put in the time but not their energy or passion. The remaining 13 percent are actively disengaged (Hodges, 2015). Not only do these teachers fail to engage with their work, but they also can actively undermine their engaged colleagues' work. Perhaps more importantly, teachers who are not engaged are far more likely to exit the profession than those who are engaged (Gallup, n.d.).

> " " Until you make your school the best part of a student's day, you will struggle with student attendance, achievement, and graduation rates. Having a high-achieving school is no accident. It is the result of purposeful, engaged teaching over time.
>
> —Eric Jensen

Engagement is a byproduct of job satisfaction and morale, and to increase or sustain engagement, schools must help teachers meet their roles and responsibilities and form their professional and personal relationships. Effective schools regularly (at least twice a year) survey staff to measure engagement, hope, optimism, relationships, self-efficacy, and the other components of job satisfaction and morale. Staff members should be involved in reviewing the survey results and determining next steps in response to areas needing improvement. Gallup has surveys for staff and students (available at https://bit.ly/2WEGyxH), as do the Search Institute (https://bit.ly/3bnnEiX) and Hope Survey (www.hopesurvey.org/). Surveys on the seeds of hope can be found in *Building a Culture of Hope* (Barr & Gibson, 2013).

Conclusion

There is a reciprocal relationship between what is best for students and what is best for staff, between how school leaders interact with teachers and staff and how staff interact with students. The ways that staff interact with students mirror the ways that administration interacts with staff, and meeting staff's needs leads to meeting students' needs. Creating a trauma-sensitive, welcoming, and optimistic school climate for students necessitates creating the same climate for staff. Staff's growth, development, pride, and confidence come from the same structures and expectations that create those characteristics in students (Benard, 1993). School personnel need administrators and colleagues who believe in them, trust them, and care about them, just as students need teachers and staff who do the same. According to Benard (1993), "It's hard [for teachers] to be caring and supportive, to have high expectations, and to involve students in decision making without support, respect, or opportunities to work collegially with others." When educators look at their students, hopefully they see a bit of themselves as young people, are reminded of their own strengths and resilience, and believe their students have the capacity to build strength and resilience.

Positive teacher job satisfaction and morale are critical to reducing the turnover churn in our high-poverty, high-minority schools, which has a negative impact on student learning. A resilient school emphasizes staff satisfaction and morale as a foundational condition for student success. By addressing compassion fatigue (see chapter 3, page 49), staff relational needs, and staff professional needs, a resilient school ensures that the best and brightest teachers and school personnel will find a good fit and choose to stay, both in the profession and in the school contexts that most need their expertise.

As described in chapter 4, page 71, resilient schools are places where, despite great odds:

- Socioeconomic and ethnic or minority achievement gaps have been closed or significantly reduced
- Students succeed in school and graduate
- Students successfully transition to postsecondary jobs or education
- Teachers and school staff maintain these remarkable achievements over time

Our extensive review of the literature, combined with our observations in schools across the United States, revealed four areas of research related to student success and resilience, reflected in the four cornerstones of the resilient school. When schools meet the academic needs of students, the social-emotional needs of students, the human needs of students and families, and the relational and professional needs of staff, they are more able to positively impact all learners, but especially those affected by poverty and trauma.

Next Steps

Please complete the following Next Steps, to integrate your experiences within your own schools and communities with the information presented in this chapter.

1. When teachers look at achievement test data, it quickly becomes evident that some teachers are much more effective than others. One way to gain strength as a team of teachers and to actively help each other is to plan professional development in which teachers most effective with certain subjects or topics are invited to share how they do it. You might also encourage teacher-to-teacher observations followed by discussion and debriefing. These types of efforts tend to build a team spirit and enrich morale.

2. A strong school staff have a strong sense of shared beliefs. You might try anonymous surveys of a few basic principles of education: Do you believe all kids can learn with adequate instruction and support? Do you believe that parents of poor children or youth care for their children and support the school?

3. Are you a member of a union, or have you participated in collective bargaining? What is your experience in your area, and how well do unions represent and support members?

4. If your district has implemented the PLC process, compare your experience to what is described.

5. Complete the modes of regulation chart (page 198) to discover more about your self-regulation strategies. Make a plan to incorporate more into your week. Share with your teaching team.

Epilogue

A Personal Note and a Vision
for Resilient Schools

We, the authors, both grew up in poverty and understand it in a deeply personal way. We both struggled up through obstacle after obstacle: family crises, job challenges, personal tragedies, and the constant companion of fear. Both of us were fortunate to not be locked into generational poverty; in fact, Bob's family was already on an upward trajectory before he was born, though no one in his family had ever graduated from high school, let alone college. Although we each had a strong sense of agency and capability instilled in us early on, neither of us had the benefits of attending what we call a *resilient school*. However, we lived in a different era, when students could put themselves through college working as a janitor or laboring in a salsa factory. We came of age at a time when working with your hands still paid enough to make ends meet and even get ahead. And we both had the advantage of being born white.

Emily Gibson was very fortunate. She and her brother grew up in a single-parent home in the middle of a redwood forest, on welfare, and with a mom debilitated by mental and physical health issues. During her childhood, the social safety net kept her family off the streets and provided enough to get by, but barely so. On the rare occasions when she didn't have to walk to school, Emily would have her mom stop a few blocks before the building so she could avoid the social embarrassment of climbing out the window of the broken car in front of her peers. Her clothes came from thrift stores and rummage sales, and her tennis shoes were often full of holes, barely hiding her stained and smelly socks. But she spent her days raising salamanders, watching birds, and building forts. As a teenager, she became enamored with horses, mucking stalls, cleaning saddles, and feeding the horses in the rain and mud, working every day just to secure one riding lesson a week. Horses have remained part of her life ever since.

Emily often explains how fortunate she is that her mother valued education, the arts, writing, nature, science—in essence, what it means to be a creative, thinking human being. Those lessons instilled in her a never-ending thirst for knowledge, which led her to her purpose: working directly with children impacted by poverty as a public school teacher. Despite overwhelming bullying and near-debilitating social rejection, somehow, with teachers' encouragement, she made it through school, though she almost dropped out in her junior year because she had a good-enough job and saw no purpose in school anymore. Her high school biology teacher and the rest of her high school science department believed in her, encouraged her, and saw the great promise of her life. In fact, her biology teacher, as he did with any student who showed passion and enthusiasm for science, always called her *Dr. Gibson*. Nearly thirty years later, *Dr. Gibson* became a reality when Emily earned her EdD from Boise State University. One of the first graduation announcements she sent was to that very same biology teacher, with the note, "Now everybody calls me Dr. Gibson!" In her career as an educator, a teacher educator, a mentor, and a coach, Emily has had the great fortune to be a catalyst for positive change and transformation. Emily's brother became a successful carpenter, bypassing college and attending trade school for his path to a good life. The Gibson siblings broke the cycle of poverty.

Bob Barr was very fortunate. He grew up in a farming family with his mom, his dad, a grandmother, and a sister. As farmers, they never had any want for food. His dad's favorite daily phrase at mealtime was "Everything on the table we either raised or baked." The Barrs came from a long line of farmers who either worked on shares with a landowner or rented land. No one in the family had ever owned their own land, until Bob's parents came along. They had very limited education, and when Bob arrived at school, his lack of reading readiness, his Texas pronunciation of words, and his inability to spell made learning a challenge. Yet, with the support and encouragement of teachers at all levels, he made it successfully through high school and then worked his way through college as a night janitor to become a high school history teacher.

While in high school, he almost came untracked, after working so hard to get a K–12 education. He and his girlfriend almost threw it all away when, at the age of sixteen, they ran off to Oklahoma to get married and had their first child at seventeen. Bob's wife was expelled from school when her pregnancy began to show; yet she returned to high school and graduated. After her children were grown enough, she went off to college at the age of thirty, completed her degree in seven years, and then earned a master's degree at Indiana University. Bob went on to complete a PhD at Purdue University, became one of twenty Ford Foundation Washington interns in education, and later became the director of teacher education at Indiana University and dean of education at Oregon State University and Boise State, all while authoring or coauthoring more than a dozen books. Further, the Barrs' two children have both earned doctoral degrees. The Barr family broke the cycle of poverty.

Both Emily and Bob found their way out of poverty through a pathway of education. Both were fortunate to have had a few very powerful teachers in their lives, teachers who believed in them, encouraged them, and helped them see a future that they never dreamed of. Yet these two success stories of breaking out of poverty could just as easily have fallen apart on any number of occasions. Both Emily and Bob know too well the quicksand of poverty that makes upward social mobility so difficult in the United States. But if they had grown up in today's world of income inequality, they may not have been so fortunate.

This book started with the recognition that poverty may well be the greatest challenge faced not just by schools but by the United States. It is surely a cancer growing dramatically in pockets of poverty all across the United States, overwhelming local schools and community agencies. Poverty will not simply go away. Without major local, state, and national efforts, it will only continue to grow (see chapter 1, page 11). In the absence of any obvious political will to address poverty through legislation, the only ray of hope is public education.

The bright and shining lights of hope are the local public schools—*resilient schools*—serving high-poverty communities. Resilient schools are not just any schools; these schools have expanded their scope and purpose to address the needs of students and staff and also families. These schools have emerged as the first line of offense in the battle against poverty; these schools have become communities' first responders to the needs of the poor. These resilient schools are emerging all across the United States in a major grassroots movement. And as they struggle to reinvent themselves to confront the needs of poverty, they are clearly redefining the role and purpose of public education in communities throughout the land.

Resilient schools are surely the future of education in high-poverty communities. They represent the hope of a better life for the students of poverty who attend those schools. It is through these schools that students have an opportunity to break out of the quicksand of generational poverty and find a pathway to a better life.

Looking back over this book, a number of powerful ideas associated with resilient schools leap out and provide direction and vision for the future. So, in conclusion, we, the authors, feel the need to emphasize them once more. Among the many ideas identified and discussed for helping students gain personal resilience and find a pathway to a better life, the following points are worth revisiting.

Like quicksand, poverty is nearly impossible to escape without resilience and an internal locus of control, as well as executive function skills. Children living in poverty without strong internal and external protective factors need outside help and support to find a way out of poverty. It can be a tricky thing, finding and keeping to that pathway out of the quicksand. In the United States, children born into poverty are almost set up to fail from the outset. From our research and work, we know that the most important skills children living in poverty can gain in public schools are social-emotional regulation and executive function skills. Without self-regulation and executive function skills, students exposed to chronic stress and trauma will likely continue in cyclic failure, which they will likely pass down to their children. From our research and work, we also know that the most important policies and programs to help young adults exit the cycle of poverty are those that provide high school and postsecondary education and training for knowledge-based jobs. Without education and training, low-income students are likely sentenced to the roles of the working poor.

These most important things are deeply intertwined, for the outcomes of one are not possible without the outcomes of the other. It is unlikely a student will pursue and complete postsecondary opportunities without having executive function and self-regulation skills to initiate and sustain the pursuit. As we conclude, we would like to remind readers of the other key ideas conveyed in this book necessary to breaking the cycle of poverty. These include listening to student voices; meeting the emotional challenges of students; becoming trauma-informed, trauma-sensitive schools; increasing engagement and personal connections; and teaching hope and finding a vision for a better life.

Listening to Student Voices

Throughout this book, we have highlighted the importance of listening to student voices. Research (see, for example, Damon, 2008; Gallup, 2017; Hope Survey, 2018; Quaglia, n.d.; and the Centergy Project at www.thecentergyproject.com) makes it clear that we have much to learn from students if only we listen. But it is not enough for teachers and school staff to listen to students and solicit their views and opinions. They must take action after collecting and analyzing the results. Students will only share honestly and openly when they trust the adults who seek their views, and they will watch closely to see if the adults hear and act on their voices. Schools must listen to students, and they must learn from the students and let the student voices lead to visible action in order to improve life and learning in the schools. The power of student voices is immense and can only improve schools and schooling.

Meeting the Emotional Challenges of Students

Comprehensive student surveys, follow-up discussions, and interviews evidence the high levels of anxiety, depression, fear, anger, and other emotional challenges faced by students today. Many of these feelings can be traced back to the traumas and stresses of lives lived in poverty, on the outskirts of hope. Neuroscience tells us these emotions can dramatically interfere with teaching and learning (for example, Cole et al., 2005). If schools have any chance of closing the achievement gap, keeping students learning and graduating, and having students make personal plans for after high school, the core area of schools' work lies in social-emotional learning and needs: hope, optimism, engagement, and self-regulation.

In addition, students seem to cry out for related mental health services that only counselors or other mental health providers can deliver. While school outreach centers provide for students' and their families' basic needs (food, clothing, housing, and health), someone also needs to address students' emotional needs. Principals frequently explain that their high school counselors—tasked with academic as well as personal counseling—have a caseload of several hundred students and there is so little they can realistically do. And school budgets continue to shrink in most districts. Yet the Marietta Student Life Center in Georgia found agencies and organizations in the community that were able to provide eight to twelve additional counselors, student support staff, and mental health providers to address students' foundational emotional needs. All other efforts to improve academic performance and graduation rates depend on meeting students' emotional and mental health needs.

Becoming Trauma-Informed, Trauma-Sensitive Schools

School principals at all levels are quick to identify mental health issues as the primary challenge that they face with today's students. The extent to which trauma and stress permeate families and communities today is sobering, and for children living in poverty, it appears even greater. Schools must address trauma and stress to give large numbers of students any chance at all of succeeding academically and finding a better life. Too often, adults respond to students under the influence of trauma or stress with traditional discipline and withdraw belonging and positive regard, which further alienates students from the benefits of caring adults. It is absolutely essential that all school personnel and all schools become *trauma sensitive* and *trauma informed*.

Increasing Engagement and Personal Connections

Talk to almost any people who have emerged from the quicksand of poverty, and they will likely tell a story of an adult, often a teacher or school staff member, who seems to have set their life on a different trajectory. You hear it again and again: "They believed in me. They made me believe that I could do things I never dreamed of. They never gave up on me." Few things have more power in the success of children, especially children living in poor communities, than caring teachers with high expectations. Closely related to this personal connection is the feeling of personal engagement in student learning. And while engagement is associated with curricular relevance and student purpose, it is almost always associated with one or more effective teachers who connect the student to the content and the world outside the classroom.

Teaching Hope and Finding a Vision for a Better Life

Eric Jensen and Herbert Kohl, more than any other authors we quote in this book, have encouraged teachers to help students dream, gain a vision of a possible future, and have hope. Throughout their works, both Jensen and Kohl encourage teachers to talk to students about their future and about their potential, and to encourage students to understand that these dreams are within their grasp. Another author, Russell J. Quaglia (n.d.), calls for helping students find personal aspirations and helping them work to achieve those aspirations.

Perhaps the most hopeful research is that supporting the importance of hope in students' lives. We now know the power of surrounding students with an optimistic Culture of Hope. We now know that resilience and hope can be taught. Both hope and resilience emphasize helping students look to the future and envision a goal or purpose to constantly think about where they are and where they need to be—what they need to accomplish to achieve their dream and fulfill their life purpose. This teaching of hope and resilience prepares students for the world beyond high school.

Conclusion

Any realistic possibility of helping students whose lives have been impacted by poverty and potentially trauma must focus on the essential, foundational issues outlined in this epilogue. As our schools and teachers did for us in a very different time, teachers in every school are listening to their students and developing strong connections with them. They are mentoring their students, believing in them, and challenging them to reach for the opportunities—to reach for their futures.

The good news is that in spite of the very sticky quicksand of poverty, schools—particularly schools on their way to becoming resilient schools—are helping students work through their emotional and mental health needs, connect with caring and demanding adults in the school, and find purpose for their lives. These schools teach students self-regulation and executive function skills and help them build postsecondary plans for their futures. They teach students hope and how to chart a course for a better life. These schools represent hope for the students living in poverty in this country. This is our hope—that they may be the next fortunate ones.

Appendix

Additional Reports and Resources

The following reports and resources provide more thorough information on topics from this book. Visit **go.SolutionTree.com/schoolimprovement** for an online, clickable version of this appendix.

The Realities of Poverty in the United States

- **Teaching poverty certificate (https://education.ecu.edu/elmid/elmid_teachingpoverty):** At East Carolina University (n.d.), teachers can earn a certificate in teaching children in poverty. In this certificate's coursework, students learn about the cognitive, social, and emotional implications of poverty on children and families, including poverty's effects on children's development and the impact of poverty-related stress and trauma on children's learning and attention. Additionally, students learn educational and assessment strategies that address poverty-affected children's specific cognition, social-emotional learning, and development needs, and they apply them to classroom practice.

- **National Child Traumatic Stress Network (www.nctsn.org):** This network's mission is to raise the standard of care and improve access to services for traumatized children, their families, and communities throughout the United States. The network provides tremendous webinars, available for free on its website.

- **Children's Defense Fund (www.childrensdefense.org):** This is a national organization working to end child poverty. It provides vast resources for learning about the current state of poverty in each state as well as the nation, and is incredibly beneficial for gathering data. Their website states,

  CDF provides a strong, effective and independent voice for all the children of America who cannot vote, lobby, or speak for themselves. We pay particular attention to the needs of poor children, children of color and those with disabilities. CDF educates the nation about the needs of children and encourages preventive investments before they get sick, drop out of school, get into trouble or suffer family breakdown. (Children's Defense Fund, 2020)

- **Souls of Poor Folk by the Institute for Policy Studies (https://ips-dc.org /souls-of-poor-folks):** A comprehensive and historical portrait of poverty in the United States, from the original Poor People's Campaign of the 1960s to the 2010s.

- **United Nations Report on Poverty in the United States (https:// digitallibrary.un.org/record/1629536?ln=en):** This is a special report, published by the United Nations, detailing the reality of poverty in the United States.

- **Implicit biases surrounding poverty:** Paul Gorski's (2013) book *Reaching and Teaching Students in Poverty: Strategies for Erasing the Opportunity Gap* is a wonderful resource on this topic.

The Whole-Child Approach

- **National Youth-at-Risk (NYAR) Conference:** Based at Georgia Southern University, this group sponsors a journal, the *National Youth-at-Risk Journal*, and an annual conference (see https://digitalcommons.georgiasouthern.edu/ nyar for more information). The National Youth-at-Risk Conference and its journal focus on the well-being of the whole child. Its efforts focus on fostering the five Hs, which map well onto the resilient school: (1) *head* for intellectual achievement and talents, (2) *heart* for social-emotional skills, (3) *hands* for safety and protection, (4) *health* for physical and mental health, and (5) *home* for family and community support.

- **Association for Supervision and Curriculum Development (n.d.):** ASCD's whole-child symposiums are reports from a gathering of researchers, practitioners, and leaders at which they talk about the needs of the whole child. Recent reports include 2017's Symposium (available at www.ascd .org/whole-child-symposium.aspx) and 2015's Symposium (available at www.ascd.org/ASCD/pdf/siteASCD/wholechild/spring2015wcsreport.pdf). Further, an archive of past symposiums' reports and resources is also accessible (available at www.ascd.org/conferences/whole-child-symposium /past-events.aspx).

- **Aspen Institute (www.aspeninstitute.org/issues/education):** The Aspen Institute held an in-depth symposium on the whole child, with scholars, educators, leaders, and researchers. They issued a report of their findings in 2018 (available at http://nationathope.org/wp-content/uploads/2018_aspen_ final-report_full_webversion.pdf).

Trauma-Informed Practices

- **Collaborative Learning for Educational Achievement and Resilience (CLEAR; https://extension.wsu.edu/clear):** Washington State University's CLEAR provides resources and professional development on trauma-informed practices that increase educators' capacity to support student development and academic success. The Resources tab is especially helpful.

- **Trauma-sensitive schools learning modules:** The Wisconsin Department of Public Instruction (n.d.) provides outstanding online training modules for schools and educators wishing to further develop the trauma lens (available at https://dpi.wi.gov/sspw/mental-health/trauma/modules). This free online course, with fourteen modules, utilizes PBIS and response to intervention while adding the trauma-informed care values.

- **Healthy Environments and Response to Trauma in Schools (HEARTS):** The HEARTS program at the University of California San Francisco provides information on trauma-informed practices. Its resource list (available at https://hearts.ucsf.edu/resources) is excellent (UCSF HEARTS, n.d.).

- **Trauma and Learning Policy Initiative (https://traumasensitiveschools.org):** This initiative provides a treasure trove of resources for schools and educators interested in developing greater capacity for trauma-informed practices. The Trauma and Learning Policy Initiative has also published a two-volume series, *Helping Traumatized Children Learn* (Cole et al., 2005, 2013; available at https://massadvocates.org), which provides background knowledge and research on trauma's impacts on children and learning, and other resources for schools seeking to increase their effectiveness with high-trauma student populations.

- **The trauma-informed school:** A step-by-step implementation guide for administrators and school personnel (Sporleder & Forbes, 2016). This is an outstanding resource for those wishing to implement trauma-informed practices. Jim Sporleder is the former principal featured in the film about ACEs and resilience, *Paper Tigers*.

Resilience

- **Compassionate Schools:** Washington State has published a handbook titled *The Heart of Learning and Teaching: Compassion, Resiliency, and Academic Success* (Wolpow, Johnson, Hertel, & Kincaid, 2016). This free resource (available at www.k12.wa.us/CompassionateSchools/HeartofLearning.aspx) is of great value for schools wanting to work on resilience.

- ***C.A.R.E.: Strategies for Closing the Achievement Gaps, Fourth Edition:*** This free resource by the National Education Association (2011; available online at www.nea.org/assets/docs/CAREguide2011.pdf) provides lessons for grades K–12 on the four areas of CARE (culture, abilities, resilience, and effort), plus educator and paraeducator self-assessments.

- **Child and Youth Resilience Measure & Adult Resilience Measure (https://cyrm.resilienceresearch.org/how-to-use/):** These are surveys designed to measure and monitor child and youth resilience and adult resilience. They were developed by the partnership of TRACEs and Oregon State University in Bend, Oregon.

The Academic Needs of Students

- **The National Dropout Prevention Center (n.d.a):** This center keeps a clearinghouse of any and all strategies proven effective for keeping students in school and engaged (see http://dropoutprevention.org/effective-strategies).

- **America's Promise Alliance (https://www.americaspromise.org):** The America's Promise Alliance has been described as a "Marshall Plan" for American high schools. This group had two major goals for American high schools: (1) a 90 percent graduation rate by 2020, and (2) the highest college attainment rates in the world. This group is a research powerhouse on education and high school graduation, with numerous freely available reports and publications.

The Social–Emotional Needs of Students

- ***Relationships First: Creating Connections That Help Young People Thrive:*** This study (Roehlkepartain et al., 2017) provides research from the Search Institute on developmental relationships and is available for free download (http://page.search-institute.org/relationships-first).

- **Collaborative Problem Solving:** Psychologists Ross Greene and Stuart Ablon developed this approach for responding to behavior challenges in a collaborative way rather than a way that displays power or control. In brief, when students struggle with expected behavior, adults work with them from a place of curiosity (for example, "I notice that you are struggling with _____. What's up with that?"). As students share their perspectives, the adult and child work together to come up with a solution that meets both of their needs. See Ablon's work (www.thinkkids.org) and Greene's work (http://cpsconnection.com) for more information.

- **CASEL Standards:** What is SEL? Collaborative for Academic, Social, and Emotional Learning (CASEL, n.d.). The CASEL standards provide guidance for social-emotional learning content in public schools.

The Human Needs of Students and Families

- **Coalition for Community Schools (www.communityschools.org):** This coalition provides incredible information and resources for developing and maintaining community outreach schools that meet the human needs of students and families.

- **The Children's Aid Society (2011):** This society published a comprehensive guide for schools and districts wishing to begin community outreach schools titled *Building Community Schools: A Guide for Action* (available at www.theoryofchange.org/wp-content/uploads/toco_library/pdf/NCCS_ BuildingCommunitySchools.pdf).

- **Community Resource Coordinators:** Cincinnati Public Schools (2012) published *Transforming Schools, Revitalizing Neighborhoods: A Guide for Resource Coordinators.* This guide (available at www.communityschools. org/assets/1/AssetManager/Cincinnati%20CLC%20Manual%20for%20 Resource%20Coordinators.pdf) is helpful for creating and strengthening this critical role in the community outreach school.

- **National Education Association's (n.d.a). resources for community outreach schools:** *Community Schools: All Together Now!* (National Education Association, n.d.a.) is available online (see www.nea.org/ home/66319.htm). Further, *The Six Pillars of Community Schools Toolkit: NEA Resource Guide for Educators, Families, and Communities* (National Education Association, n.d.b.) is accessible at www.nea.org/assets/docs/ Comm%20Schools%20ToolKit-final%20digi-web-72617.pdf.

The Relational and Professional Needs of Staff

- *Teacher Morale, Motivation, and Professional Identity* **(Bosso, 2017):** This report of research (available at https://files.eric.ed.gov/fulltext/ ED581425.pdf) fundamentally changed how we, the authors, view teacher retention and attrition.

- *Understanding Teacher Morale* **(Senechal, et al., 2016):** This report from the Metropolitan Educational Research Consortium (available at https:// scholarscompass.vcu.edu/cgi/viewcontent.cgi?article=1055&context=merc_ pubs) dovetails nicely with the above report by Bosso (2017) to explain the relational and professional needs of staff.

Brain Research

- *Culturally Responsive Teaching and the Brain: Promoting Authentic Engagement and Rigor Among Culturally and Linguistically Diverse Students:* This book, by Zaretta Hammond (2015), provides educators with practical strategies for increasing engagement among student populations that tend to struggle with achievement in white, middle-class schools. It is an excellent source for dealing with potential implicit biases, as well.

- *Using Brain Science to Design New Pathways Out of Poverty* **(Babcock, 2014b):** This report (available at https://s3.amazonaws.com/empath-website/pdf/ Research-UsingBrainScienceDesignPathwaysPoverty-0114.pdf) connects the dots between brain science, trauma, and the transformative abilities of schools.

Disrupted Learning

Two education groups have published information about disrupted learning:

- **Oregon Education Association (n.d.),** *A Crisis of Disrupted Learning: Conditions in Our Schools and Recommended Solutions* (available at www.oregoned.org/assets/docs/DisruptedLearning_Report_2019_v5.pdf)

- **Connecticut Education Association (2019),** *Crisis in the Classroom: Disruptive Behavior. Disrupted Learning* (available at www.cea.org/ issues/press/2019/feb/22/crisis-in-the-classroom-disruptive-behavior-disrupted-learning.cfm)

Surveys for School Use

- **Comprehensive School Climate Inventory (www.schoolclimate.org/ services/measuring-school-climate-csci):** This nationally recognized survey "provides an in-depth profile of your school community's particular strengths, as well as areas for improvement" by assessing "student, parent/ guardian, and school personnel perceptions"(National School Climate Center, n.d.).

- **Gallup Student Poll (ww.gallup.com/education/233537/gallup-student-poll.aspx):** The Gallup Student Poll provides reliable research on student engagement and other factors.

- **Youth Risk Behavior Surveys (Centers for Disease Control and Prevention, 2018; available at www.cdc.gov/healthyyouth/data/yrbs/index.htm).** Two surveys, one for middle school, one for high school, measure the levels of risk behaviors among students.

- **Hope Survey (www.hopesurvey.org/):** The Hope Survey produces research, as well as surveys, on hope, resilience, and student engagement.

- **Trauma Responsive Schools Implementation Assessment (TRS-IA) Treatment and Services Adaptation Center (n.d.; available at https://traumaawareschools.org/traumaResponsiveSchools):** This assessment can help schools determine where they have strengths and where they can develop more in becoming a trauma-informed school.

References and Resources

ACEs Too High. (n.d.). Accessed at https://acestoohigh.com on April 1, 2020.

Adams, J. M. (2013). Social and emotional learning gaining new focus under Common Core. Accessed at https://edsource.org/2013/social-and-emotional-learning-gaining-new-traction-under-common-core/32161 on February 21, 2020.

Adelman, C. (1999). Answers in the tool box. Academic intensity, attendance patterns, and bachelor's degree attainment. Washington, DC: National Institute on Postsecondary Education, Libraries, and Lifelong Learning. Accessed at https://eric.ed.gov/?id=ED431363 on February 21, 2020.

Administration for Children and Families (n.d.). Secondary traumatic stress: What is secondary traumatic stress? Washington, DC: U.S. Department of Health and Human Services.

Allard, S. (2018, May 31). Why poverty is rising faster in suburbs than in cities. Accessed at https://theconversation.com/why-poverty-is-rising-faster-in-suburbs-than-in-cities-97155 on February 21, 2020.

Alston, P. (2017, December 15). Statement on visit to the USA, by professor Philip Alston, United Nations special rapporteur on extreme poverty and human rights. Accessed at www.ohchr.org/EN/NewsEvents/Pages/DisplayNews.aspx?NewsID=22533 on October 24, 2019.

American Institutes for Research. (2008). Afterschool programs make a difference: Findings from the Harvard Family Research Project. Accessed at www.sedl.org/pubs/sedl-letter/v20n02/afterschool_findings.html on October 8, 2019.

Aspen Institute. (2018). *From a nation at risk to a nation at hope: Recommendations from the National Commission on Social, Emotional, and Academic Development*. Washington, DC: Author. Accessed at http://nationathope.org/wp-content/uploads/2018_aspen_final-report_full_webversion.pdf on October 24, 2019.

Association for Experiential Education. (n.d.). What is experiential education? Accessed at www.aee.org/what-is-ee on October 24, 2019.

Association for Supervision and Curriculum Development. (n.d.). Whole child. Accessed at www.ascd.org/whole-child.aspx on October 24, 2019.

Association for Supervision and Curriculum Development. (2007). *The learning compact redefined: A call to action. A report of the commission on the whole child.* Alexandria, VA: Author. Accessed at www.ascd.org/ASCD/pdf/Whole%20 Child/WCC%20Learning%20Compact.pdf on February 21, 2020.

Association for Supervision and Curriculum Development. (2015). *Poverty and education: From a war on poverty to the majority of public school students living in poverty—A report on the spring 2015 ASCD Whole Child Symposium.* Alexandria, VA: Author. Accessed at www.ascd.org/ASCD/pdf/siteASCD/ wholechild/spring2015wcsreport.pdf on October 8, 2019.

Autio, E. (2019, January). *A crisis of disrupted learning: Conditions in our schools and recommended solutions.* Portland, OR: Oregon Education Association. Accessed at www.oregoned.org/assets/docs/DisruptedLearning_ Report_2019_v5.pdf on October 24, 2019.

Azerrad, D. (2016). How equal should opportunities be? Accessed at www.nationalaffairs.com/publications/detail/how-equal-should-opportunities-be on October 7, 2019.

Babcock, E. (2014a). Poverty and brain science. Accessed at www.empathways.org/ approach/poverty-brain-science on October 23, 2019.

Babcock, E. (2014b). *Using brain science to design new pathways out of poverty.* Boston: Crittenton Women's Union. Accessed at https://s3.amazonaws.com/empath-website/pdf/Research-UsingBrainScienceDesignPathwaysPoverty-0114.pdf on October 7, 2019.

Babcock, E. (2018, March). *Using brain science to transform human services and increase personal mobility from poverty.* Washington, DC: U.S. Partnership on Mobility From Poverty. Accessed at www.mobilitypartnership.org/ using-brain-science-transform-human-services-and-increase-personal-mobility-poverty on October 7, 2019.

Bach, N. (2019, January 29). Millions of Americans are one missed paycheck away from poverty, report says. Accessed at https://fortune.com/2019/01/29/americans-liquid-asset-poor-propserity-now-report on October 7, 2019.

Balfanz, R., & Legters, N. (2004, September). *Locating the dropout crisis: Which high schools produce the nation's dropouts? Where are they located? Who attends them?* Baltimore: Center for Research on the Education of Students Placed at Risk. Accessed at http://citeseerx.ist.psu.edu/viewdoc/download?doi=10.1 .1.393.862&rep=rep1&type=pdf on October 7, 2019.

Barkan, S. E. (2016). *Social problems: Continuity and change.* Minneapolis: University of Minnesota Libraries.

Barnum, M. (2018, September 26). Want to boost test scores and increase grad rates? One strategy: Look outside schools and help low-income families. Accessed at www.chalkbeat.org/posts/us/2018/09/26/research-boost-test-score-help-families on October 7, 2019.

Barr, R. D., & Gibson, E. L. (2013). *Building a culture of hope: Enriching schools with optimism and opportunity.* Bloomington, IN: Solution Tree Press.

Barr, R. D., & Parrett, W. H. (1995). *Hope at last for at-risk youth.* Boston: Allyn & Bacon.

Barr, R. D., & Parrett, W. (1997). *How to create alternative, magnet, and charter schools that work.* Bloomington, IN: Solution Tree Press.

Barr, R. D., & Parrett, W. H. (2001). *Hope fulfilled for at-risk and violent youth: K–12 programs that work* (2nd ed.). Boston: Allyn & Bacon.

Barr, R. D., & Parrett, W. H. (2007). *The kids left behind: Catching up the under-achieving children of poverty.* Bloomington, IN: Solution Tree Press.

Barr, R. D., & Parrett, W. H. (2008). *Saving our students, saving our schools: 50 proven strategies for helping underachieving students and improving schools* (2nd ed.). Thousand Oaks, CA: Corwin Press.

Barth, P., Haycock, K., Jackson, H., Mora, K., Ruiz, P., Robinson, S., et al. (Eds.). (1999). *Dispelling the myth: High poverty schools exceeding expectations.* Washington, DC: The Education Trust. Accessed at https://files.eric.ed.gov/fulltext/ED445140.pdf on October 7, 2019.

Beacon Broadside. (2017, December 24). Martin Luther King, Jr.'s "A Christmas Sermon on Peace" still prophetic 50 years later. Accessed at www.beaconbroadside.com/broadside/2017/12/martin-luther-king-jrs-christmas-sermon-peace-still-prophetic-50-years-later.html on October 8, 2019.

Beatty, A. (2010). *Student mobility: Exploring the impacts of frequent moves on achievement—Summary of a workshop.* Washington, DC: National Academies Press. Accessed at www.nap.edu/read/12853/chapter/1 on October 7, 2019.

Beaumont, L. R. (2009). Learned helplessness: Why bother? Accessed at www.emotionalcompetency.com/helpless.htm on October 7, 2019.

Bellis, M. A., Hughes, K., Ford, K., Hardcastle, K. A., Sharp, C. A., Wood, S., et al. (2018, June 26). Adverse childhood experiences and sources of child-hood resilience: A retrospective study of their combined relationships with child health and educational attendance. *BMC Public Health, 18.* Accessed at https://doi.org/10.1186/s12889-018-5699-8 on February 21, 2020.

Benard, B. (1991, August). *Fostering resiliency in kids: Protective factors in the family, school, and community.* Washington, DC: U.S. Department of Education. Accessed at https://files.eric.ed.gov/fulltext/ED335781.pdf on October 7, 2019.

Benard, B. (1993). Fostering resiliency in kids. *Educational Leadership, 51*(3). Accessed at www.ascd.org/publications/educational-leadership/nov93/vol51/num03/Fostering-Resiliency-in-Kids.aspx on October 7, 2019.

Bender, W. N. (2002). *Differentiating instruction for students with learning disabilities: Best teaching practices for general and special educators.* Thousand Oaks, CA: Corwin Press.

Benson, P. L. (1997). *All kids are our kids: What communities must do to raise caring and responsible children and adolescents.* San Francisco: Jossey-Bass.

Berlin, R., & Davis, R. B. (1989). Children from alcoholic families: Vulnerability and resilience. In T. F. Dugan & R. Coles (Eds.), *The child in our times: Studies in the development of resiliency* (pp. 81–105). New York: Brunner/Mazel.

Better Together. (2017, Spring). *Central Oregon community report.* Redmond, OR: Author. Accessed at www.strivetogether.org/wp-content/uploads/2017/07/Better-Together-Central-Oregon-Community-Report-2017.pdf on October 7, 2019.

Better Together. (2018, Fall). *Central Oregon community report.* Redmond, OR: Author. Accessed at http://bettertogethercentraloregon.org/files/2018/11/Community-Report-2018_FNL-Online.pdf on October 7, 2019.

Birdsong, K. (2016, January 26). 10 facts about how poverty impacts education [Blog post]. Accessed at www.scilearn.com/blog/10-facts-about-how-poverty-impacts-education on October 7, 2019.

Blad, E. (2016, February 24). Community schools blunt the impacts of poverty in Vancouver, Wash. Education Week Leaders to Learn From. Accessed at https://leaders.edweek.org/profile/steve-webb-and-tom-hagley-superintendent-chief-of-staff-community-schools/ on February 21, 2020.

Blad, E., & Harwin, A. (2017, January 24). Black students more likely to be arrested at school. Accessed at www.edweek.org/ew/articles/2017/01/25/black-students-more-likely-to-be-arrested.html on October 7, 2019.

Blow, C. M. (2015, January 28). Reducing our obscene level of child poverty. Accessed at www.nytimes.com/2015/01/28/opinion/charles-blow-reducing-our-obscene-level-of-child-poverty.html on October 7, 2019.

Boghani, P. (2017, November 22). How poverty can follow children into adulthood. Accessed at www.pbs.org/wgbh/frontline/article/how-poverty-can-follow-children-into-adulthood on October 7, 2019.

Bonilla-Santiago, G. (2014). *The miracle on Cooper Street: Lessons from an inner city.* Bloomington, IN: Archway Publishing.

Bonilla-Santiago, G. (2017, January 24). Education: Key to breaking cycle of poverty. Accessed at www.huffingtonpost.com/gloria-bonilla-santiago/education-key-to-breaking_b_14369716.html on October 7, 2019.

Bookbinder, H. (1989, August 20). Did the war on poverty fail? Accessed at www.nytimes.com/1989/08/20/opinion/did-the-war-on-poverty-fail.html on October 7, 2019.

Bosso, D. (2017, May). *Teacher morale, motivation and professional identity: Insight for educational policymakers from state teachers of the year.* Philadelphia: National Network of State Teachers of the Year. Accessed at https://files.eric.ed.gov/fulltext/ED581425.pdf on October 7, 2019.

Boyes-Watson, C., & Pranis, K. (2015). *Circle forward: Building a restorative school community.* St. Paul, MN: Living Justice Press.

Bracey, G. (2002). What students do in the summer. *Phi Delta Kappan, 83*(7), 497–498.

Brendtro, L. K., Brokenleg, M., & Van Bockern, S. (2019). *Reclaiming youth at risk: Futures of promise* (3rd ed.). Bloomington, IN: Solution Tree Press.

Broader, Bolder Approach to Education. (n.d.). Accessed at www.boldapproach.org/case-study/vancouver-public-schools on October 7, 2019.

Brown, C. (2019). A good run for unskilled workers. Accessed at www.axios.com/low-skilled-unemployment-rate-falling-3efa1f82-ab2d-4c03-9212-9379dec0abd3.html on February 21, 2020.

Bruno, J. E. (2002, July). *The geographical distribution of teacher absenteeism in large urban school district settings: Implications for school reform efforts aimed at promoting equity and excellence in education.* Accessed at www.semanticscholar.org/paper/The-Geographical-Distribution-of-Teacher-in-Large-Bruno/9cbcf660ab6faf41121f1dd9e67059c7eee5853c on October 7, 2019.

Bryant, A. L., & Kelley, K. (2006). Preface. In B. K. Perkins (ED.), *Where we learn: The CUBE survey of urban school climate* (p. 11). Alexandria, VA: National School Boards Association.

Budge, K. M., & Parrett, W. H. (2018). *Disrupting poverty: Five powerful classroom practices.* Alexandria, VA: Association for Supervision and Curriculum Development.

Buffum, A., Mattos, M., & Malone, J. (2017). *Taking action: A handbook for RTI at Work (How to implement response to intervention in your school).* Bloomington, IN: Solution Tree Press.

Buffum, A., Mattos, M., & Weber, C. (2012). *Simplifying response to intervention: Four essential guiding principles.* Bloomington, IN: Solution Tree Press.

Bureau of Labor Statistics. (2017, May 22). 69.7 percent of 2016 high school graduates enrolled in college in October 2016. Accessed at www.bls.gov/opub/ted/2017/69-point-7-percent-of-2016-high-school-graduates-enrolled-in-college-in-october-2016.htm on October 7, 2019.

Burke, D. L. (1997). *Looping: Adding time, strengthening relationships.* Champaign, IL: ERIC Clearinghouse on Elementary and Early Childhood Education. Accessed at www.ericdigests.org/1998-2/looping.htm on October 7, 2019.

Burns, M. (2015, July 14). Path out of poverty? Education plus neuroscience [Blog post]. Accessed at www.scilearn.com/blog/path-out-poverty-education-plus-neuroscience on October 7, 2019.

Burns, M. (2016, January 6). How poverty affects school success. Accessed at www.smartbrief.com/original/2016/01/how-poverty-affects-school-success on October 7, 2019.

C. K. (2018, March 1). A never-ending war: Poverty in America—America's welfare programmes are not the problem. Accessed at www.economist.com/democracy-in-america/2018/03/01/poverty-in-america on October 7, 2019.

Calderon, V. J., & Jones, J. M. (2018, September 28). Superintendents say engagement, hope best measures of success. Accessed at www.gallup.com/education/243224/superintendents-say-engagement-hope-best-measures-success.aspx on October 7, 2019.

Camera, L. (2018). In most states, poorest school districts get less funding. Accessed at www.usnews.com/news/best-states/articles/2018-02-27/in-most-states-poorest-school-districts-get-less-funding on February 21, 2020.

Campbell, D. (2016). *The art of being there: Creating change, one child at a time.* Boise, ID: Ampelon.

Caringi, J. C. (2012). What do we know about STS in schools? Current research findings from Montana. Accessed at https://learn.nctsn.org/course/view.php?id=232 on October 7, 2019.

Carnevale, A. P., Smith, N., & Strohl, J. (2013, June). *Recovery: Job growth and education requirements through 2020.* Washington, DC: Center on Education and the Workforce. Accessed at https://cew.georgetown.edu/cew-reports/recovery-job-growth-and-education-requirements-through-2020 on October 7, 2019.

Carter, S. C. (2000). *No excuses: Lessons from 21 high-performing, high-poverty schools.* Washington, DC: The Heritage Foundation. Accessed at https://files.eric.ed.gov/fulltext/ED440170.pdf on February 21, 2020.

Carver-Thomas, D., & Darling-Hammond, L. (2017). *Teacher turnover: Why it matters and what we can do about it* [Research brief]. Accessed at https://learningpolicyinstitute.org/sites/default/files/product-files/Teacher_Turnover_BRIEF.pdf on October 7, 2019.

CASEL. (n.d.). What is SEL? Accessed at https://casel.org/what-is-sel/ on February 21, 2020.

Center for Poverty Research. (2018). What is "deep poverty"? Accessed at https://poverty.ucdavis.edu/faq/what-deep-poverty on February 21, 2020.

Center for Promise. (2017, March 28). *Youth in poverty six times more likely to experience detrimental levels of adversity than higher-income peers* [Press release]. Accessed at www.americaspromise.org/press-release/youth-poverty-six-times-more-likely-experience-detrimental-levels-adversity-higher on October 8, 2019.

Center on the Developing Child. (n.d.). Key concepts: Resilience. Accessed at https://developingchild.harvard.edu/science/key-concepts/resilience on October 8, 2019.

Centers for Disease Control and Prevention. (n.d.). Adverse childhood experiences (ACEs). Accessed at www.cdc.gov/violenceprevention/acestudy/index.html on October 7, 2019.

Centers for Disease Control and Prevention. (2018). Youth Risk Behavior Surveillance System (YRBSS). Accessed at www.cdc.gov/healthyyouth/data/yrbs/index.htm on October 8, 2019.

Chawla, K. (2014, May 19). I-Team: Classrooms of fear—PTSD for teachers. Accessed at www.wafb.com/story/25556879/iteam-classrooms-of-fear-ptsd-for-teachers on October 7, 2019.

Chenoweth, K. (2007). *"It's being done": Academic success in unexpected schools.* Cambridge, MA: Harvard Education Press.

Chenoweth, K. (2009). *How it's being done: Urgent lessons from unexpected schools.* Cambridge, MA: Harvard Education Press.

Cherry, K. (2019a, September 29). *Characteristics of resilient people.* Accessed at www.verywellmind.com/characteristics-of-resilience-2795062 on October 7, 2019.

Cherry, K. (2019b, September 13). *Locus of control and your life: Are you in control of your destiny?* Accessed at www.verywellmind.com/what-is-locus-of-control-2795434 on October 7, 2019.

Child Trends. (2018). Children in working poor families. Accessed at www.childtrends.org/?indicators=children-in-working-poor-families on February 21, 2020.

Child Trends. (2019, March, 7). Adverse childhood experiences. Accessed at www.childtrends.org/?indicators=adverse-experiences on February 21, 2020.

Children's Aid Society. (2005). *Schools: The perfect place to address the needs of the whole child.* New York: Author. Accessed at https://files.eric.ed.gov/fulltext/ED499356.pdf on October 7, 2019.

Children's Aid Society. (2011). *Building community schools: A guide for action.* New York: National Center for Community Schools. Accessed at www.theoryofchange.org/wp-content/uploads/toco_library/pdf/NCCS_BuildingCommunitySchools.pdf on October 8, 2019.

Children's Defense Fund. (2015). *Ending child poverty now.* Washington, DC: Author. Accessed at www.childrensdefense.org/wp-content/uploads/2018/06/Ending-Child-Poverty-Now.pdf on October 7, 2019.

Children's Defense Fund. (2020). Our mission. Accessed at www.childrensdefense.org/about/who-we-are/our-mission/ on February 21, 2020.

Cincinnati Public Schools. (2012). *Transforming schools revitalizing neighborhoods: A guide for resource coordinators.* Cincinnati, OH: Cincinnati City School District. Accessed at www.communityschools.org/assets/1/AssetManager/Cincinnati%20CLC%20Manual%20for%20Resource%20Coordinators.pdf on October 24, 2019.

Clotfelter, C. T., Ladd, H. F., & Vigdor, J. L. (2009). *Are teacher absences worth worrying about in the U.S.?* (Working Paper No. 24). Washington, DC: Urban Institute. Accessed at www.urban.org/sites/default/files/publication/33381/1001286-Are-Teacher-Absences-Worth-Worrying-about-in-the-U-S-.PDF on October 7, 2019.

Coalition for Community Schools. (n.d). *Exhibit 3: Indicators of capacity.* Accessed at comunityschools.org/assets/1/AssetManager/Indicators%20of%20 Capacity%20-%20Results%20Framework.pdf on March 24, 2020.

Coalition for Community Schools. (2019). Accessed at www.communityschools.org/ on February 21, 2020.

Coalition for Community Schools. (2020). Community school results. Accessed at www.communityschools.org/results/ on February 20, 2020.

Cohen, R. (2003, September 4). Houston's disappearing dropouts. Accessed at www.washingtonpost.com/archive/opinions/2003/09/04/hous-tons-disappearing-dropouts/4be59aba-a857-49c9-acb0-5511c835592e /?utm_term=.b7fe40ee1581 on October 7, 2019.

Cole, S. F., Eisner, A., Gregory, M., & Ristuccia, J. (2013). *Helping traumatized children learn: Creating and advocating for trauma-sensitive schools* (Vol. 2). Boston: Massachusetts Advocates for Children. Accessed at https:// traumasensitiveschools.org/tlpi-publications/download-a-free-copy-of-a-guide-to-creating-trauma-sensitive-schools on October 7, 2019.

Cole, S. F., O'Brien, J. G., Gadd, M. G., Ristuccia, J., Wallace, D. L., & Gregory, M. (2005). *Helping traumatized children learn: A report and policy agenda* (Vol. 1). Boston: Massachusetts Advocates for Children. Accessed at https:// traumasensitiveschools.org/tlpi-publications/download-a-free-copy-of-help-ing-traumatized-children-learn on October 7, 2019.

Coleman, J. S. (1966). *Equality of educational opportunity.* Washington, DC: National Center for Educational Statistics. Accessed at https://files.eric.ed.gov/fulltext/ ED012275.pdf on October 7, 2019.

Comer, J. P., Haynes, N. M., Joyner, E. T., & Ben-Avie, M. (Eds.). (1996). *Rallying the whole village: The Comer process for reforming education.* New York: Teachers College Press.

Connecticut Education Association. (2019, Feb, 22). Crisis in the classroom: Disruptive behavior. Disrupted learning. Accessed at www.cea.org/issues/ press/2019/feb/22/crisis-in-the-classroom-disruptive-behavior-disrupted-learning.cfm on February 21, 2020.

Costa, R. (2012). *Clinical risk factors, signs, prevention, and treatment of STS in educa-tors.* Accessed at https://learn.nctsn.org/course/view.php?id=232 on October 7, 2019.

Cotton, K., & Wikelund, K. R. (1989). *Parent involvement in education.* Portland, OR: Education Northwest. Accessed at http://educationnorthwest.org/sites/

default/files/resources/parent-involvement-in-education-508.pdf on February 21, 2020.

Coyhis, D. L. (2008). *Understanding the purpose of life: 12 teachings for native youth.* Colorado Springs, CO: Coyhis.

Crotty, J. M. (2013, March 13). Motivation matters: 40% of high school students chronically disengaged from school. Accessed at www.forbes.com/sites/jamesmarshallcrotty/2013/03/13/motivation-matters-40-of-high-school-students-chronically-disengaged-from-school/#7dbe57206594 on October 7, 2019.

Damon, W. (2008). *The path to purpose: How young people find their calling in life.* New York: Free Press.

Darling-Hammond, L., & Cook-Harvey, C. M. (2018). *Educating the whole child: Improving school climate to support student success* [Research brief]. Palo Alto, CA: Learning Policy Institute. Accessed at https://learningpolicyinstitute.org/sites/default/files/product-files/Educating_Whole_Child_BRIEF.pdf on October 7, 2019.

Data Resource Center for Child and Adolescent Health. (2012). *National survey of children's health: Data query from the Child and Adolescent Health Measurement Initiative.* Baltimore: Author. Accessed at www.childhealthdata.org/browse/survey/results?q=2614&r=1 on October 8, 2019.

Dautovic, G. (2019). Automation and job loss statistics in 2020—The robots are coming. Accessed at https://fortunly.com/statistics/automation-job-loss-statistics#gref on February 21, 2020.

Deaton, A. (2018, January 24). The U.S. can no longer hide from its deep poverty problem. Accessed at www.nytimes.com/2018/01/24/opinion/poverty-united-states.html on October 7, 2019.

DeSilver, D. (2018, August 7). For most U.S. workers, real wages have barely budged in decades. Accessed at www.pewresearch.org/fact-tank/2018/08/07/for-most-us-workers-real-wages-have-barely-budged-for-decades on October 7, 2019.

Developmental Studies Center. (1996). *Ways we want our class to be: Class meetings that build commitment to kindness and learning/Ideas from the child development project.* Oakland, CA: Developmental Studies Center.

Dickler, J. (2019, September 5). Tuition-free college is now a reality in nearly 20 states. Accessed at www.cnbc.com/2019/03/12/free-college-now-a-reality-in-these-states.html on October 7, 2019.

Dizikes, P. (2016, April 11). New study shows rich, poor have huge mortality gap in U.S. Accessed at http://news.mit.edu/2016/study-rich-poor-huge-mortality-gap-us-0411 on October 7, 2019.

Donovan, T. (2008). The importance of algebra for everyone. *Focus on Basics: Connecting Research & Practice, 9*(A), 35–37. Accessed at www.ncsall.net/fileadmin/resources/fob/2008/fob_9a.pdf on February 21, 2020.

Dorado, J., & Zakrzewski, V. (2013, October 30). How to support stressed-out teachers. Accessed at https://greatergood.berkeley.edu/article/item/how_to_support_stressed_out_teachers on October 7, 2019.

Drake, S. M. (2012). *Creating standards-based integrated curriculum: The common core state standards edition* (3rd. ed.). Thousand Oaks, CA: Corwin Press.

Drake, S. M., & Burns, R. C. (2004). Meeting standards through integrated curriculum. Alexandria, VA: ASCD.

Drug Policy Alliance. (2018, January). *The drug war, mass incarceration and race.* Accessed at www.drugpolicy.org/resource/drug-war-mass-incarceration-and-race-englishspanish on October 7, 2019.

Dryfoos, J. G. (1996). Full-service schools. *Educational Leadership, 53*(7), 18–23. Accessed at www.ascd.org/publications/educational_leadership/apr96/vol53/num07/Full-Service_Schools.aspx on October 7, 2019.

Dryfoos, J. G. (1998). *Full-service schools: A revolution in health and social services for children, youth, and families.* San Francisco: Jossey-Bass.

Dryfoos, J. G. (2000). *Evaluation of community schools: Findings to date.* Washington, DC: Coalition for Community Schools. Accessed at www.communityschools.org/assets/1/AssetManager/Evaluation%20of%20Community%20Schools_joy_dryfoos.pdf on October 7, 2019.

Dryfoos, J. G. (2008). Centers of hope. *Educational Leadership, 65*(7), 38–43. Accessed at www.ascd.org/publications/educational-leadership/apr08/vol65/num07/Centers-of-Hope.aspx on October 7, 2019.

DuFour, R. (2004). What is a professional learning community? *Educational Leadership, 61*(8), 6–11. Accessed at www.ascd.org/publications/educational-leadership/may04/vol61/num08/What-Is-a-Professional-Learning-Community%C2%A2.aspx on October 7, 2019.

DuFour, R., DuFour, R., Eaker, R., & Karhanek, G. (2010). *Raising the bar and closing the gap: Whatever it takes.* Bloomington, IN: Solution Tree Press.

DuFour, R., DuFour, R., Eaker, R., Many, T., & Mattos, M. (2016). *Learning by doing: A handbook for Professional Learning Communities at Work* (3rd ed.). Bloomington, IN: Solution Tree Press.

DuFour, R., & Marzano, R. J. (2011). *Leaders of learning: How district, school, and classroom leaders improve student achievement.* Bloomington, IN: Solution Tree Press.

Durante, F., & Fiske, S. T. (2017). How social-class stereotypes maintain inequality. Accessed at www.ncbi.nlm.nih.gov/pmc/articles/PMC6020691/ on February 21, 2020.

East Carolina University. (n.d.). Teaching children in poverty certificate. Accessed at http://catalog.ecu.edu/preview_program.php?catoid=15&poid=4085 on October 24, 2019.

Eaton, D. K., Kann, L., Kinchen, S., Ross, J., Hawkins, J., Harris, W. A., et al. (2006, August). Youth risk behavior surveillance—United States, 2005. *Journal of School Health, 76*(7), 353–372. Accessed at https://doi.org/10.1111/j.1746-1561.2006.00127.x on February 21, 2020.

Eberstadt, N. (2016, September 22). America's unseen social crisis: Men without work. Accessed at https://time.com/4504004/men-without-work on October 10, 2019.

Economic Policy Institute. (n.d.). The state of working America key numbers: Poverty. Accessed at www.stateofworkingamerica.org/fact-sheets/poverty on October 7, 2019.

The Economist. (2019, November 27). Why are Americans' lives getting shorter? Accessed at https://www.economist.com/graphic-detail/2019/11/27/why-are-americans-lives-getting-shorter on February 21, 2020.

Edelman, M. W. (2014, September 19). The high moral and economic cost of child poverty in America. Accessed at www.childrensdefense.org/child-watch-columns/health/2014/the-high-moral-and-economic-cost-of-child-poverty-in-america on October 7, 2019.

The Education Trust. (1999). Ticket to nowhere: The gap between leaving high school and entering college and high-performance jobs. *Thinking K–16, 3*(2). Accessed at http://edtrust.org/wp-content/uploads/2013/10/k16_fall99.pdf on October 7, 2019.

The Education Trust. (2005). *The power to change: High schools that help all students achieve.* Washington, DC: Author. Accessed at https://edtrust.org/wp-content/uploads/2013/10/ThePowerToChange.pdf on October 7, 2019.

Elgart, M. A. (2017). *The impact of poverty on education.* Accessed at www.advanced.org/source/ceo-message-its-about-poverty-not-race on October 7, 2019.

Elias, M. (2013). The school-to-prison pipeline. Accessed at www.tolerance.org/mag-azine/spring-2013/the-schooltoprison-pipeline on October 7, 2019.

Entwisle, D. R., Alexander, K. L., & Olson, L. S. (2000). Summer learning and home environment. In R. D. Kahlenberg (Ed.), *A notion at risk: Preserving public education as an engine for social mobility* (pp. 9–30). New York: Century Foundation Press.

Epstein, J. L. (2011). *School, family, and community partnerships: Preparing educators and improving schools* (2nd ed.). New York: Routledge.

Evans, L. (1997). Understanding teacher morale and job satisfaction. *Teaching and Teacher Education, 13*(8), 831–845.

Family Access Network. (n.d.). The Family Access Network (FAN). Accessed at https://familyaccessnetwork.org/about/ on February 21, 2020.

Fashola, O. S. (2002). *Building effective afterschool programs.* Thousand Oaks, CA: Corwin Press.

Felitti, V. J., Anda, R. F., Nordenberg, D., Williamson, D. F., Spitz, A. M., Edwards, V., et al. (1998, May). Relationship of childhood abuse and household dysfunction to many of the leading causes of death in adults: The adverse childhood experiences (ACE) study. *American Journal of Preventive Medicine, 14*(4), 245–258. Accessed at https://doi.org/10.1016/S0749-3797(98)00017-8 on February 21, 2020.

Fight for $15. (n.d.). About us. Accessed at https://fightfor15.org/ on October 7, 2019.

Finley, T. (2017, October 30). Are you at risk for secondary traumatic stress? Accessed at www.edutopia.org/article/are-you-risk-secondary-traumatic-stress on October 7, 2019.

Firth, P. (2014, September 8). Homelessness and academic achievement: The impact of childhood stress on school performance. Accessed at http://firesteelwa.org/2014/09/homelessness-and-academic-achievement-the-impact-of-child-hood-stress-on-school-performance/ on February 21, 2020.

FirstGEN Fellows. (2014). FirstGEN nonprofits. Accessed at http://firstgenfellows.org/first-generation-college-student-links on October 8, 2019.

Fletcher, R., & Portalupi, J. (2001). *Writing workshop: The essential guide.* Portsmouth, NH: Heinemann.

Fontenot, K., Semega, J., & Kollar, M. (2018, September). *Income and poverty in the United States: 2017* (Report No. P60-263). Washington, DC: U.S. Census Bureau. Accessed at www.census.gov/library/publications/2018/demo/p60-263.html on October 8, 2019.

Frankel, M. (2001). *Growing resilient children.* Accessed at http://toolsforliferesources. com/wp-content/uploads/2013/12/Resilient-children.pdf on October 8, 2019.

Gallup. (n.d.). Build engaged and thriving schools. Accessed at www.gallup.com/ education/227657/improve-k-12.aspx on October 8, 2019.

Gallup. (2017). *2016 Gallup student poll: A snapshot of results and findings.* Accessed at www.sac.edu/research/PublishingImages/Pages/research-studies/2016%20 Gallup%20Student%20Poll%20Snapshot%20Report%20Final.pdf on October 8, 2019.

GAP Report. (2017). GAP Report on housing. Accessed at https://nlihc.org/gap on February 21, 2020.

Garbarino, J., Dubrow,N., Kostelny, K., & Pardo, C. (1992). *Children in danger: Coping with the consequences of community violence.* San Francisco: Jossey-Bass.

Garmezy, N. (1991). Resilience and vulnerability to adverse developmental outcomes associated with poverty. *American Behavioral Scientist, 34*(4), 416–430.

Garmezy, N. (1993). Children in poverty: Resilience despite risk. *Psychiatry: Interpersonal and Biological Processes, 56*(1), 127–136.

Gibson, E. L., & Barr, R. D. (2015). Building a culture of hope for youth at risk: Supporting learners with optimism, place, pride, and purpose. *National Youth-At-Risk Journal, 1*(1). Accessed at https://doi.org/10.20429/ nyarj.2015.010103 on October 8, 2019.

Gibson, E. L., & Barr, R. D. (2017). Building a culture of hope: Exploring implicit biases against poverty. *National Youth-At-Risk Journal, 2*(2). Accessed at https://doi.org/10.20429/nyarj.2017.020203 on October 8, 2019.

Gilens, M., & Page, B. I. (2014). Testing theories of America politics: Elites, interest groups, and average citizens. *Perspectives on Politics, 12*(3), 564–581. Accessed at www.cambridge.org/core/journals/perspectives-on-politics/article/testing-theories-of-american-politics-elites-interest-groups-and-average-citizens/623 27F513959D0A304D4893B382B992B/core-reader on February 21, 2020.

Given, B. K. (2002). *Teaching to the brain's natural learning systems.* Alexandria, VA: Association for Supervision and Curriculum Development.

Goodreads. (n.d.a). Fred Rogers quotes. Accessed at www.goodreads.com/author/ quotes/32106.Fred_Rogers on October 24, 2019.

Goodreads. (n.d.b). James Baldwin quotes. Accessed at www.goodreads.com/author/ quotes/10427.James_Baldwin on October 24, 2019.

Gorman, L. (2006). Why poverty persists. Accessed at www.nber.org/digest/jun06/w11681.html on October 8, 2019.

Gorski, P. C. (2007). The question of class. *Teaching Tolerance, 31*, 26–29. Accessed at www.tolerance.org/magazine/spring-2007/the-question-of-class on October 8, 2019.

Gorski, P. C. (2008). The myth of the culture of poverty. *Educational Leadership, 65*(7), 32–36. Accessed at www.ascd.org/publications/educational-leadership/apr08/vol65/num07/The-Myth-of-the-Culture-of-Poverty.aspx on February 21, 2020.

Gorski, P. C. (2012). Perceiving the problem of poverty and schooling: Deconstructing the class stereotypes that mis-shape education practice and policy. *Equity & Excellence in Education, 45*(2), 302–319.

Gorski, P. C. (2013). *Reaching and teaching students in poverty: Strategies for erasing the opportunity gap.* New York: Teachers College Press.

Green, E. L., & Waldman, A. (2018, December 28). "I feel invisible": Native students languish in public schools. Accessed at www.nytimes.com/2018/12/28/us/native-american-education.html on October 8, 2019.

Greene, R. W. (2008). *Lost at school: Why our kids with behavioral challenges are falling through the cracks and how we can help them.* New York: Scribner.

Gunn, J. (2018a, July 19). How teachers can practice self-care for long-term health and wellness [Blog post]. Accessed at https://education.cu-portland.edu/blog/lifestyle/teacher-health-wellness-resources on October 8, 2019.

Gunn, J. (2018b, June 22). Self-care for teachers of traumatized students [Blog post]. Accessed at https://education.cu-portland.edu/blog/classroom-resources/self-care-for-teachers on October 8, 2019.

Gurwitch, R. (2012). Self-care: One of the hardest activities after crisis events. Accessed at https://learn.nctsn.org/course/view.php?id=232 on October 8, 2019.

Guskey, T. R. (2010). Lessons of mastery learning. *Educational Leadership, 68*(2), 52–57. Accessed at www.ascd.org/publications/educational-leadership/oct10/vol68/num02/Lessons-of-Mastery-Learning.aspx on October 8, 2019.

Gutierrez, L. (2018, December 12). Lily the Muppet returns to "Sesame Street," and now she's homeless. Accessed at www.charlotteobserver.com/news/nation-world/national/article222991165.html on October 8, 2019.

Hammond, Z. (2015). *Culturally responsive teaching and the brain: Promoting authentic engagement and rigor among culturally and linguistically diverse students.* Thousand Oaks, CA: Corwin Press.

Hansen, S. (2017, August 28). Resilience cannot be learned. Accessed at https://
resiliencei.com/2017/08/resilience-cannot-learned/ on April 14, 2020.

Hanson, K. (2009, October 24). What exactly is hope and how can you measure it?
Accessed at http://positivepsychology.org.uk/hope-theory-snyder-adult-scale
on October 8, 2019.

Hanson, T. L., & Kim, J. (2007, September). *Measuring resilience and youth development: The psychometric properties of the Healthy Kids Survey* (Issues &
Answers Report, REL 2007–No. 034). Washington, DC: U.S. Department
of Education. Accessed at https://ies.ed.gov/ncee/edlabs/regions/west/pdf/
REL_2007034.pdf on October 8, 2019.

Harris, K. R., Graham, S., Mason, L. H., & Friedlander, B. (2008). *Powerful writing
strategies for all students.* Baltimore: Brookes.

Hart, B., & Risley, T. R. (1995). *Meaningful differences in the everyday experience
of young American children.* Baltimore: Brookes. Accessed at https://search.
proquest.com/openview/c3ffc4660038587372a496029eef7b6a/1?pq-
origsite=gscholar on October 8, 2019.

Heacox, D. (2002). *Differentiating instruction in the regular classroom: How to reach
and teach all learners, grades 3–12.* Minneapolis, MN: Free Spirit.

Healy, M. (2014, July 10). The resilient child: Can your child bounce back from
failure? [Blog post]. Accessed at www.psychologytoday.com/us/blog/creative-
development/201407/the-resilient-child on October 8, 2019.

Hechinger Report. (2011). Why school leadership matters. Accessed at https://hech-
ingerreport.org/why-school-leadership-matters/ on February 21, 2020.

Heick, T. (2013, September 24). 6 proposals for improving teacher morale [Blog
post]. Accessed at www.edutopia.org/blog/proposals-for-improving-teacher-
morale-terry-heick on October 8, 2019.

Henderson, N. (2012). *The resiliency workbook: Bounce back stronger, smarter and
with real self-esteem.* Solvang, CA: Resiliency in Action. Accessed at www.
resiliency.com/products/the-resiliency-workbook on October 8, 2019.

Henderson, N. (2013). Havens of resilience. *Educational Leadership, 71*(1), 22–27.
Accessed at www.ascd.org/publications/educational-leadership/sept13/vol71/
num01/Havens-of-Resilience.aspx on October 8, 2019.

Henderson, N., & Milstein, M. M. (2003). *Resiliency in schools: Making it happen for
students and educators* (Updated ed.). Thousand Oaks, CA: Corwin Press.

Hodges, T. (2015, February 26). Six things the most engaged schools do differently [Blog post]. Accessed at https://news.gallup.com/opinion/gallup/181751/six-things-engaged-schools-differently.aspx on October 8, 2019.

Hodges, T. (2016, August 31). Student hope, engagement as important as graduation rates [Blog post]. Accessed at https://news.gallup.com/opinion/gallup/195248/student-hope-engagement-important-graduation-rates.aspx on October 8, 2019.

Hodges, T. (2018, August 30). U.S. superintendents challenged to find, keep good teachers. Accessed at www.gallup.com/education/241796/superintendents-challenged-find-keep-good-teachers.aspx on October 8, 2019.

Hodgkinson, H. L. (1989). *The same client: The demographics of education and service delivery systems.* Washington, DC: Institute for Educational Leadership. Accessed at https://files.eric.ed.gov/fulltext/ED312757.pdf on October 8, 2019.

Hope Survey. (2018). Supporting research. Accessed at www.hopesurvey.org/supporting-research on October 8, 2019.

Hoynes, H. (2012, April). *Poverty: Facts, causes and consequences.* Accessed at https://gspp.berkeley.edu/assets/uploads/faculty/customtab/Hoynes-Poverty-Inequality-4-13-12.pdf on October 8, 2019.

Hoynes, H., Page, M. E., & Stevens, A. H. (2006). Poverty in America: Trends and explanations. *Journal of Economic Perspectives, 20*(1), 47–68.

Hughes, K., Bellis, M. A., Hardcastle, K., Sethi, D., Butchart, A., Mikton, C., et al. (2017). The effect of multiple adverse childhood experiences on health: A systematic review and meta-analysis. *The Lancet: Public Health, 2*(8), 356–366.

Hughes, M., & Tucker, W. (2018, March–April). Poverty as an adverse childhood experience. *North Carolina Medical Journal, 79*(2), 124–126.

Huitt, W. (2007). Maslow's hierarchy of needs. Accessed at http://www.edpsycinteractive.org/topics/conation/maslow.html on February 21, 2020.

Hydon, S., Wong, M., Langley, A. K., Stein, B. D., & Kataoka, S. H. (2015). Preventing secondary traumatic stress in educators. *Child and Adolescent Psychiatric Clinics of North America, 24*(2), 319–333.

Ingrum, A. (2006). High school dropout determinants: The effect of poverty and learning disabilities. *The Park Place Economist, 14*(1), 73–79. Accessed at https://digitalcommons.iwu.edu/parkplace/vol14/iss1/16 on October 8, 2019.

IRIS Center. (2019). SRSD: Using learning strategies to enhance student learning [Module]. Nashville, TN: Vanderbilt University. Accessed at https://iris.peabody.vanderbilt.edu/module/srs/#content on October 24, 2019.

Isaacs, J. B. (2012, March). Starting school at a disadvantage: The school readiness of poor children. Accessed at www.brookings.edu/research/starting-school-at-a-disadvantage-the-school-readiness-of-poor-children/ on February 21, 2020.

Jacobs, T. (2018). New research debunks the upward mobility myth. Accessed at https://psmag.com/economics/new-research-debunks-the-upward-mobility-myth on February 21, 2020.

Janosko, J. (2019). Poverty is down—but concerns about homelessness remain up. Accessed at https://endhomelessness.org/poverty-is-down-but-concerns-about-homelessness-remain-up/ on February 21, 2020.

Jennings, P. A. (2018a, November 14). Changing how educators see negative experiences in the classroom. Accessed at www.kqed.org/mindshift/52402/changing-how-educators-see-negative-experiences-in-the-classroom on October 8, 2019.

Jennings, P. A. (2018b). *The trauma-sensitive classroom: Building resilience with compassionate teaching.* New York: Norton.

Jensen, E. (n.d.a). Why "cross your fingers and hope for the best" is actually great advice. Accessed at www.jensenlearning.com/cross-your-fingers-and-hope-for-the-best on October 8, 2019.

Jensen, E. (n.d.b). How are kids from poverty different and what do the differences suggest we can do about it? Accessed at www.brainbasedlearning.net/how-are-kids-from-poverty-different/ on February 21, 2020.

Jensen, E. (2009). *Teaching with poverty in mind: What being poor does to kids' brains and what schools can do about it.* Alexandria, VA: Association for Supervision and Curriculum Development.

Jensen, E. (2013). *Engaging students with poverty in mind: Practical strategies for raising achievement.* Alexandria, VA: Association for Supervision and Curriculum Development.

Jensen, E. (2019). *Poor students, rich teaching: Seven high-impact mindsets for students from poverty* (Rev. ed.). Bloomington, IN: Solution Tree Press.

Johnson, L. B. (1964, January 8). *First State of the Union address.* Accessed at www.americanrhetoric.com/speeches/lbj1964stateoftheunion.htm on October 8, 2019.

Joseph, N., Waymack, N., & Zielaski, D. (2014, June). *Roll call: The importance of teacher attendance.* Washington, DC: National Council on Teacher Quality. Accessed at www.nctq.org/dmsView/RollCall_TeacherAttendance on October 8, 2019.

Kenneally, B. (2018). *Upstate girls: Unraveling Collar City.* New York: Regan Arts.

Kinkade, L. (2018, June 22). America's poor becoming more destitute under Trump, UN report says. Accessed at www.cnn.com/2018/06/22/us/america-poverty-un-report/index.html on October 8, 2019.

Klitsch, S. (2010). Beyond the basics: How extracurricular activities can benefit foster youth. *National Center for Youth Law Newsletter, XXIX*(4). Accessed at https://youthlaw.org/publication/beyond-the-basics-how-extracurricular-activities-can-benefit-foster-youth/ on February 21, 2020.

Kohl, H. R. (1967). *Thirty-six children: Innovations in education.* New York: New American Library.

Kohl, H. R. (1994). *"I won't learn from you" and other thoughts on creative maladjustment.* New York: New Press.

Kohl, H. R. (1998). *The discipline of hope: Learning from a lifetime of teaching.* New York: New Press.

Konnikova, M. (2016, February 11). How people learn to become resilient. Accessed at www.newyorker.com/science/maria-konnikova/the-secret-formula-for-resilience on October 8, 2019.

Korball, H., & Jian, Y. (2018). Basic facts about low-income children: Children under 18 years, 2016. Accessed at www.nccp.org/publications/pub_1194.html on February 21, 2020.

Kozol, J. (2005). *The shame of the nation: The restoration of apartheid schooling in America.* New York: Crown.

Kremer, K. P., Maynard, B. R., Polanin, J. R., Vaughn, M. G., & Sarteschi, C. M. (2015, March). Effects of after-school programs with at-risk youth on attendance and externalizing behaviors: A systematic review and meta-analysis. *Journal of Youth and Adolescence, 44*(3), 616–636. Accessed at www.ncbi.nlm.nih.gov/pmc/articles/PMC4597889/ on February 21, 2020.

Kris, D. F. (2018, December 2). How to build a trauma-sensitive classroom where all learners feel safe. Accessed at www.kqed.org/mindshift/52566/how-to-build-a-trauma-sensitive-classroom-where-all-learners-feel-safe on October 8, 2019.

Kuhfeld, M. (2018a, September 4). Summer learning loss: Does it widen the achievement gap? [Blog post]. Accessed at www.nwea.org/blog/2018/summer-learning-loss-does-it-widen-the-achievement-gap on October 8, 2019.

Kuhfeld, M. (2018b, July 16). Summer learning loss: What we know and what we're learning [Blog post]. Accessed at www.nwea.org/blog/2018/summer-learning-loss-what-we-know-what-were-learning on October 8, 2019.

Lambert, L. (2002). A framework for shared leadership. *Educational Leadership, 59*(8), 37–40. Accessed at www.ascd.org/publications/educational-leadership/

may02/vol59/num08/A-Framework-for-Shared-Leadership.aspx on October 8, 2019.

Lander, J. (2018, September 26). Helping teachers manage the weight of trauma: Understanding and mitigating the effects of secondary traumatic stress for educators [Blog post]. Accessed at www.gse.harvard.edu/news/uk/18/09/helping-teachers-manage-weight-trauma on October 8, 2019.

Larson, M. R., & Kanold, T. D. (2016). *Balancing the equation: A guide to school mathematics for educators and parents.* Bloomington, IN: Solution Tree Press.

Learning Forward. (n.d.). ESSA and professional learning. Accessed at https://learningforward.org/get-involved/essa on October 24, 2019.

Lezotte, L. W., & Snyder, K. M. (2011). *What effective schools do: Re-envisioning the correlates.* Bloomington, IN: Solution Tree Press.

Lieb, D. A. (2018, December 30). 2019: Minimum wage rising in 20 states and numerous cities. Accessed at www.ktvb.com/article/news/nation/2019-minimum-wage-rising-in-20-states-and-numerous-cities/277-f6044884-2b33-45bd-bdf3-f8a54a1b48fe on October 8, 2019.

Liew, J., & McTigue, E. M. (2010). Educating the whole child: The role of social and emotional development in achievement and school success. In L. E. Kattington (Ed.), *Handbook of Curriculum Development* (pp. 465–478). Hauppauge, NY: Nova Sciences Publishers, Inc.

Lindsey, D. (2009). *Child poverty and inequality: Securing a better future for America's children.* New York: Oxford University Press.

Litvinov, A. (2019). K–12 public schools: Our crumbling, critical infrastructure. *NEA Today, 37*(3). Accessed at www.nea.org/home/74479.htm on February 21, 2020.

Logan, J. A. R., Justice, L. M., Yumus, M., & Chaparro-Moreno, L. J. (2019, March 20). When children are not read to at home: The million word gap. *Journal of Developmental & Behavioral Pediatrics.* Accessed at www.readingrockets.org/research/topic/parent_engagement on February 21, 2020.

Lopez, S. (2009). *Gallup student poll national report.* Washington, DC: Gallup. Accessed at www.americaspromise.org/sites/default/files/d8/legacy/bodyfiles/GSP%20National%20Report.pdf on October 8, 2019.

Lopez, S. (2018a, November 28). Must reads: For children trapped in poverty, breaking free is getting harder. Accessed at www.latimes.com/local/california/la-me-california-poverty-suburbs-homeless-part4-20181128-htmlstory.html on October 23, 2019.

Lopez, S. (2018b, November 25). Must reads: Hidden in L.A. suburbia, wrenching poverty preys on children and destroys dreams. Accessed at www.latimes.com/local/california/la-me-california-poverty-suburbs-homeless-part1-20181125-htmlstory.html on October 23, 2019.

Loschert, K. (2017, April 7). Why a high school diploma alone no longer guarantees career success. Accessed at https://all4ed.org/why-a-high-school-diploma-alone-no-longer-guarantees-career-success/ on February 21, 2020.

Losen, D. J., & Whitaker, A. (2018, August). *11 million days lost: Race, discipline, and safety at U.S. public schools (part 1)*. New York: American Civil Liberties Union. Accessed at https://aclu.org/sites/default/files/field_document/final_11-million-days_ucla_aclu.pdf on October 10, 2019.

Lynch, M. (2014, May 30). High school dropout rate: Causes and costs. Accessed at www.huffingtonpost.com/matthew-lynch-edd/high-school-dropout-rate_b_5421778.html on October 8, 2019.

MacCallum, N. (2017). *Building resiliency: Effective management of vicarious trauma and secondary traumatic stress* [Webinar]. San Francisco, CA: Family Resource Centers Network of California. Accessed at www.frcnca.org/wp-content/uploads/2019/03/Building-Resiliency-webinar-version-3.13.19.pdf on February 21, 2020.

MacDorman, M. F., Mathews, T. J., Mohangoo, A. D., & Zeitlin, J. (2014). *International comparisons of infant mortality and related factors: United States and Europe, 2010. National Vital Statistics Reports, 63*(5), 1–6. Accessed at https://www.cdc.gov/nchs/data/nvsr/nvsr63/nvsr63_05.pdf on February 21, 2020.

Mader, J. (2017, October 31). New research finds it hasn't gotten easier for poor kids to catch up. Accessed at https://hechingerreport.org/new-research-finds-hasnt-gotten-easier-poor-kids-catch/ on February 21, 2020.

Maier, A., Daniel, J., & Oakes, J. (2017). *Community schools as an effective school improvement strategy: A review of the evidence* [Research brief]. Palo Alto, CA: Learning Policy Institute. Accessed at learningpolicyinstitute.org/sites/default/files/product-files/Community_Schools_Effective_BRIEF.pdf on October 8, 2019.

Maslow, A. H. (1970). *Motivation and personality* (2nd ed.). New York: Harper & Row.

Mead, S. (n.d.). 7 key characteristics of resilient children [Blog post]. Accessed at www.whitbyschool.org/passionforlearning/7-key-characteristics-of-resilient-children on October 8, 2019.

Melnick, H., Cook-Harvey, C. M., & Darling-Hammond, L. (2017, April). *Encouraging social and emotional learning in the context of new accountability.* Palo Alto, CA: Learning Policy Institute.

Michell, M. (2018, October 24). Intervention vs. remediation: What's the difference? [Blog post]. Accessed at https://blog.edmentum.com/intervention-vs-remediation-what%E2%80%99s-difference on October 24, 2019.

Miller, R. T., Murnane, R. J., & Willett, J. B. (2007, August). *Do teacher absences impact student achievement? Longitudinal evidence from one urban school district* (Working Paper No. 13356). Cambridge, MA: National Bureau of Economic Research. Accessed at www.nctq.org/nctq/research/1190910822841.pdf on October 8, 2019.

Mind Tools Content Team. (n.d.). Burnout self-test: Checking yourself for burnout. Accessed at www.mindtools.com/pages/article/newTCS_08.htm on October 24, 2019.

Mishel, L., Gould, E., & Bivens, J. (2015, January 6). Wage stagnation in nine charts. Accessed at www.epi.org/publication/charting-wage-stagnation on October 8, 2019.

Moore, K. A., Redd, Z., Burkhauser, M., Mbwana, K., & Collins, A. (2009, April). *Children in poverty: Trends, consequences, and policy options.* Washington, DC: Child Trends. Accessed at www.childtrends.org/wp-content/uploads/2013/11/2009-11ChildreninPoverty.pdf on October 8, 2019.

Morgan, I., & Amerikaner, A. (2018). Funding gaps, 2018. Accessed at https://edtrust.org/resource/funding-gaps-2018/ on February 21, 2020.

Mui, Y. Q. (2016, May 25). The shocking number of Americans who can't cover a $400 expense. Accessed at www.washingtonpost.com/news/wonk/wp/2016/05/25/the-shocking-number-of-americans-who-cant-cover-a-400-expense/?utm_term=.a8569302a80d on October 8, 2019.

Multnomah County. (2020). SUN community schools. Accessed at https://multco.us/sun/sun-community-schools on February 21, 2020.

Murphy, J., & Torre, D. (2014). *Creating productive cultures in schools: For students, teachers, and parents.* Corwin Press, Thousand Oaks, CA.

Nadasen, P. (2017, December 21). Extreme poverty returns to America. Accessed at www.washingtonpost.com/news/made-by-history/wp/2017/12/21/extreme-poverty-returns-to-america/?utm_term=.12f1f09cc262 on October 8, 2019.

National Academies of Sciences, Engineering, and Medicine. (2019). *Shaping summertime experiences: Opportunities to promote healthy development and well-being for children and youth.* Washington, DC: The National Academies Press. Accessed at https://doi.org/10.17226/25546 on February 21, 2020.

National Alliance to End Homelessness. (2018). *Family homelessness in the United States: A state-by-state snapshot.* Washington, DC: Author. Accessed at https://endhomelessness.org/resource/family-homelessness-in-the-united-states-state-by-state-snapshot on October 8, 2019.

National Center for Children in Poverty. (2017, February 10). Study: American children have a 43% chance of being born into poverty. Accessed at www.mintpressnews.com/study-american-children-have-a-43-chance-of-being-born-into-poverty/224792 on October 8, 2019.

National Center for Education Statistics. (n.d.). Fast facts: Graduation rates. Accessed at https://nces.ed.gov/fastfacts/display.asp?id=40 on October 8, 2019.

National Child Traumatic Stress Network. (n.d.). Secondary traumatic stress. Accessed at www.nctsn.org/trauma-informed-care/secondary-traumatic-stress on October 8, 2019.

National Commission on Teaching and America's Future. (2016). *What matters now: A new compact for teaching and learning.* Arlington, VA: Author. Accessed at https://files.eric.ed.gov/fulltext/ED572506.pdf on October 8, 2019.

National Conference of State Legislatures. (2019, June). Youth homelessness overview. Accessed at www.ncsl.org/research/human-services/homeless-and-runaway-youth.aspx on October 8, 2019.

National Council of Juvenile and Family Court Judges. (2006, October 24). Finding your ACE score. Accessed at www.ncjfcj.org/publications/finding-your-ace-score/ on February 21, 2020.

National Council of Teachers of Mathematics. (2014). *Principles to actions: Ensuring mathematical success for all.* Reston, VA: Author.

National Dropout Prevention Center. (n.d.a). Effective strategies. Accessed at http://dropoutprevention.org/effective-strategies on October 24, 2019.

National Dropout Prevention Center. (n.d.b). *Five attributes of resilience (RICCO).* Accessed at https://dropoutprevention.org/wp-content/uploads/2015/05/RICCO_Chart-Marty.pdf on October 10, 2019.

National Education Association. (n.d.a). Community schools: All together now! Accessed at www.nea.org/home/66319.htm on October 8, 2019.

National Education Association. (n.d.b). *The six pillars of community schools toolkit: NEA resource guide for educators, families, and communities.* Washington,

DC: Author. Accessed at www.nea.org/assets/docs/Comm%20Schools%20
ToolKit-final%20digi-web-72617.pdf on October 8, 2019.

National Education Association. (2011). *C.A.R.E.: Strategies for closing the achieve-ment gaps* (4th ed.). Washington, DC: Author. Accessed at www.nea.org/
assets/docs/CAREguide2011.pdf on October 24, 2019.

National Education Association. (2016). *Backgrounder: Students from pov-erty*. Washington, DC: Author. Accessed at www.nea.org/assets/docs/
Backgrounder_Students%20from%20poverty_online.pdf on October 8, 2019.

National Governors Association Center for Best Practices & Council of Chief
State School Officers. (2010a). *Common Core State Standards for English
language arts and literacy in history/social studies, science, and technical sub-jects*. Washington, DC: Authors. Accessed at www.corestandards.org/assets/
CCSSI_ELA%20Standards.pdf on October 24, 2019.

National Governors Association Center for Best Practices & Council of Chief State
School Officers. (2010b). *Common Core State Standards for mathematics*.
Washington, DC: Authors. Accessed at www.corestandards.org/assets/
CCSSI_Math%20Standards.pdf on October 24, 2019.

National Low Income Housing Coalition. (2019, March). The gap: A shortage of
affordable rental homes. Accessed at https://nlihc.org/gap on October 8,
2019.

National Research Council and Institute of Medicine. (2010). *Student mobility:
Exploring the impacts of frequent moves on achievement: Summary of a work-shop*. Washington, DC: The National Academies Press.

National School Climate Center. (n.d.). Measuring school climate (CSCI). Accessed
at www.schoolclimate.org/services/measuring-school-climate-csci on
October 24, 2019.

Nelson, J., Lott, L., & Glenn, H. S. (2013). *Positive discipline in the classroom:
Developing mutual respect, cooperation, and responsibility in your classroom*
(Rev. 4th ed.). Roseville, CA: Prima.

Newell, R. J., & Van Ryzin, M. J. (2007). Growing hope as a determinant of school
effectiveness. *Phi Delta Kappan, 88*(6), 465–471.

Newell, R. J., & Van Ryzin, M. J. (2009). *Assessing what really matters in schools:
Creating hope for the future*. Lanham, MD: Rowman & Littlefield.

NGSS Lead States. (2013). *Next Generation Science Standards: For states, by states*.
Washington, DC: The National Academies Press.

Noble, K. G., Houston, S. M., Brito, N. H., Bartsch, H., Kan, E., Kuperman, J. M., et al. (2015). Family income, parental education and brain structure in children and adolescents. *Nature Neuroscience, 18,* 773–778.

Noble, K. G., Norman, M. F., & Farah, M. J. (2005). Neurocognitive correlates of socioeconomic status in kindergarten children. *Developmental Science, 8*(1), 74–87.

November, A. (2011, March). *TEDxNYED—Alan November* [Video file]. Accessed at https://novemberlearning.com/educational-resources-for-educators/videos/tedxnyed-alan-november on October 8, 2019.

November, A. (2012). *Who owns the learning? Preparing students for success in the digital age.* Bloomington, IN: Solution Tree Press.

Oakes, J., Maier, A., & Daniels, J. (2017). *Community schools: An evidence-based strategy for equitable school improvement.* Boulder, CO: National Education Policy Center, and Washington, DC: Learning Policy Institute. Accessed at https://learningpolicyinstitute.org/sites/default/files/product-files/Community_Schools_Evidence_Based_Strategy_BRIEF.pdf on February 21, 2020.

Olen, H. (2018, October 3). Donald Trump's grotesque fraud [Blog post]. Accessed at www.washingtonpost.com/blogs/post-partisan/wp/2018/10/03/donald-trumps-grotesque-fraud on October 24, 2019.

Oregon Education Association. (n.d.). Educator stories: Disrupted learning environments. Accessed at www.todaysoea.org/articles/educator-stories-disrupted-learning-environments on October 8, 2019.

Osler, J. (2007). *A guide for integrating issues of social and economic justice into mathematics curriculum.* Accessed at www.radicalmath.org/docs/SJMathGuide.pdf on February 21, 2020.

Parrett, W. H., & Budge, K. M. (2012). *Turning high-poverty schools into high-performing schools.* Alexandria, VA: Association for Supervision and Curriculum Development.

Parrett, W. H., & Budge, K. M. (2015, December 10). What can schools do to address poverty? [Blog post]. Accessed at www.edutopia.org/blog/what-can-schools-do-to-address-poverty-william-parrett-kathleen-budge on October 7, 2019.

Patterson, J. L., & Kelleher, P. (2005). *Resilient school leaders: Strategies for turning adversity into achievement.* Alexandria, VA: Association for Supervision and Curriculum Development.

PBLWorks. (n.d.). What is PBL? Accessed at www.pblworks.org/what-is-pbl on October 24, 2019.

Pennsylvania Community of Practice. (2018, May). *Alignment of the PBIS framework and trauma informed classrooms/trauma sensitive schools.* Accessed at https://intranet.bloomu.edu/documents/mcdowell/pk12/AlignmentPBISTraumaInfCare.pdf on February 21, 2020.

Perma, D. M., & Davis, J. R. (2006). *Aligning standards and curriculum for classroom success* (2nd ed.). Thousand Oaks, CA: Corwin Press.

Perry, B. D. (2002). Neurodevelopmental impact of violence in childhood. In D. H. Schetky & E. P. Benedek (Eds.), *Principles and practice of child and adolescent forensic psychiatry* (pp. 191–203). Washington, DC: American Psychiatric Association.

Pink, D. H. (2009). *Drive: The surprising truth about what motivates us.* New York: Riverhead Books.

Podolsky, A., Kini, T., Bishop, J., & Darling-Hammond, L. (2016). *Solving the teacher shortage: How to attract and retain excellent educators* [Research brief]. Palo Alto, CA: Learning Policy Institute. Accessed at https://learningpolicyinstitute.org/sites/default/files/product-files/Solving_Teacher_Shortage_Attract_Retain_Educators_BRIEF.pdf on October 8, 2019.

Powell, R. R., Zehm, S. J., & Kottler, J. A. (1995). *Classrooms under the influence: Addicted families, addicted students.* Newbury Park, CA: Corwin Press.

PowerQuotations (n.d). Quote by Woodrow T. Wilson. Accessed at powerquotations.com/quote/it-is-easier-to-change on March 24, 2020.

Pressman, S. (2018, September 12). The range of poverty in America. Accessed at www.usnews.com/news/healthiest-communities/articles/2018-09-12/poverty-in-america-new-census-data-paint-an-unpleasant-picture on October 8, 2019.

Provini, C. (2012). Best practices for professional learning communities. Accessed at https://www.educationworld.com/a_admin/best-practices-for-professional-learning-communities.shtml on February 21, 2020.

Public Schools First. (2016, September 1). The facts on child poverty. Accessed at www.publicschoolsfirstnc.org/resources/fact-sheets/the-facts-on-child-poverty on October 8, 2019.

Quaglia, R. J. (n.d.). Five things I've learned. Accessed at www.thefivethings.org/russell-j-quaglia/index.html on October 8, 2019.

Quinn, D. M., & Polikoff, M. (2017, September). Summer learning loss: What is it, and what can we do about it? Accessed at www.brookings.edu/research/

summer-learning-loss-what-is-it-and-what-can-we-do-about-it on October 8, 2019.

Quinn, J. (2011). Introduction: Every school a community school—The vision becomes reality. In Children's Aid Society, *Building community schools: A guide for action* (pp. vii–ix). New York: National Center for Community Schools. Accessed at www.theoryofchange.org/wp-content/uploads/toco_library/pdf/NCCS_BuildingCommunitySchools.pdf on October 8, 2019.

Radford, J. (2019, June 17). Key findings about U.S. immigrants. Accessed at www.pewresearch.org/fact-tank/2019/06/17/key-findings-about-u-s-immigrants on October 8, 2019.

Rank, M. R. (2005). *One nation, underprivileged: Why American poverty affects us all.* New York: Oxford University Press.

Rasmussen, K. (1998). Looping: Discovering the benefits of multiyear teaching. *ASCD Education Update, 40*(2). Accessed at www.ascd.org/publications/newsletters/education-update/mar98/vol40/num02/Looping.aspx on October 8, 2019.

Ratcliffe, C., & Kalish, E. (2017). *Escaping poverty: Predictors of persistently poor children's economic success.* Washington, DC: U.S. Partnership on Mobility From Poverty. Accessed at www.urban.org/sites/default/files/publication/90321/escaping-poverty.pdf on October 8, 2019.

Ratcliffe, C., & McKernan, S. (2010). *Childhood poverty persistence: Facts and consequences.* Washington, DC: Urban Institute. Accessed at www.urban.org/sites/default/files/publication/32926/412126-childhood-poverty-persistence-facts-and-consequences.pdf on October 8, 2019.

Ratcliffe, C., & McKernan, S. (2012). *Child poverty and its lasting consequence.* Washington, DC: Urban Institute. Accessed at www.urban.org/UploadedPDF/412659-Child-Poverty-and-Its-Lasting-Consequence-Paper.pdf on October 10, 2019.

Rebora, A. (2018). Perspectives: Recruitment, retention, and resilience. *Educational Leadership, 75*(8), 7. Accessed at www.ascd.org/publications/educational-leadership/may18/vol75/num08/Recruitment,-Retention,-and-Resilience.aspx on October 8, 2019.

Robinson, R. (2018). *Implementing a culture of care.* Professional development workshop presented at Bend-La Pine Schools professional development day, Bend, Oregon.

Roehlkepartain, E., Pekel, K., Syvertsen, A., Sethi, J., Sullivan, T., & Scales, P. (2017). *Relationships first: Creating connections that help young people thrive.*

Minneapolis, MN: Author. Accessed at http://page.search-institute.org/relationships-first on October 24, 2019.

Rothstein, R. (2008). Whose problem is poverty? *Educational Leadership, 65*(7), 8–13. Accessed at www.ascd.org/publications/educational-leadership/apr08/vol65/num07/Whose-Problem-Is-Poverty%C2%A2.aspx on October 8, 2019.

Rotter, J. B. (1975). Some problems and misconceptions related to the construct of internal versus external control of reinforcement. *Journal of Consulting and Clinical Psychology, 43*(1), 56–67.

Rowe, M. L. (2018). Understanding socioeconomic differences in parents' speech to children. *Child Development Perspectives, 12*(2), 122–127. Accessed at https://onlinelibrary.wiley.com/doi/abs/10.1111/cdep.12271 on October 8, 2019.

Rumberger, R. W. (2015, June). *Student mobility: Causes, consequences, and solutions.* Accessed at https://nepc.colorado.edu/sites/default/files/pb_rumberger-student-mobility.pdf on February 21, 2020.

Rutter, M. (1985). Resilience in the face of adversity: Protective factors and resistance to psychiatric disorder. *The British Journal of Psychiatry, 147*, 598–611. Accessed at https://psycnet.apa.org/doi/10.1192/bjp.147.6.598 on February 21, 2020.

Saady, B. (2018, August 13). Throwing children away: The school-to-prison pipeline. Accessed at www.theamericanconservative.com/articles/throwing-children-away-the-school-to-prison-pipeline on October 8, 2019.

Saakvitne, K. W., & Pearlman, L. A. (1996). *Transforming the pain: A workbook on vicarious traumatization.* New York: Norton.

Sainato, M. (2017, July 18). U.S. prison system plagued by high illiteracy rates. Accessed at https://observer.com/2017/07/prison-illiteracy-criminal-justice-reform on October 8, 2019.

Sarason, S. B. (1971). *The culture of the school and the problem of change.* Boston: Allyn & Bacon.

Sarkar, S., Barnes, S. G., & Noffke, A. (Eds.). (2018). *The souls of poor folk: Auditing America 50 years after the Poor People's Campaign challenged racism, poverty, the war economy/militarism and our national morality.* Washington, DC: Institute for Policy Studies. Accessed at https://ips-dc.org/wp-content/uploads/2018/04/PPC-Audit-Full-410835a.pdf on October 8, 2019.

Sauter, M. B., Stebbins, S., & Frohlich, T. C. (2017, April 7). Cities hit hardest by extreme poverty. Accessed at https://247wallst.com/special-report/2017/04/07/cities-hit-hardest-by-extreme-poverty-2/5 on October 8, 2019.

Schear, T. (2016, November 29). *Addressing trauma in community schools* [Webinar]. Accessed at www.communityschools.org/assets/1/AssetManager/ Addressing%20Trauma%20in%20Community%20Schools%20Webinar. pdf on October 8, 2019.

Schorr, L. (1992). Service integration and beyond: The challenge of integrating education and human services: Strategies to strengthen Northwest families. Accessed at https://tinyurl.com/weoqj3o on February 21, 2020.

Schorr, L., & Schorr, D. (1989). *Within our reach: Breaking the cycle of disadvantage.* New York: Anchor Books.

Search Institute. (n.d.). The developmental assets framework. Accessed at www. search-institute.org/our-research/development-assets/developmental-assets-framework on October 24, 2019.

Search Institute. (2016, July). *The developmental relationships framework.* Minneapolis, MN: Author. Accessed at www.search-institute.org/developmental-relation-ships/developmental-relationships-framework on October 24, 2019.

Seligman, M. E. P. (2007). *The optimistic child: A proven program to safeguard children against depression and build lifelong resilience.* Boston: Houghton Mifflin.

Senechal, J., Sober, T., Hope, S., Johnson, T., Burkhalter, F., Castelow, T., et al. (2016, December). *Understanding teacher morale.* Richmond, VA: Metropolitan Educational Research Consortium. Accessed at https://scholarscompass. vcu.edu/cgi/viewcontent.cgi?article=1055&context=merc_pubs on October 8, 2019.

The Sentencing Project. (2018). *Report of the Sentencing Project to the United Nations special rapporteur on contemporary forms of racism, racial discrimination, xenophobia, and related intolerance: Regarding racial disparities in the United States criminal justice system.* Accessed at www.sentencingproject.org/publications/ un-report-on-racial-disparities/ on February 21, 2020.

Sharot, T. (2011, June 6). The optimism bias. Accessed at http://content.time.com/ time/health/article/0,8599,2074067,00.html on April 14, 2020.

Shulman, L. S. (1998). Theory, practice, and the education of professionals. *Elementary School Journal, 98*(5), 511–526.

Siegel, D. J., & Bryson, T. P. (2011). *The whole-brain child: 12 revolutionary strategies to nurture your child's developing mind.* New York: Delacorte Press.

Skinner, R., & Chapman, C. (1999, September). *Service-learning and community service in K–12 public schools* (NCES 1999-043). Washington, DC: National Center for Education Statistics. Accessed at https://nces.ed.gov/ pubs99/1999043.pdf on October 24, 2019.

Slade, S., & Griffith, D. (2013). A whole child approach to student success. *KEDI Journal of Educational Policy, 10*(3), 21–35.

Smith, H. (2005). *Comer School Development Program: James Comer interview* [Radio broadcast transcript]. Accessed at www.pbs.org/makingschoolswork/sbs/csp/jamescomer.html on October 8, 2019.

Smith, J. M., Fien, H., & Paine, S. C. (2008). When mobility disrupts learning. *Educational Leadership, 65*(7), 59–63. Accessed at www.ascd.org/publications/educational-leadership/apr08/vol65/num07/When-Mobility-Disrupts-Learning.aspx on February 21, 2020.

Snyder, C. R. (1995). Conceptualizing, measuring, and nurturing hope. *Journal of Counseling and Development, 73*(3), 355–360.

Snyder, C. R., Shorey, H. S., Cheavens, J., Pulvers, K. M., Adams, V. H., III, & Wiklund, C. (2002). Hope and academic success in college. *Journal of Educational Psychology, 94*(4), 820–826. Accessed at https://psycnet.apa.org/record/2002-06506-016 on October 8, 2019.

Souers, K. (2016). *Fostering resilient learners: Strategies for creating a trauma-sensitive classroom.* Alexandria, VA: Association for Supervision and Curriculum Development.

Sparks, S. D. (2016a, June 27). 1 in 4 teachers miss 10 or more school days, analysis finds. Accessed at www.edweek.org/ew/articles/2016/06/27/1-in-4-teachers-miss-10-or.html?r=94535099 on October 8, 2019.

Sparks, S. D. (2016b, August 11). Student mobility: How it affects learning. Accessed at www.edweek.org/ew/issues/student-mobility/index.html on February 21, 2020.

Sporleder, J., & Forbes, H. T. (2016). *The trauma-informed school: A step-by-step implementation guide for administrators and school personnel.* Boulder, CO: Beyond Consequences Institute.

Sprenger, M. (2013). *Teaching the critical vocabulary of the Common Core: 55 words that make or break student understanding.* Alexandria, VA: Association for Supervision and Curriculum Development.

Stamm, B. H. (2009). *Professional quality of life scale (ProQOL): Compassion satisfaction and compassion fatigue, version 5.* Accessed at http://proqol.org/uploads/ProQOL_5_English_Self-Score_3-2012.pdf on October 8, 2019.

Stamm, B. H. (2010). *The concise ProQOL manual* (2nd ed.). Accessed at https://proqol.org/uploads/ProQOLManual.pdf on October 8, 2019.

Stevens, A. (2018). Employment and poverty. Accessed at https://econofact.org/employment-and-poverty on February 21, 2020.

Stiggins, R. (2001). *Student-involved classroom assessment.* Upper Saddle River, NJ: Prentice Hall.

Stiggins, R. (2017). *The perfect assessment system.* Alexandria, VA: Association for Supervision and Curriculum Development.

Strasser, D. (2014). An open letter on teacher morale. *Educational Leadership, 71*(5), 10–13. Accessed at www.ascd.org/publications/educational-leadership/feb14/vol71/num05/An-Open-Letter-on-Teacher-Morale.aspx on October 8, 2019.

Stringfield, S. & Teddlie, C. (1988, October). *A time to summarize: The Louisiana school effectiveness study.* Accessed at www.ascd.org/ASCD/pdf/journals/ed_lead/el_198810_stringfield.pdf on February 21, 2020.

Suitts, S. (2013, October). *A new majority update: Low income students in the South and nation.* Atlanta, GA: Southern Education Foundation. Accessed at www.southerneducation.org/wp-content/uploads/2019/02/New-Majority-2013.pdf on October 8, 2019.

Suitts, S. (2015, January). *A new majority: Low income students now a majority in the nation's public schools—Research bulletin.* Atlanta, GA: Southern Education Foundation. Accessed at www.southerneducation.org/wp-content/uploads/2019/02/New-Majority-Update-Bulletin.pdf on October 8, 2019.

Sutcher, L., Darling-Hammond, L., & Carver-Thomas, D. (2016). *A coming crisis in teaching? Teacher supply, demand, and shortages in the U.S.* [Research brief]. Palo Alto, CA: Learning Policy Institute. Accessed at https://learningpolicyinstitute.org/sites/default/files/product-files/A_Coming_Crisis_in_Teaching_BRIEF.pdf on October 8, 2019.

Taylor, K. (2017, May 30). Poverty's long-lasting effects on students' education and success. Accessed at www.insightintodiversity.com/povertys-long-lasting-effects-on-students-education-and-success on October 7, 2019.

Teddlie, C., & Stringfield, S. (1993). *Schools make a difference: Lessons learned from a ten-year study of school effects.* New York: Teachers College Press.

Teicher, J. G. (2014, July 17). A new way to talk about poverty in Troy, New York. Accessed at https://slate.com/culture/2014/07/brenda-ann-kenneally-documents-life-below-the-poverty-line-in-troy-york-in-her-documentary-project-upstate-girls.html on October 8, 2019.

Tileston, D. W., & Darling, S. K. (2008). *Why culture counts: Teaching children of poverty.* Bloomington, IN: Solution Tree Press.

Toch, T., & Headden, S. (2014, September 3). How to motivate students to work harder. Accessed at www.theatlantic.com/education/archive/2014/09/how-to-get-insecure-students-to-work-harder/379500 on October 8, 2019.

Tomlinson, C. A. (2017). *How to differentiate instruction in academically diverse classrooms* (3rd ed.). Alexandria, VA: Association for Supervision and Curriculum Development.

Tomlinson, C. A. (2018). One to grow on: A teacher lost in the pipeline. *Educational Leadership*, *75*(8), 92–93. Accessed at www.ascd.org/publications/educational-leadership/may18/vol75/num08/A-Teacher-Lost-in-the-Pipeline.aspx on October 8, 2019.

TRACEs Central Oregon. (n.d.). *Measuring strengths to nurture resilience in central Oregon*. Accessed at http://tracesco.org/wp-content/uploads/2018/05/TRACEs_Measuring-Strengths_1pager.pdf on October 24, 2019.

Trauma and Learning Policy Initiative. (2019, January 30). Whole school approach: The importance of community. Accessed at https://traumasensitiveschools.org/whole-school-approach-the-importance-of-community on October 8, 2019.

Treatment and Services Adaptation Center. (n.d.). What is the TRS-IA? Accessed at https://traumaawareschools.org/traumaResponsiveSchools on October 24, 2019.

Tyler, R. W. (1949). *Basic principles of curriculum and instruction*. Chicago: University of Chicago Press.

UCSF HEARTS. (n.d.). Resources. Accessed at https://hearts.ucsf.edu/resources on October 24, 2019.

U.S. Bureau of Labor Statistics (2019). Employment projections: Occupations with the most job growth. Accessed at www.bls.gov/emp/tables/occupations-most-job-growth.htm on February 21, 2020.

U.S. Census Bureau. (n.d.). Poverty. Accessed at www.census.gov/topics/income-poverty/poverty.html on October 8, 2019.

U.S. Department of Education. (2015). Every student succeeds act (ESSA). Accessed at www.ed.gov/essa?src=rn on February 21, 2020.

U.S. Department of Education. (2016). Education department releases guidance on homeless children and youth. Accessed at www.ed.gov/news/press-releases/education-department-releases-guidance-homeless-children-and-youth on February 21, 2020.

U.S. Department of Education. (2019). Chronic absenteeism in the nation's schools: A hidden educational crisis. Accessed at www2.ed.gov/datastory/chronicabsenteeism.html on October 8, 2019.

United Way of Central Indiana. (n.d.). Accessed at https://uwci.org/our-work/education on October 8, 2019.

Varlas, L. (2008). Full-service community schools. Accessed at www.ascd.org/publications/newsletters/policy_priorities/summer08/num54/full/Full-Service_Community_Schools.aspx on October 8, 2019.

Varner, C., Mattingly, M., & Grusky, D. (2017). *The facts behind the visions*. Accessed at https://inequality.stanford.edu/sites/default/files/Pathways_Spring2017_Facts-Behind-Visions.pdf on October 8, 2019.

Vasconcelos, K. (2017, April 4). 3 ways poverty impacts children learning to read [Blog post]. Accessed at www.scilearn.com/blog/3-ways-poverty-impacts-children-learning-read on October 8, 2019.

Waterford.org. (2018, November 1). How parent involvement leads to student success. Accessed at www.waterford.org/education/how-parent-involvment-leads-to-student-success/on February 21, 2020.

Webb, S. T., & Hagley, T. R. (2019, August). Cultivating community schools. Accessed at http://my.aasa.org/AASA/Resources/SAMag/2019/Aug19/Webb-Hagley.aspx on February 21, 2020.

Weis, A. C. (2017). *Resilience self-reflection*. Accessed at https://apps.carleton.edu/studenthealth/assets/Resilience_Self_Reflection.pdf on October 24, 2019.

Weiss, E. (2016, February 17). Case study: Vancouver Public Schools. Broader, bolder approach. Accessed at www.boldapproach.org/index.html@p=129.html on February 21, 2020.

Weiss, E., & Reville, P. (2019). *Broader, bolder, better: How schools and communities help students overcome the disadvantages of poverty*. Cambridge, MA: Harvard Education Press.

Werner, E. E., & Smith, R. S. (1992). *Overcoming the odds: High risk children from birth to adulthood*. Ithaca, NY: Cornell University Press.

White, G. B. (2017, April 27). Escaping poverty requires almost 20 years with nearly nothing going wrong. Accessed at www.theatlantic.com/business/archive/2017/04/economic-inequality/524610 on October 8, 2019.

Willison, S., & Gibson, E. (2011). Graduate school learning curves: McNair scholars' postbaccalaureate transitions. *Equity & Excellence in Education, 44*(2), 153–168.

Winebrenner, S. (2001). *Teaching gifted kids in the regular classroom: Strategies and techniques every teacher can use to meet the academic needs of the gifted and talented.* Minneapolis, MN: Free Spirit.

Wisconsin Department of Public Instruction. (n.d.). Trauma-sensitive schools online professional development [Module]. Accessed at https://dpi.wi.gov/sspw/mental-health/trauma/modules on October 24, 2019.

Wolfe, P. (2001). *Brain matters: Translating research into classroom practice.* Alexandria, VA: Association for Supervision and Curriculum Development.

Wolpow, R., Johnson, M. M., Hertel, R., & Kincaid, S. O. (2016, May). *The heart of learning and teaching: Compassion, resiliency, and academic success.* Olympia, WA: Compassionate Schools. Accessed at www.k12.wa.us/sites/default/files/public/compassionateschools/pubdocs/theheartoflearningandteaching.pdf on October 24, 2019.

Youth Law Center. (2019, January). *Closing the extracurricular gap: Prioritizing extracurricular activities as a key intervention for children and youth in foster care and juvenile justice.* San Francisco, CA: Youth Law Center. Accessed at https://ylc.org/wp-content/uploads/2019/01/YLC-Extracurriculars-Report-2019.pdf on February 21, 2020.

Zakariya, S. B. (2015). *Learning to read, reading to learn: Why third grade is a pivotal year for mastering literacy.* Alexandria, VA: Center for Public Education. Accessed at www.nsba.org/sites/default/files/reports/NSBA_CPE_Early_Literacy_Layout_2015.pdf on October 8, 2019.

Zalaznick, M. (2017, November 8). Schools provide community coverage. Accessed at http://districtadministration.com/schools-provide-community-coverage on October 8, 2019.

Zemelman, S., Daniels, H., & Hyde, A. (2005). *Best practice: Today's standards for teaching and learning in America's schools* (3rd ed.). Portsmouth, NH: Heinemann.

Zohar, A., Degani, A., & Vaaknin, E. (2001). Teachers' beliefs about low-achieving students and higher order thinking. *Teaching and Teacher Education, 17,* 469–485. Accessed at http://academic.sun.ac.za/mathed/174/teacherslow-achievers.pdf on October 8, 2019.

Index

A

Ablon, S., 142, 220
absenteeism
    community outreach and, 158
    compassion fatigue and secondary
        traumatic stress and, 62
    human needs of students and
        families and, 155
    impacts of poverty and, 34–36, 46
    staff turnover and attrition and, 52
academic majors, 149, 150
academic needs
    about, 95–97
    additional reports and resources
        for, 220
    conclusion, 118
    data, assessment, and accountability
        and, 100–102
    effective teachers and the Power of
        We and, 99–100
    extra time for instruction and
        support and, 105–107
    field notes on, 102, 103, 106, 107,
        112, 113, 114–115
    parent and guardian involvement
        and, 112–115
    positive interpersonal relationships
        and, 109–112
    progress monitoring and remediation
        and, 103–105
    rigorous, aligned curriculum and,
        102–103
    social-emotional needs and, 97
    targeted reading and mathematics
        and, 108–109
    trauma-informed practices and,
        115–118
    visionary leadership and, 98–99
academic preparation, 32–34, 46
academic success, 95, 144, 147
accountability, 96, 100–102, 202
administrators, 98–99. *See also* impacts
    of poverty on school staff;
    leadership
Advancement via Individual
    Determination (AVID), 103
adverse childhood experiences (ACE). *See*
    also stress; trauma
    behavior challenges and, 32, 37–40, 46
    executive function skills and, 44
    research on poverty and resilience
        and, 84–85
    schoolwide community and, 137
    trauma-informed practices and, 115
after-school programs, 106, 171
agency, sense of, 202, 204, 206–207
AllThingsPLC, 206
Alston, P., 14
America's Promise Alliance, 220
Aspen Institute, 87, 88, 218
assessment and addressing academic
    needs, 96, 100–102
Association for Supervision and
    Curriculum Development
    (ASCD), 15, 87, 218
atmosphere, 113, 130, 131
attendance, 35. *See also* absenteeism

B

Barr, R., 212–213
basic human needs. *See* human needs of
    students and families
before-school programs, 106, 171

behavior challenges
    adverse childhood experiences and,
        32, 37–40, 46
    secondary traumatic stress and, 62
behavior supports, 117
beliefs, 130–131
belonging
    ideas for fostering, 195
    Maslow's hierarchy of needs and,
        128, 134
    research on, 135
    seeds of hope and, 127, 134–139,
        194–195
Bend, OR
    community outreach and, 182, 185
    encouraging optimism and, 193
    field notes on, 196, 197
    suburban poor and, 17
Better Together, 161, 182, 183
biases, 12, 98, 111
blue-collar workers, 22–23, 33
Boise, ID
    community outreach and, 5, 6, 161,
        168–169
    field notes on, 134, 174, 175–176,
        181, 193–194
    suburban poor and, 17
Bonilla-Santiago, G., 160
brain research. *See* neuroscience
Brainiacs Club, 124
*Broader, Bolder, Better: How Schools
    and Communities Help Students
    Overcome the Disadvantages of
    Poverty* (Weiss and Reville), 88
Budge, K., 13
Building a Culture of Hope (Barr and
    Gibson), 7, 89, 127

C

*C.A.R.E.: Strategies for Closing the
    Achievement Gap* (National
    Education Association), 220
careers. *See also* employment; wages
    career clusters, 149, 150
    career exploration, 149
    career interests, 136, 138–139

CASEL Standards, 221
caseworkers, 107
celebrations, 130, 133–134, 199
Center on the Developing Child, 71
Centergy Project, 159, 164
Centers for Disease Control and
    Prevention, 83
Chenoweth, K., 102, 132
Child Trauma Academy, 84
Children's Aid Society, 177, 180, 221
Children's Defense Fund, 26, 27, 217
chronic adversity, 39
city poverty, 15
class meetings, 141, 142, 143
classroom circles, 141, 143
Coalition for Community Schools, 160,
    172, 180, 184, 185, 221
cocurricular activities, 138
cognitive needs, 128
collaborative and proactive solutions, 142
Collaborative Learning for Educational
    Achievement and Resilience
    (CLEAR), 219
collaborative problem solving, 142,
    220–221
College and Career Readiness Standards, 123
Commission on the Whole Child, 85, 87
Common Core State Standards, 46, 123
community
    communitywide celebrations, 130,
        133–134
    protective factors and, 79
    schoolwide community, 136,
        137–138
community development, 169, 171
community outreach/community
    outreach schools
    about, 5, 187
    advisory boards/board of directors
        and, 163, 175
    community partners and, 168,
        176–181
    emergence of, 157–162
    examples of, 161
    facilities for, 174
    funding for, 157, 182–184

long-term impact of, 184–188
monitoring outcomes of, 157,
    181–182
resilient schools and, 156
resource center coordinators and,
    172–173
school as a hub of coordination and,
    165–171
setting up, 157
terms for, 160
tools for assessing outcomes, 183
community partners, 168, 176–181
community schools. *See* community
    outreach/community outreach
    schools
Community Schools Coordinators
    Network, 181
Community Schools Leaders
    Network, 180
compassion fatigue, 60–62. *See also*
    secondary traumatic stress
competence, 75, 76, 141
Comprehensive School Climate
    Inventory, 222
Connecticut Education Association, 222
consistency, 141
core classes, 102–103
country poverty, 15
creativity, 77
criminal justice system, 25–26
*Culturally Responsive Teaching and the
    Brain: Promoting Authentic
    Engagement and Rigor Among
    Culturally and Linguistically
    Diverse Students* (Hammond),
    222
Culture of Hope
    developing, 125
    institutional culture and, 124–126
    Maslow's hierarchy of needs and, 127
    resilient schools and, 89–90
    seed 1, 130–134, 192–193
    seed 2, 134–139, 194–195
    seed 3, 139–143, 196–197
    seed 4, 144–147, 197, 199
    seed 5, 147–151, 199–200

seeds of hope within, 129
social-emotional needs and, 43, 122,
    127–129
teaching hope and finding a vision
    for a better life and, 216
curriculum, 96, 102–103

D

Damon, W., 148
data, 96, 100–102, 187–188
deep poverty, 16
developmental risk factors and assets,
    83–84
disrupted learning, 63–65, 222
dropouts/dropout rate
    criminal justice system and, 25
    literacy and, 33, 108
    poverty and, 3, 44
Dryfoos, J., 85, 157
DuFour, R., 97, 104, 205, 206

E

Edelman, J., 3
education. *See also* impacts of poverty on
        teaching and learning; schools
    family education and, 169, 171
    parent and guardian education, 114
    poverty epidemic and, 22–23, 24–25
    and who are the poor, 17
Education Trust, 102
employment. *See also* careers; wages
    challenges of poverty and, 19
    Children's Defense Fund and, 27
    family education and, 171
    family housing and workforce
        support and, 178
    poverty epidemic and, 22–23
    state of poverty in the United States
        and, 15
Ending Child Poverty Now (Children's
    Defense Fund), 26
engagement
    emotional challenges of students
        and, 215
    personal connections and, 215

staff's professional needs and, 202, 204, 208

student leadership and responsibility and, 145–146

whole-child strategies and, 87

English language learners, 33, 171

enrichment activities, 105

Every Student Succeeds Act (ESSA), 101, 102, 207

executive function skills

cycle of poverty and, 4, 213–214

independent learning and, 116

protective factors and, 79

role of in ending poverty, 43–46

seeds of hope and, 128

expectations

optimism and hope and, 130, 132

positive reinforcement and, 110–111

pride, self-esteem, and self-confidence and, 144

trauma-informed practices and, 116

external locus of control

dependent learners and, 116

executive functions and, 44

field notes on, 43

impacts of poverty and, 46

learned helplessness and, 40–41

seeds of hope and, 128

external/environmental protective factors, 78–80. *See also* protective factors

extracurricular activities, 138

extreme poverty, 16

F

families. *See also* human needs of students and families; parents/guardians

early family intervention and support, 107

identifying needs of, 157, 162–164

research on poverty and resilience in education and, 85

school as surrogate family, 136–137

Family Access Network (FAN), 185

family access networks. *See* community outreach/community outreach schools

family community resource centers. *See* community outreach/community outreach schools

family education, 169, 171

family mobility, 18, 35, 155, 158, 186

family services and supports, 169, 169–170

fight-flight-freeze mode, 4, 39, 40

fit, concept of, 55, 192

food

challenges of poverty and, 19, 162

Children's Defense Fund and, 26, 27

family services and supports and, 169

food scarcity, 155

weekend backpacks and, 166, 167

Free and Reduced Lunch, 1

Friends of the Children, 72–73

From a Nation at Risk to a Nation of Hope (Aspen Institute), 88

full-service schools, 85, 86, 157, 160. *See also* community outreach/community outreach schools

funding gap, 19, 24–25

future, planning/dreaming for

optimism and hope and, 133

sense of purpose and, 150–151

teaching hope and finding a vision for a better life, 216

G

Gallup Student Poll, 223

generational poverty, 14, 42

Georgia, 164, 171, 172. *See also* Marietta Student Life Center

Gibson, E., 211–212

goals

academic needs and, 99–100

optimism and hope and, 133

sense of purpose and, 200

student learning goals, 105

Gorski, P., 12, 13, 109

graduation rate. *See also* dropouts/
        dropout rate
    community outreach and, 159, 160,
        181–182
    needs of families and, 164
    parent and guardian involvement
        and, 112
    pathways to the future and, 150
    seeds of hope within a Culture of
        Hope and, 129
Greene, R., 142, 220
guaranteed curriculum, 103. *See also*
        curriculum

H

Hammond, Z., 84
health care
    challenges of poverty and, 18–19,
        162
    effects of poverty and, 3
    family education and, 171
    family services and supports and, 169
Healthy Environments and Response to
        Trauma in Schools (HEARTS), 219
Heart of Learning and Teaching:
        Compassion, Resiliency, and
        Academic Success (Wolpow,
        Johnson, Hertel, and Kincaid), 219
high-poverty, high performing schools
    community outreach and, 157
    curriculum and, 102
    expectations and, 132
    human needs of students and
        families and, 156
    mastery learning perspective and, 96
    relationships and, 109
        research on poverty and
            resilience in education and, 84
    seeds of hope and, 128
    social-emotional factors and, 122
    trauma-informed practices and, 115
    visionary leadership and, 98
    wraparound educational programs and,
        171
high-poverty communities, 89, 213

home visits, 107, 114
homelessness. *See also* housing
    absenteeism, illness, and interrupted
        education and, 35, 36
    family housing and workforce
        support and, 178
    poverty and, 3, 18
    rate of, 36
hope. *See also* Culture of Hope
    emotional challenges of students
        and, 215
    ideas for encouraging, 193
    institutional culture and, 124–126
    role of in ending poverty, 26–28
    seeds of hope and, 127, 130–134,
        192–193
    social-emotional needs and, 123–127
    teaching hope, 126–127, 216
    whole-school model and, 89
Hope Survey, 208, 223
housing, 18, 26, 27, 178. *See also*
        homelessness
human needs of students and families
    about, 155–157
    additional reports and resources for,
        221
    community outreach. *See* community
        outreach/community outreach
        schools
    conclusion, 188–189
    field notes on, 158–159, 159, 165, 167,
        168, 169–170, 172, 174–175, 176,
        178–179, 179–180, 181, 188
    identifying needs of families and,
        162–164
    poverty and, 2
    school as a hub of coordination,
        165–171
human services, 130, 134

I

Idaho. *See* Boise, ID
illness and impact of poverty, 34–36
immigrants, 17, 168

impacts of poverty on school staff. *See
       also* staff; teachers
    about, 49–50
    conclusion, 66
    field notes on, 50–51, 51–52, 55–56,
       56–57, 59, 60, 61–62, 64
    staff exposure to trauma and, 57–66
    staff turnover and attrition and,
       50–57
impacts of poverty on teaching and learning
    about, 31–32
    absenteeism, illness, and interrupted
       education and, 34–36
    academic preparation and, 32–34
    adverse childhood experiences and
       behavior challenges and, 37–40
    conclusion, 46–47
    executive function skills and, 43–46
    field notes on, 35, 41–42, 43
    learned helplessness and, 40–43
    learning loss over school breaks and,
       36–37
income inequality, 21–22
independence, 75, 76
independent learning, 116–117
Institute for Educational Leadership, 180
institutional culture, 124–126
instruction. *See also* impacts of poverty
       on teaching and learning; teaching
    academic needs and, 96
    extra time for, 105–107
    trauma-informed practices and,
       115–116
Integrated Student Supports (ISS), 186.
       See also community outreach/
       community outreach schools
interests, 136, 138, 149
internal locus of control, 75, 76, 80, 213
internal protective factors, 75–78. *See also*
       protective factors
interrupted education, 34–36, 46
interventions, 103–105
introduction
    about, 1–2
    epidemic of poverty, 3–4
    field notes on, 4

    our aim, 6–8
    resilience, 4–6

J

Jensen, E., 13, 42, 84, 133, 216
job satisfaction
    belonging and, 194
    research on poverty and resilience in
       education and, 85–86
    seeds of hope and, 192
    staff's professional needs and, 202
    structural supports and, 204–208

K

Kentucky, 159, 172
*Kids Left Behind: Catching Up the
       Underachieving Children of
       Poverty, The* (Barr and Parrett), 122
kindergarten, 106, 171
Kohl, H., 216

L

language-based teaching, 117–118
leadership
    compassion fatigue and secondary
       traumatic stress and, 62
    developing shared vision and, 111
    student leadership and responsibility,
       144, 145–146
    visionary leadership, 96, 98–99
LEAP Academy University, 160
learned helplessness
    impacts of poverty and, 40–43, 46
    relationships and, 109
    research on poverty and resilience in
       education and, 85
    social-emotional needs and, 122
learning. *See also* impacts of poverty on
       teaching and learning
    academic learning and social-
       emotional learning, 126
    independent learning, 116–117
    learning labs, 105

learning loss over school breaks, 36–37, 46

learning options, 149, 150

small-group learning environments, 137

literacy, 25, 33, 108. *See also* reading/ reading readiness

M

Marietta Student Life Center, 161, 164, 172, 215

Marzano, R., 97

Maslow's hierarchy of needs

belonging and, 134

confidence and self-esteem and, 144

Culture of Hope and, 127

human needs of students and families and, 156

optimism and hope and, 130

pyramid of, 128

self-actualization and, 147

mastery learning perspective, 96

mathematics, 97, 103, 106–109

meetings

class meetings, 141, 142, 143

optimism and hope in staff meetings, 193

PLCs and, 205–206

mental health

belonging and, 135

emotional challenges of students and, 215

family services and supports and, 170

poverty and, 59, 162

public-sector partners and, 178

schools and, 2

mindfulness exercises, 141, 142, 143

morale

belonging and, 194

engagement and, 208

optimism and, 56–57, 192

research on poverty and resilience in education and, 85–86

structural supports and, 204–208

multitiered system of supports (MTSS), 103–104

N

National Center for Community Schools, 180, 184

National Child Traumatic Stress Network, 217

National Dropout Prevention Center, 75, 220

National Education Association, 172, 221

National Youth-at-Risk Conference, 218

neuroscience, 84, 222

Next Generation Science Standards, 123

No Child Left Behind (NCLB), 100–101, 102, 202

Northwest Regional Education Laboratory, 73, 85

nutrition. *See also* food

O

Ohio, 17, 161

optimism

Culture of Hope and, 125

emotional challenges of students and, 215

ideas for encouraging, 193

morale and, 56–57

protective factors and, 75, 77

seeds of hope and, 127, 130–134, 192–193

whole-school model and, 89

Oregon. *See* Bend, OR

Oregon Education Association, 63, 65, 222

P

parents/guardians. *See also* families

academic needs and, 97, 112–115

challenges of poverty and, 162

literacy and, 109

parent and guardian education, 114

parental involvement, 113

Parrett, W., 13

Path to Purpose: How Young People Find Their Calling in Life, The (Damon), 148

PeaceJam Foundation, 147

Perry, B., 84

personal connections, 144, 145, 215. See
    also relationships
personal note and a vision for
    resilient schools
    about, 211–214
    conclusion, 216
    increasing engagement and personal
        connections and, 215
    meeting the emotional challenges of
        students and, 214–215
    student voice and, 214
    teaching hope and finding a vision
        for a better life and, 216
    trauma-informed, trauma-sensitive
        schools and, 215
physiological needs, 128, 130
place, sense of and seeds of hope, 127,
    134–139, 194–195
place-based poverty, 14
positive behavioral interventions and
        supports (PBIS), 117, 137, 141,
    142, 193
positive reinforcement, 110–111, 144
postsecondary education and training
    access to, 45
    executive function skills and self-
        regulation and, 214
    pathways to the future and, 150, 151
    resilient schools and, 209
    seeds of hope and, 129
post-traumatic stress disorder (PTSD), 58
poverty. *See also* impacts of poverty on
        school staff; impacts of poverty
        on teaching and learning
    about, 11
    additional reports and resources for,
        217–218
    adverse childhood experiences and, 38
    benefits of growing up poor, 110
    conclusion, 29
    cost of, 28
    effects of, 3
    field notes on, 15–16, 18, 19, 21, 23,
        24, 28
    growth of, 213
    issues associated with, 162

need for educators to understand the
    effects of, 12–13
research on poverty and resilience in
    education, 82–84
role of hope in ending, 26–28
state of poverty in the United States,
    14–26
stereotypes of the poor, 14–15
types of, 14
poverty rate, 1, 3, 14, 17
Power of We, 96, 99–100, 204, 206
preschool, 3, 106, 171
pride
    ideas for fostering, 199
    seeds of hope and, 127, 144–147,
    197, 199
primary trauma, 57, 63–66. *See also*
    secondary traumatic stress;
    trauma
private-sector partners, 178
professional development, 204, 207
professional identity, 204, 206–207
professional learning communities (PLC)
    academic needs and, 100
    PLC at Work, 199
    Power of We and, 206
    professional development and, 207
    structural supports and, 204–206
professional needs. *See* staff's relational
    and professional needs
progress monitoring
    academic needs and, 96, 103–105
    sense of pride, self-esteem, and self-
        confidence and, 144, 147
    progress and, 102
protective factors
    assets and, 83
    cycle of poverty and, 213
    external/environmental protective
        factors, 78–81
    internal protective factors, 75–78
    resilient students and resilient schools
        and, 73–75
    schools and, 132
    self-righting capacity of learners to
        build resilience and, 81–82

social-emotional needs and, 141, 143

Public Schools First, 44

public-sector partners, 178

purpose, sense of
  ideas for fostering, 200
  seeds of hope and, 127, 147–151,
    199–200

Q

Quaglia, R., 135, 140, 148, 216

R

*Reaching and Teaching Students in
    Poverty: Strategies for Erasing the
    Opportunity Gap* (Gorski), 13, 218

reading/reading readiness. *See also* literacy
  academic needs and, 97, 106–109
  community outreach and, 158, 186

READS for Summer Learning, 37

relationships. *See also* personal
    connections; staff's relational and
    professional needs
  academic needs and, 97, 109–112
  adverse childhood experiences and,
    39
  protective factors and, 75
  secondary traumatic stress and, 62
  support for staff and, 89
  trauma-sensitive relationships, 111

*Relationships First: Creating Connections
    that Help Young People Thrive*
    (Roehlkepartain), 220

remediation, 96, 103–105

research on poverty and resilience in
    education
  about, 82–83
  childhood trauma and adversity and,
    84–85
  developmental risk factors and assets
    and, 83–84
  high-poverty, high performing
    schools and, 84
  needs of families and, 85
  school staff attrition, job satisfaction,
    and morale and, 85–86

social-emotional needs of the whole
    child and, 85
  trauma and stress neuroscience and, 84

research on resilient students and resilient
    schools
  about, 71–73
  conclusion, 91–92
  field notes on, 72–73, 78, 80–81,
    81–82
  framework of a resilient school,
    89–91
  protective factors for resilience in
    youth, 73–82
  research on poverty and resilience in
    education, 82–86
  research on resilience in youth, 73
  whole-school model, 86–89

resilience
  about, 4–6
  additional reports and resources for,
    219–220
  building, 72
  definition of, 71
  fostering staff resilience, 200–202
  physiological needs and, 156
  self-righting capacity of learners to
    build resilience, 81–82

resilient schools
  about, 2–3
  community outreach and, 156
  definition of, 5, 209
  personal note and a vision for. *See*
    personal note and a vision for
    resilient schools

resilient schools framework, 91, 96. *See
    also* academic needs; human
    needs of students and families;
    social-emotional needs; staff's
    relational and professional needs

respect, 130, 131

response to intervention (RTI), 104

restorative justice/restorative discipline,
    142, 193

reteaching, 104–105

Reville, P., 13, 186

S

safety, 128, 130, 131
Sarason, S., 124, 125
school breaks, 36–37, 46
school counselors, 215
school readiness, 32–34, 46, 105
schools. *See also* community outreach/
     community outreach schools
     as hub of coordination, 157, 165–171
     protective factors and, 79–80, 132
     school as surrogate family, 136,
         136–137
     schoolwide community, 136,
         137–138
Schools Uniting Neighborhoods (SUN),
     161, 185
school-to-prison pipeline, 26
Schorr, L., 85
Search Institute, 75, 83, 208
secondary trauma. *See* secondary
     traumatic stress
secondary traumatic stress. *See also*
         primary trauma; trauma
     definition of, 57
     post-traumatic stress disorder
         (PTSD) and, 58
     response to, 62–63
     signs of, 60–62
     staff exposure to trauma and, 58–60
     teachers and, 49
     tools for measuring, 63
seeds of hope. *See* Culture of Hope
self-actualization, 128, 147
self-care, 200–201, 201–202
self-confidence
     ideas for fostering, 199
     Maslow's hierarchy of needs and, 144
     seeds of hope and, 127, 144–147,
         197, 199
self-esteem
     ideas for fostering, 199
     Maslow's hierarchy of needs and, 1
         28, 144
     seeds of hope and, 127, 144–147,
         197, 199

self-regulation
     adverse childhood experiences and, 39
     emotional challenges of students
         and, 215
     ideas for fostering, 196–197
     modes of, 198
     postsecondary education and
         training and, 214
     seeds of hope and, 127, 139–143,
         196–197
     self-regulation tools, 141, 143
sensory rooms/labs, 143
service learning projects, 144, 146–147
Shame of the Nation, The (Kozol), 64
situational poverty, 14
social safety nets, 3, 23–24, 45
social-emotional learning, 126, 141, 142
social-emotional needs
     about, 121–123
     academic needs and, 97
     additional reports and resources for,
         220–221
     conclusion, 151
     Culture of Hope and, 127–151
     emotional challenges of students and,
         214–215
     emphasis on hope and, 123–127
     field notes on, 122–123, 124, 126,
         131–132, 133, 134, 138, 146, 147
     schools and, 2
     whole-school model and, 87
social-emotional regulation, 214
Souls of Poor Folk (Institute for Policy
     Studies), 218
staff. *See also* impacts of poverty on
         school staff; teachers
     fostering staff resilience, 200–202
     and identifying needs of students,
         164
staff exposure to trauma
     about, 57–58
     disrupted learning environments and,
         63–66
     secondary traumatic stress, 58–63
staff mobility, 112
staff turnover and attrition
     about, 50–53

compassion fatigue and secondary traumatic stress and, 62

factors related to teacher shortage and, 53–54

morale as a form of optimism and, 56–57

research on poverty and resilience in education and, 85–86

staff's relational and professional needs and, 192

teacher job satisfaction and morale and, 54–56

staff's relational and professional needs about, 191

additional reports and resources for, 221–222

conclusion, 208–209

field notes on, 192, 193–194, 195, 196, 197, 206, 207

fostering staff resilience and, 200–202

meeting staff's professional needs and, 202–208

secondary traumatic stress and, 62

supporting staff with seeds of hope, 192–200

whole-school model and, 89

state of poverty in the United States about, 14–15

challenges of poverty and, 18–20

poverty epidemic and, 20–26

who are the poor and, 16–17

Stiggins, R., 123

stress. *See also* adverse childhood experiences (ACE); secondary traumatic stress; trauma

emotional challenges of students and, 214–215

research on poverty and resilience in education and, 84

trauma-informed, trauma-sensitive schools and, 215

student achievement

community outreach and, 158

competence and, 141

expectations and positive reinforcement and, 110

protective factors and, 79

staff turnover and attrition and, 51, 52

staff unity and, 100

student leadership, 145–146

student voice, 164, 214

suburban poor, 17

success, 130, 132–133, 147

Suitts, S., 2

summer learning loss, 36–37

summer programs, 37, 106–107

support

academic needs and, 96

extra time for instruction and, 105–107

fostering staff resilience and, 200–201

transitions and, 139

surveys, 200, 204, 208, 222–223

T

talents, 136, 138, 149

Teacher Morale, Motivation, and Professional Identity Research (Bosso), 221

teachers. *See also* impacts of poverty on school staff; staff

academic needs and, 99–100

looping teachers, 109

need for educators to understand the effects of, 12–13

needs of students and, 164

policy rollout and, 203–204

teacher job satisfaction and morale, 54–56

teacher mobility, 112

teacher shortage, 53–54

teaching. *See also* impacts of poverty on teaching and learning; instruction

aspects of, 54–55

language-based teaching, 117–118

teaching hope, 126–127

teaching poverty certification, 217

Teaching with Poverty in Mind (Jensen), 42

Thirty-Six Children (Kohl), 64

transitions, 136, 139, 141

trauma. *See also* secondary traumatic
      stress; staff exposure to trauma
      adverse childhood experiences and
          behavior challenges and, 38–40
      effects of, 4, 115, 139–140
      emotional challenges of students and,
          214–215
      human needs of students and
          families and, 155
      poverty and, 162
      rate of, 58
      research on poverty and resilience in
          education and, 84–85
      trauma-informed practices, 115–118
      trauma-sensitive relationships, 111
      whole-school model and, 88–89

Trauma and Learning Policy Initiative,
      88–89, 219

Trauma Responsive Schools
      Implementation Assessment
      (TRS-IA), 223

trauma-informed practices
      academic needs and, 97
      additional reports and resources
          for, 219
      schools and, 215

trauma-informed schools/trauma-
      sensitive schools
      belonging and, 135
      schools and, 215
      schoolwide community and, 137
      trauma-informed practices and,
          115–118
      whole-school model and, 88–89

trust, 130, 131

U

Understanding Teacher Morale (Senechal),
      55, 203, 222

*United Nations Report on Poverty in the
      United States,* 218

United Way, 161, 177, 184

U.S. Department of Education, 36

*Using Brain Science to Design New
      Pathways Out of Poverty*
      (Babcock), 222

V

Vancouver, WA
      after-school programs and, 106
      community outreach and, 5, 6, 161,
          182, 184, 185–186
      field notes on, 167, 178–179, 179–
          180, 181, 207
      suburban poor and, 17

vicarious trauma. *See* secondary traumatic
      stress

voice
      student voice, 164, 214
      teacher voice, 203–204, 206–207

W

wages. *See also* careers; employment
      challenges of poverty and, 19
      Children's Defense Fund and, 26
      poverty epidemic and, 21, 22–23

War on Poverty, 20, 23, 45

Washington. *See* Vancouver, WA

Weiss, E., 13, 186

who are the poor, 16–17

whole child, social-emotional needs of, 85

whole-child approach
      additional reports and resources for,
          218
      research on poverty and resilience in
          education and, 85
      resilient schools and, 2, 90

whole-school model
      hope and optimism and, 89
      resilient students and resilient schools
          and, 86
      school- or districtwide framework
          and, 87–88
      social-emotional needs and, 87
      staff's relational and professional
          needs and, 89
      trauma-sensitive schools and, 88–89
      whole-child approach and, 87

Wilson, W., 125

Within Our Reach: Breaking the Cycle of Disadvantage (Schorr and Schorr), 85

wraparound educational programs, 169, 171

Y

Youth Risk Behavior Surveys, 223

Building a Culture of Hope
Robert D. Barr and Emily L. Gibson
Discover a blueprint for turning low-performing schools into cultures of hope. The authors draw from their own experiences working with high-poverty, high-achieving schools to illustrate how to support students with an approach that considers social as well as emotional factors.
BKF503

Turning Your School Around
Robert D. Barr and Debra L. Yates
Learn a step-by-step protocol for the self-guided audit that focuses on the most crucial areas of school improvement identified in _The Kids Left Behind_, the nationally recognized work by Robert D. Barr and William H. Parrett.
BKF295

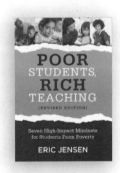

Poor Students, Rich Teaching, Revised Edition
Eric Jensen
You have the power to change the lives of students from poverty. Rely on the new edition of Dr. Eric Jensen's best-selling book _Poor Students, Rich Teaching_ and its companion handbook to help you fully embrace the mindsets that lead to richer teaching.
BKF887

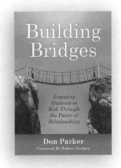

Building Bridges
Anthony Muhammad
Research shows that discipline problems are one of the greatest challenges in education. In _Building Bridges_, author Don Parker shows educators how to address this issue head-on, to build teacher-student relationships and create a welcoming learning environment that promotes engagement and achievement.
BKF793

GL⬤BAL **PD**

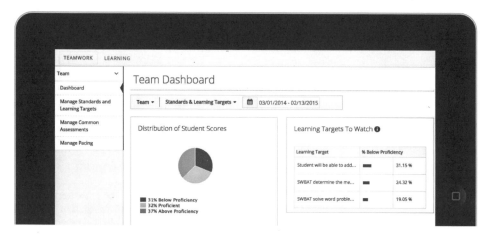

The **Power to Improve**
Is in Your Hands

Global PD gives educators focused and goals-oriented training from top experts. You can rely on this innovative online tool to improve instruction in every classroom.

- Get unlimited, on-demand access to guided video and book content from top Solution Tree authors.

- Improve practices with personalized virtual coaching from PLC-certified trainers.

- Customize learning based on skill level and time commitments.

▶ **REQUEST A FREE DEMO TODAY**
SolutionTree.com/GlobalPD

▲ Solution Tree